P A T A G O

PATAGONIA

NATURAL HISTORY, PREHISTORY AND ETHNOGRAPHY AT THE UTTERMOST END OF THE EARTH

◆

EDITED BY COLIN McEWAN, LUIS A. BORRERO AND ALFREDO PRIETO

PRINCETON UNIVERSITY PRESS
PRINCETON, NEW JERSEY

The Trustees of the British Museum gratefully acknowledge the generous joint sponsorship by the Governments of Argentina and Chile in support of this book and the exhibition.

First published in 1997 in the United States of America and Canada by Princeton University Press, 41 William Street, Princeton, New Jersey 08540

First published in 1997 by British Museum Press
A division of The British Museum Company Ltd
46 Bloomsbury Street
London WC1B 3QQ

ISBN 0-691-05849-0

Designed by Harry Green

Typeset in Palatino and Futura
Printed in Italy by Petruzzi
Origination by Bright Arts, Hong Kong

http://pup.princeton.edu
10 9 8 7 6 5 4 3 2 1
(Pbk.)

Frontispiece Two Selk'nam women wearing guanaco cloaks, *c.* 1914.

Contents

Foreword

by the Ambassadors of Argentina and Chile to the United Kingdom

The Embassies of Argentina and Chile to the United Kingdom feel privileged to cooperate with the Museum of Mankind in supporting the exhibition about Patagonia. This joint sponsorship is a further expression of the strong feelings of interdependence and shared interest which now exist between both countries.

Patagonia is a region of superlatives and extremes. It appears on maps as remote and mysterious, almost untouched by man, with immense pampas, wooded mountains, majestic cordilleras, lakes of turquoise waters, fjords and colossal glaciers. Beaten remorselessly by cold winds from the south, with long and cruel winters, it was a harsh habitat for its aboriginal peoples. Today they are almost gone. Like the poet we can ask, 'Stone on stone, the man, where was he? Air on air, the man, where was he?' Aónikenk, Selk'nam, Kawéskar, Yámana. Those were the names of these peoples. They were almost wiped out by alcohol, disease and confinement, and by colonists anxious to make way for sheep or cattle ranches. Their heritage is scarce but it is enough to show us how they were able to survive for centuries, adapted to their rugged environment. And that is the aim of the exhibition and this book that accompanies it.

Few subjects could serve better than Patagonia to illustrate the historic links between Argentina, Chile and the United Kingdom. The historic first navigation through the Strait was made by Magallanes, followed by the pioneering expeditions of Juan Ladrillero and Sarmiento de Gamboa and the Spaniards Malaspina and Cordoba Laso de la Vega. Later, many British navigators, explorers and scientists voyaged to Patagonia. Among these were Thomas Cavendish, John Byron, James Cook, Philip Parker King and, of course, Robert Fitzroy and his celebrated scientist on board, Charles Darwin.

We are proud that the last exhibition to be held at the Museum of Mankind takes as its subject a region so dear to Chile and Argentina. Looking back at our past, at the peoples who lived, toiled and struggled in Patagonia over the centuries, our desire to cooperate and grow together in peace in the future should be increased.

It has been an honour to be associated with this project.

ROGELIO PFIRTER
Ambassador of Argentina

MARIO ARTAZA
Ambassador of Chile

Introduction

by Colin McEwan, Luis A. Borrero and Alfredo Prieto

Even to many Chileans and Argentinians Patagonia can seem a wild, remote realm which has given rise to ambition, adventure, grief and folly in equal measure. How much more so viewed from afar by Europeans in the early days of exploration when distance helped magnify accounts of the native Patagonians to 'giant' proportions. For voyagers and settlers alike the region has exerted an enduring allure and spawned a colourful skein of tales which often blend fact and fiction. One part of the story, however, remains painfully incomplete and that is the largely unwritten history of its original inhabitants.

The essays in this volume do not attempt to retell the personal travails woven into such classic narratives of recent Patagonian history as Lucas Bridges' *Uttermost Part of the Earth*, nor do they delve into the whys and wherefores of missionary endeavours. Still less are they a homage to a host of latter-day travellers. Rather, they pursue an elusive history of peoples fleetingly glimpsed through fragmentary archaeological, textual and pictorial sources. Together they seek to contribute to the task of reconstituting a world that has nearly vanished.

The arrival of the earliest human settlers in Fuego-Patagonia over ten thousand years ago marked the culmination of man's long journey to people the globe. The descendants of these original peoples came to be known by various names. The Aónikenk were the southernmost group of continental steppe hunters known collectively as Tehuelche. Closely related to them both linguistically and in terms of their hunting way of life were the Selk'nam (or Ona) and Mannenkenk (Haush) who inhabited the grassland expanses of northern and south-eastern Isla Grande de Tierra del Fuego. The canoe Indians that frequented the labyrinthine waterways of the Fuegian archipelagos can be divided into two broad groups. The Yámana (or Yahgan) were concentrated around the Canal Beagle[1] and the islands to the south, while the Kawéskar (also known as Alakaluf or Halakwulup) ranged throughout the remote western islands as far north as Golfo de Penas.

Each of these groups possessed tools and weapons skilfully adapted for survival in the face of a harsh and uncompromising climate. Far from being culturally 'impoverished', we know that they also nurtured rich oral traditions and a range of vocabulary matching most other cultures. This forces us to ask the same question that Darwin asked of himself, steeped as he was in a Victorian world view: can we recognise our own humanity in these other human beings? With hindsight we can also try to ask another, more intractable question, namely what did the Fuegians make of Darwin and his companions? Can we imagine the impressions made on those who witnessed the arrival of the strange vessels and their eclectic human cargo, not to mention the succession of craft that had visited these shores intermittently in the preceding three centuries? How is 'communication' effected under such circumstances? Who can judge whom? Here the labels of 'primitive' and 'civilised' begin to dissolve under the weight of mutual incomprehension. When Darwin recorded that the Fuegians were 'the most miserable wretches on earth' he invested them with a stigma that has endured ever since. He was perhaps scarcely aware that the people he came into contact with were already suffering the irreversible consequences of contact with sealers and whalers. If this most attentive observer of the natural world had stayed longer on Tierra del Fuego he would surely have noted the impact that the decimation of the seal colonies was beginning to have on the Yámana way of life.

Darwin did witness the return of the Fuegians that Fitzroy had taken to England and we know that certain scenes made a deep impression, contributing indirectly to his still unformed theory of evolution. But what can we know of how Fuegia Basket, York Minster and Jemmy Button felt, and what they thought?

The essays gathered here touch upon these and many related questions. Much of their interest lies in the way in which they connect with each other. It is unthinkable, for example, to try and reconstruct the archaeology of Patagonia without a thorough grounding in its natural history. Patient mapping and interpretation of the glacial geomorphology now enables us to identify when a tenuous land crossing to Isla Grande de Tierra del Fuego was possible. In turn archaeological survey helps trace the lineaments of man's presence ever further south. Ultimately, the perspective that archaeology offers in reconstructing subsistence patterns must be compared with the ethnography of the historical period which provides vital clues to ethnic distributions. Nevertheless, archaeology and ethnography represent quite different ways of 'reading' human activities and making inferences about the past. On the one hand the projectile points recovered from archaeological excavations that tell us about hunting techniques can't speak, while on the other the myths and stories recounted by shamans leave little in the way of a material record that is accessible to archaeology. Agreement between the two disciplines can never be complete, as some unresolved questions posed here make clear. Furthermore, the ethnographic sources themselves comprise events, beliefs and practices almost invariably recorded by 'outsiders'. So, too, there must be a place for dissecting the assumptions underlying familiar texts and images that can so easily exercise a seductive certainty.

We hope that this compilation of material from diverse disciplines will beg at least as many questions as it answers, and that it will encourage specialists and non-specialists alike to reach beyond familiar ways of seeing and interpreting this world. We trust, too, that it may inspire others to attempt the chapters that are not yet written.

1 Spanish toponyms are used throughout the volume. The English equivalents of some of the best known toponyms are given in fig. 1.

THE CONTRIBUTORS

Gillian Beer is Edward VII Professor of English Literature at the University of Cambridge, President of Clare Hall and a Trustee of the British Museum. Her books include *Darwin's Plots* (1983), *Arguing with the Past* (1989), *Can the Native Return?* (1989), *Forging the Missing Link: Interdisciplinary Stories* (1992) and *Open Fields: Science in Cultural Encounter* (1996).

Mateo Martinic B. is founder and Director of the Instituto de la Patagonia, Universidad de Magallanes, Chile. He has received international recognition for his many publications on the history of the Magellan Region, which include *Presencia de Chile en la Patagonia Austral (1843–1879), Voyagers to the Strait of Magellan, Historia de la Region Magallanica* and *Los Aónikenk, Historia y Cultura.*

Luis Alberto Borrero is senior archaeologist at the Consejo Nacional de Investigaciones Científicas y Tecnicas (CONICET) and Assistant Professor at the Universidad de Buenos Aires, Argentina. He has conducted archaeological surveys and excavations in the Argentinian provinces of Neuquén, Río Negro, Chubut, Santa Cruz and Tierra del Fuego, and in Magallanes, Chile. He has written a number of articles and a book, *Los Selk'nam (Ona): Su Evolución Cultural.*

Anne Chapman is Research Associate at the Centre National de la Recherche Scientifique (CNRS) and the Musée de l'Homme. She devoted much of her anthropological research to the study of the Selk'nam and Yámana in Tierra del Fuego, Chile and Argentina. Among her many publications is *Drama and Power in a Hunting Society: The Selk'nam of Tierra del Fuego* (1982) and she has created important documentary records, including a film, *The Ona People: Life and Death in Tierra del Fuego.* She has just completed a volume tracing the history of European contact, *On the Back of Beyond. Cape Horn – Indians, Explorers and Missionaries 1578–1900.*

Chalmers Clapperton is Professor of Geography at the University of Aberdeen, Scotland. He is author of *The Quaternary Geology and Geomorphology of South America* (1993), a landmark volume that reflects the range of his geomorphological field research in Andean South America. His recent work has addressed the chronology and dynamics of deglaciation in southern Patagonia and the Estrecho de Magallanes.

Andy Currant is Curator of Quaternary Mammals at the Natural History Museum, London and an Honorary Research Fellow of Royal Holloway and Bedford New College, University of London. He has recently been involved in collaborative work on fragmentary genetic material recovered from the extinct ground sloth (*Mylodon darwinii*) which inhabited the Cueva del Milodon at the end of the last ice age.

Jean-Paul Duviols is Professor of Literature and Latin American Civilisations at the Université de Paris IV, Sorbonne. Among many publications he has authored *L'Amérique espagnole vue et rêvée (Les livres de voyages de Colomb á Bougainville, 1492–1767)* and co-authored *Le Théâtre du Nouveau Monde (Les grands voyages de Theodore de Bry).*

Robert McCulloch is a Research Fellow at the University of Edinburgh. His work centres on the application of pollen analysis, tephrachronology and glacial geomorphology to the study of environmental change in Patagonia and north-west Europe.

Colin McEwan is curator of South American collections at the Museum of Mankind (the British Museum), London. He has excavated extensively in Latin America, including Patagonia. Among his previous publications is *Ancient Mexico in the British Museum* (1994).

Francisco Mena is a staff archaeologist at the Museo Chileno de Arte Precolombino. He has conducted archaeological surveys and excavation in Chilean Patagonia and has published articles on long-term human adaptations in the region.

Alfredo Prieto is an archaeologist on the faculty of the Instituto de la Patagonia, Universidad de Magallanes, Chile. He has conducted field research in Ultima Esperanza and on Tierra del Fuego. He is author of *Arqueria Selk'nam: La Guerra y la Paz en la Tierra del Fuego* and co-author of *Perspectiva Arqueologica de los Selk'nam.*

Jorge Rabassa is Professor of Geography at the University of Comahue at Neuquén, Argentina and has served as State Congressman for Tierra del Fuego (1991–5). He is a past director of the Centro Austral de Investigaciones Científicas (CADIC, CONICET) (1986–90) and is presently visiting Professor in the Department of Geology, University of Barcelona, Spain. He has conducted research projects in Argentina, Chile, Brazil, USA, Spain, South Africa, Colombia and the Antarctic Peninsula, has published more than two hundred scientific papers and serves on the editorial boards of a number of major scientific journals, among these as editor-in-chief of *Quaternary of South America & Antarctic Peninsula.*

Michael Taussig is Professor of Anthropology at Columbia University, New York. Among his many articles and books on the anthropology of contact in South America are *Shamanism, Colonialism and the Wild Man: A Study in Terror and Healing* (1987) and *Mimesis and Alterity: A Particular History of the Senses* (1993). His most recent book is *Magic and the State.*

ACKNOWLEDGEMENTS

We wish to thank warmly Ambassador Rogelio Pfirter of Argentina and Ambassador Mario Artaza of Chile for the role they have played in securing the joint commitment from their respective governments to support the exhibition at the Museum of Mankind and this book which accompanies it. We are grateful to the Cultural Ministries of both countries for enabling Luis Borrero and Alfredo Prieto to make a study visit to London in February this year. Jacqueline Tichauer (Cultural Attaché for the Embassy of Chile) and Samuel Ortiz Basualdo (Cultural Attaché for the Embassy of Argentina) have also done much 'behind the scenes' to help and we particularly appreciate their practical support, friendship and enthusiasm.

A project of this complexity realised within a tight schedule makes demands on all involved. We thank the many institutions acknowledged in the picture credits, and especially the following individuals: Mireille Simoni Abbat, Lesley Adkins, Isabel Anderton, Sumru Aricanli, Eduardo Armstrong, Aldo Audisio, Janet Backhouse, Peter Barber, Stuart Blake, Jorge Eduardo Brousse, Staffan Brunius, Juan José Cascardi, Sara Ciruzzi, Robin Cocks, Barbara Conklin, Stephen Dale, Emma Dean, Lothar Drager, Berete Due, Muguette Dumont, Eliana Duran, Elizabeth Edwards, Nora Franco, M. Fugazzola, José Antonio Perez Gollan, Richard Haas, Diana Hamer, Francis Herbert, Elizabeth Horn, Héctor Lahitte, José Luis Lanata, Ann de Lara, Ted Leyenaar, Jean Marshall, Magdalena Mieri, Craig Morris, Kazuyasu Ochiai, Paul Ossa, Catherine Owens, Margarita Alvarado Perez, Joachim Piepke, Daniel Quiroz, Corinna Raddatz, Charles Rees, Emmanuela de Rege, Rodolfo A. Raffino, Norma Rosso, Joanna Scadden, Sofia Correa Sutil, Brian Theynne, Sanna Törneman, Ana Avalos Venezuela, Geoffrey West and Nancy Young. We also appreciate the interest and assistance offered by the Royal Geographical Society, the Anglo-Argentine Society, the Anglo-Chilean Society and Gloria Carnevalli (Embassy of Venezuela).

From our very first discussions Emma Way, Head of British Museum Press, has given unqualified backing for the book. Harry Green (the designer) and Julie Young (the production manager) have brought great care and attention to detail in knitting together the text and graphic material. Liz Errington's cartographic skills have been indispensable. We especially thank Rhonda Klevansky, who generously made available a superb range of photographs, and David Williams and Adriana Meirelles for drafting a number of illustrations.

Amidst a challenging period the skilled staff of the Museum have contributed unstinting support: Dave Agar, Anne Alexander, Dean Baylis, Sue Beeby, Alison Deeprose, Renée Evans, Jean Goodey, Carmen Grannum-Symister, Allan Hills, John Lee, Alan Loader, Lucia Navascues M., David Noden, Pippa Pearce, Saul Peckham, Harry Persaud, Michael Row, Susan Vacarey, Iris Walsh, Barbara Wills and Helen Wolfe. Clara Bezanilla has assisted ably with the archival research, in addition to supervising the handling of material for conservation and photography. Dr John Mack (Keeper, Department of Ethnography) has responded willingly as needs have arisen.

Two people above all have helped bring the book to fruition. We are extremely grateful to our editor Joanna Champness for her expertise and equanimity, and to Marcia Arcuri who as Research Assistant for the project has brought an indefatigable dedication to the myriad tasks that have been asked of her.

KEY DATES AND EVENTS

(BP = years before present)

c. 21,000–19,000 BP	Last Glacial Maximum (LGM) ice limits
c. 14,000–8,000 BP	Period during which a land crossing from continental Patagonia to Isla Grande de Tierra del Fuego was possible
c. 11,000–10,000 BP	Earliest evidence for human presence on Tierra del Fuego
c. 8,000 BP	Rising sea level forms the Estrecho de Magallanes
c. 6,000 BP	Evidence for maritime adaptation on Canal Beagle
c. 2,500 BP–contact	Human occupation of Isla Grande de Tierra del Fuego and the Fuegian archipelagos becomes increasingly widespread

Selected Voyages to the Magellan Region (Sixteenth to Twentieth Centuries)

1519–21	Hernando de Magallanes traverses the Strait that now bears his name
1523	Garcie de Laoise
1525	Francisco Jofré de Loayza & Juan Sebastian Elcano
1527–9	Alvaro de Sayavedra
1534	Simon de Alcazaba
1537	León Pancaldo
1539–41	Alonso de Camargo
1553	Francisco de Ulloa & Francisco Cortez de Ojea
1557	Juan Ladrillero
1578	Francis Drake
1579 & 1584	Pedro Sarmiento de Gamboa
1586	Walter Raleigh
1587 & 1591	Thomas Cavendish
1589	John Chidley & Andrew Merrick
1594	Richard Hawkins
1599	Simon de Corde, Jacob de Mahu & Seebald de Weert
1599	Olivier van Noort
1615	Joris van Spielbergen, Lemaire & Schouter
1615–18	Bartolomé García & Gonzalo de Nodal
1623	Jacques l'Hermite
1670	John Narborough
1741	George Anson
1766	John Byron
1766	Wallis & Carteret
1766	Louis Antoine, comte de Bougainville
1769 & 1774	James Cook
1785 & 1788	Antonio de Córdoba
1822	James Weddell
1826–30	Philip Parker King; Robert Fitzroy brings four Fuegians back to England
1831–6	Voyage of the *Beagle*, commanded by Robert Fitzroy, accompanied by Charles Darwin. Three Fuegians returned to Tierra del Fuego in 1833
1837–40	Jules Dumont-d'Urville
1855	William Parker Snow
1859	Thomas Bridges arrives and in 1869 founds the first mission at Ushuaia
1875	HMS *Challenger* commanded by Charles W. Thomson
1876	Mme Annie Allnut Brassey
1878–9	HMS *Alert* commanded by George Nares, accompanied by Coppinger
1882–3	French expedition to Cabo de Hornos with P. Hyades & J. Deniker
1888–92	Isla Bayly Mission
1892–1906	Tekenika Mission on Isla Hoste
1889–1911	San Rafael Mission on Isla Dawson
1907–16	Río Douglas Mission
1919–24	The Salesian missionary and ethnographer Martin Gusinde works on Tierra del Fuego and publishes *Die Feuerland-Indianer* (1931)
1948	E. Lucas Bridges publishes *Uttermost Part of the Earth*

1 The Natural Setting

The Glacial and Post-Glacial Environmental History of Fuego-Patagonia

Robert D. McCulloch
Chalmers M. Clapperton
Jorge Rabassa
Andrew P. Currant

Introduction

Fig 1 The physical geography of Patagonia.

Patagonia, including Tierra del Fuego, is a huge territory of more than 900,000 square kilometres, located between latitude 39° and 55° South in South America. The topography of southern Patagonia and Tierra del Fuego is dominated in the west and south by the rugged Andean mountain chain, and in the east by dissected plateaux giving way to low plains. The continuous marine waterway of the Estrecho de Magallanes separates Patagonia from Isla Grande de Tierra del Fuego, and the Canal Beagle cuts Tierra del Fuego from the outer islands (fig. 1). This framework largely reflects the tectonic structure of the region, dominated by subduction of the Pacific oceanic crustal plate beneath the South American continent and active strike-slip faulting between plate fragments in the Estrecho de Magallanes/Canal Beagle area. Granitic intrusions and metamorphic rocks underlie much of the mountainous terrain, forming spectacular peaks in specific areas like Cerro Fitzroy, Torres del Paine and the Sarmiento massif, all of which rise well above 2,000 m. Late Mesozoic and Tertiary sedimentary strata create more tabular relief in the plateaux that decline eastwards, as in the Peninsula Brunswick. Throughout the 1.6 million years of the Pleistocene[1] the western part of this region has been periodically buried beneath massive ice-fields that grew over the highest and wettest ground along the Pacific margin. Powerful ice-streams draining eastward excavated large lake basins like Lago Buenos Aires, Lago Argentino and Lago Sarmiento in Patagonia, and Lago Fagnano in Tierra del Fuego. The large marine embayments of Seno Skyring, Seno Otway and Bahía Inútil have a similar origin. Ice-streams draining to the west and south cut the deep fjords that have split up so much of the western area into a mosaic of islands (figs 2 and 4). In contrast to this striking glacial scenery superimposed on the structurally controlled topography, the imprint of glaciation to the east is more subtle, where vast amounts of glacial and glaciofluvial deposits form rolling terrain composed of morainic ridges and mounds, and these merge into immense plains of outwash gravels extending to the Atlantic (fig. 3).

The regional climate of the area is strongly affected by the westerly storm tracks coupled with precipitation induced by the high western flanks of the Andean Cordillera.

76°
72°
68°
64°
60°
40°
44°
48°
52°
LA PAMPA
Bahía Blanca
ARAUCANÍA
NEUQUÉN
R. Neuquén
R. Colorado
R. Negro
Valdivia
Lakes Region
R. Limay
RÍO NEGRO
Carmen de Patagones
Puerto Montt
R. Arroyo Verde
Golfo San Matías
Península Valdés
ISLA DE CHILOÉ
CORDILLERA DE LOS ANDES
CHUBUT
R. Chubut
R. Chico
ISLAS CHONOS
Golfo San Jorge
R. Ibáñez
LAGO BUENOS AIRES
R. Deseado
Golfo de Penas
R. Pinturas
SANTA CRUZ
Puerto Eden
Cerro Fitzroy
ISLA WELLINGTON
R. Chico
R. Santa Cruz
ISLA MADRE DE DIOS
LAGO ARGENTINO
LAGO SARMIENTO
R. Coig
Torres del Paine
Seno Ultima Esperanza
Puerto Natales
R. Gallegos
Río Gallegos
Seno Skyring
Seno Otway
Strait of Magellan
Estrecho de Magallanes
Porvenir
Punta Arenas
Península Brunswick
Bahía Inútil (Useless Bay)
ISLA GRANDE DE TIERRA DEL FUEGO
ISLA SANTA INÉS
ISLA DAWSON
LAGO FAGNANO (KAMÍ)
Península Brecknock
Ushuaia
Pto. Halberton
Estrecho de le Maire
ISLA DE LOS ESTADOS
Pto Williams
ISLA NAVARINO
Canal Beagle (Beagle Channel)
ISLA HOSTE
Cabo de Hornos (Cape Horn)
Map of South America
PATAGONIA

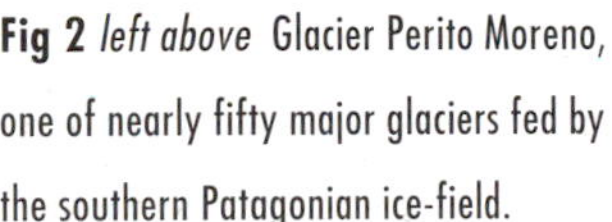

Fig 2 *left above* Glacier Perito Moreno, one of nearly fifty major glaciers fed by the southern Patagonian ice-field.

Fig 3 *left* Lago Argentino and the pampas grassland beyond.

Fig 4 An iceberg recently calved off Glacier Grey, Torres del Paine National Park, Chile.

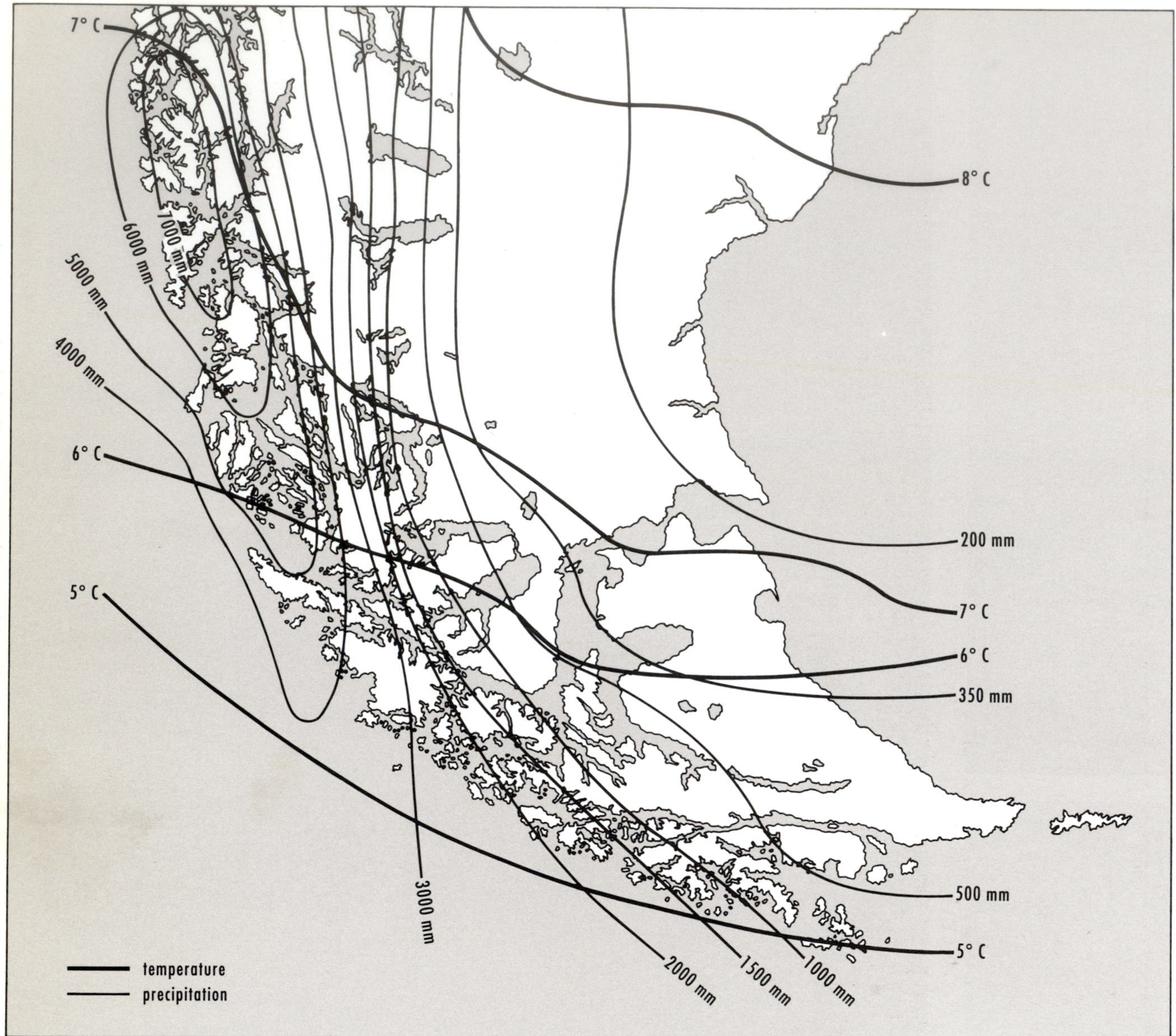

Fig 5 Distribution of mean annual temperature and precipitation in Patagonia.

Fig 6 *opposite* Principal vegetation zones in Patagonia.

This produces a strong, east-west gradient with annual precipitation of 4,000–7,000 mm falling on the western slopes of the cordillera at 50° South, whereas less than 800 mm fall on the eastern side in Argentina due to the rainshadow effect (fig. 5). Influenced by the low sea surface temperatures of the Humboldt Current offshore, these cold and humid air masses give rise to the Patagonian ice-fields and large glaciers in the Cordillera Darwin. These are the largest ice-fields in the southern hemisphere outside of Antarctica.

The vegetation patterns of Patagonia are closely related to the temperature and precipitation gradients (fig. 6). High winds and high rainfall (2,000–5,000 mm per annum) extending along the west coast as far north as *c.* 48° South support broad areas of Magellanic moorland which is composed predominantly of bog communities and

Magellanic moorland
Forest (predominantly *Nothofagus betuloides*)
Patagonian steppe
Ice-fields and glaciers

Fig 7 Cöigue Forest, composed principally of southern beech (*Nothofagus betuloides*), Chile.

dwarf shrubs.[2] Where precipitation is between 800–4,000 mm per annum, an evergreen rainforest dominated by *Nothofagus betuloides* (southern beech) occurs in sheltered areas (fig. 7). This species grows close to the margins of the Patagonian ice-fields. In areas of lower precipitation the deciduous *Nothofagus pumilio* is often present in mixed woodland. In addition, *Empetrum rubrum*, *Berberis ilicifolia*, *Gunnera magellanica* and *Senecio acanthifolius* commonly form part of the understorey shrub and herb layer, especially where the canopy is more open.

Deciduous forest of *Nothofagus pumilio* and *Nothofagus antarctica* occurs along the eastern flanks of the Andean Cordillera up to an altitude of *c.* 500 m, where precipitation is between 400–800 mm per annum (fig. 9). Here the forest canopy is more open, especially on the eastern forest margins where *Embothrium coccineum*, *Berberis buxifolia* and *Pernettya mucronata* persist with isolated stands of *Drimys winteri* and *Maytenus magellanica* woodland.[3] Within the forest zone, but where areas are free from trees, an *Empetrum rubrum–Bolax gummifera* heath is present in places, and where there is sufficient water *Sphagnum* bogs occur. The forest vegetation gives way eastwards, as precipitation falls below *c.* 400 mm per annum, to the shrub-grassland of the Patagonian steppe. This is dominated by the rough tussock grasses of *Festuca gracillima* and *Festuca magellanica* (fig. 8). The dryness of the region is exacerbated by the combination of high evaporation and persistent westerly winds.

Thus far we have described the geological history of Fuego-Patagonia, its topography, vegetation and the present-day climate. However, recent glacial and palaeoecological research suggests the environment of Fuego-Patagonia has periodically undergone significant changes over time-scales of thousands of years.

Fig 8 Tussock grass vegetation, Pedra Buena, San Julian, Santa Cruz Province.

Fig 9 *opposite* Waterfall on the Río Paine, with Torres del Paine in the background. Chile.

The glacial history

Fig 10 Last Glacial Maximum (LGM) ice limits in Patagonia, *c.* 21,000–19,000 BP.

Long before the Americas were colonised by humans, the landscape of Fuego-Patagonia was affected by repeated glacier advances that shaped the water-filled basins and major river channels that exist today. The largest expansion of the ice-fields occurred around one million years BP.[4] The most recent research suggests that the maximum expansion was probably between 1.138 and 0.994 MA BP.[5] A continuous ice mass composed of confluent glaciers from the major Andean catchments advanced as far as the Atlantic Ocean south of Río Gallegos and northern Tierra del Fuego. Limits of this massive glacier were mapped in 1932 by Caldenius, who named the glacial event the *Initio* Glaciation. Caldenius erroneously interpreted the limits as representing an earlier phase of the last glaciation or part of the penultimate glaciation (see discussion later in this chapter). After about 760,000 BP the climate of the world appears to have settled into cycles of colder glacial intervals which endured for about 100,000 years, during which the world's great ice-sheets advanced, followed by warmer interglacial conditions which lasted for little more than 10,000–15,000 years, when the ice-sheets decayed. This means that the landscape of Fuego-Patagonia has been influenced by glacial processes for about 85–90% of the last 800,000 years.

During each glacier advance rock debris was carried by ice and meltwater to the glacier snout and this material was 'bulldozed' into arcuate ridges, termed moraines. These accumulated as conspicuous moraine belts and define the former limits of each glacier advance. Maps of the moraines indicate that glaciers advanced less distance eastward during successive glaciations, probably because of a combination of tectonic uplift and subsequent glacial erosion of the basins in the west. Glacier advances during the Pleistocene formed the moraines surrounding most of the large water-filled basins of Patagonia. Morainic deposits of the middle Pleistocene formed the peninsula at Punta Dungeness and the Primera Angostura in the Estrecho de Magallanes as well as parts of the islands at the eastern end of the Canal Beagle.[6]

The last glacial cycle

Analyses of cores sampled from ocean sediments and from polar ice suggest that the last glacial interval commenced about 115,000 BP as the global climate began to cool. The first major cooling occurred between *c.* 75,000–60,000 BP and it is believed that large glaciers from the ice-cap centred over Cordillera Darwin and adjacent mountains advanced more than 170 km along the Estrecho de Magallanes and deposited the sequence of sediments underlying the Segunda Angostura.[7] Streamlined hills of glacial sediments (known as drumlins) in the vicinity of Laguna Cabeza del Mar may also have been formed at this time.[8] The curving moraine belt can be traced almost continuously northward from the Estrecho de Magallanes to the bays around Puerto Natales. The outermost ridges of moraine belts in Tierra del Fuego, as around Bahía Inútil, Lago Fagnano and at Punta Moat, east of Puerto Harberton in the Canal

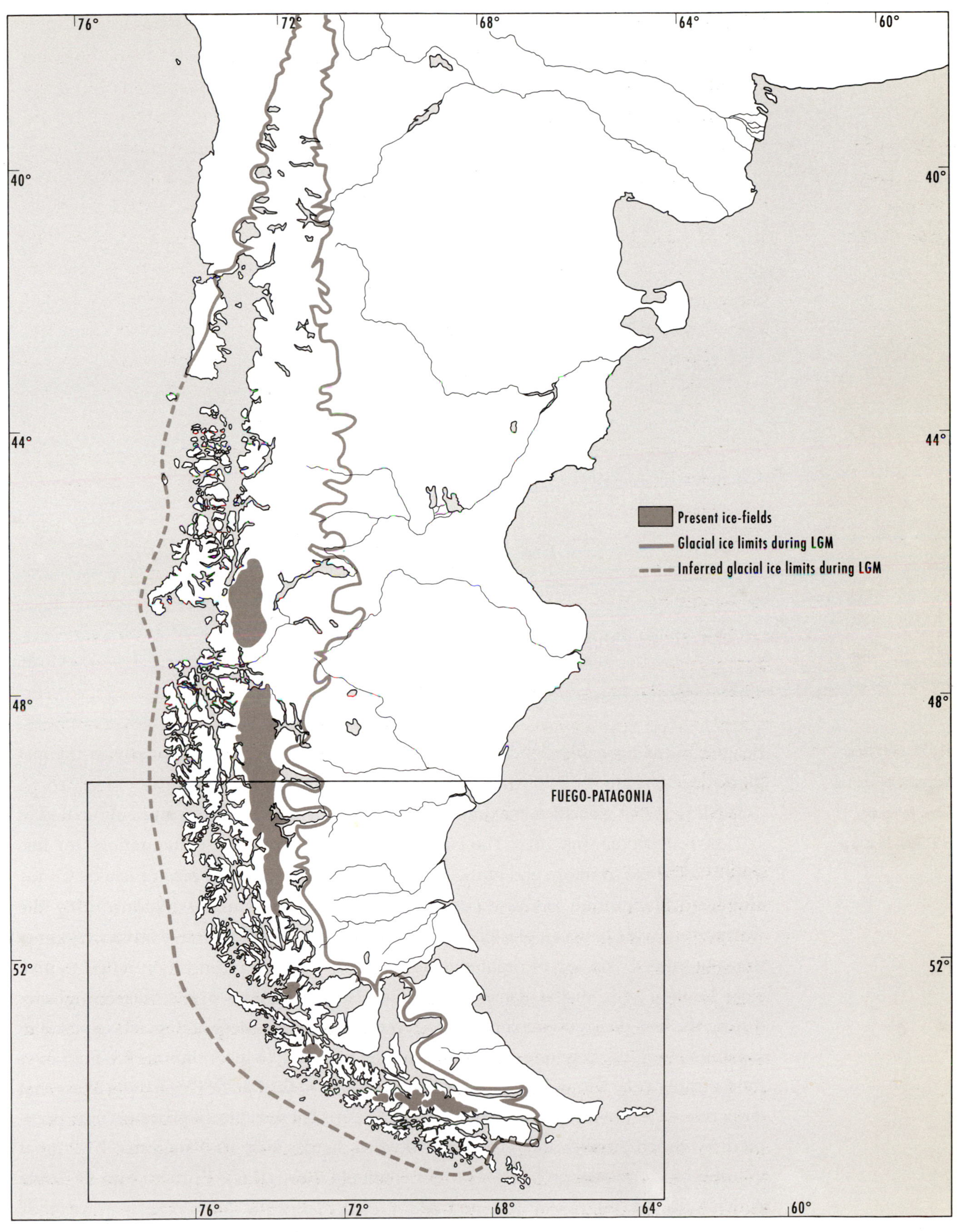
76°
72°
68°
64°
60°
40°
40°
44°
44°
48°
48°
52°
52°
Present ice-fields
Glacial ice limits during LGM
Inferred glacial ice limits during LGM
FUEGO-PATAGONIA
76°
72°
68°
64°
60°

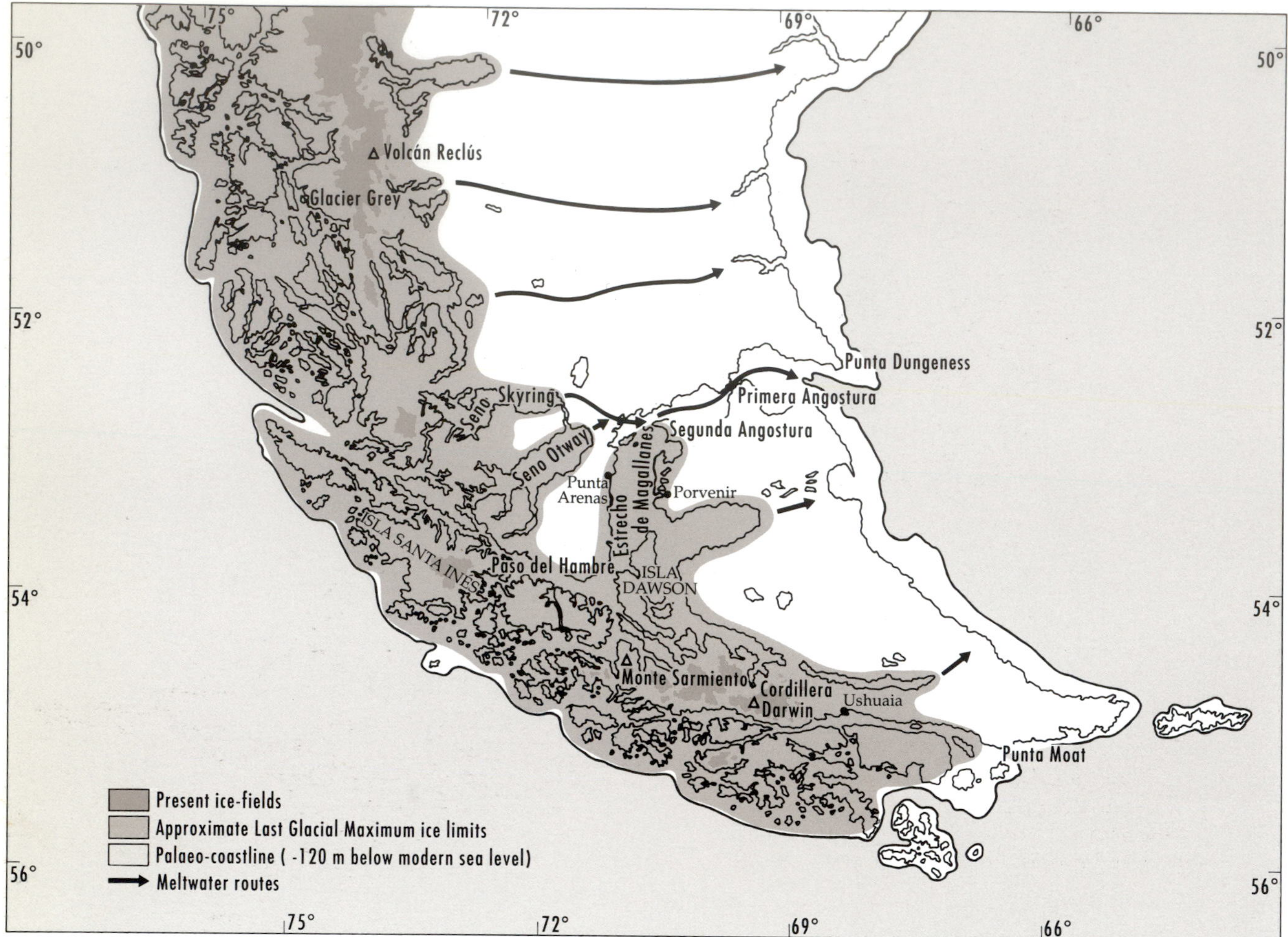

Fig 11 Last Glacial Maximum ice limits in Fuego-Patagonia, *c.* 21,000–19,000 BP.

Beagle,[9] were probably deposited during this large glacier advance early in the last glacial cycle.

The last global glaciation maximum began about 28,000 years ago and culminated at *c.* 21,000–19,000 BP (fig. 10).[10] The best-dated sequence of glacier fluctuations for this interval is at the southern end of the Chilean Lakes Region, in the area of Isla de Chiloé and Lago Llanquihue. Because peat bogs and trees grew in this region during the warmer intervals between glacier advances, the deposits of successive advances sometimes lie directly on top of organic material. This has been radiocarbon-dated to give close limiting ages for the glacier oscillations. The fluctuations of the Magellan glacier during the last glaciation maximum produced stacked sequences of deposits exposed in sea cliffs along the Segunda Angostura. As the presence of a continuous ice-field over the Cordillera Darwin would have blocked drainage to the Pacific Ocean, it is likely that large rivers carried meltwater to the Atlantic Ocean. These cut huge channels now occupied by much smaller modern rivers flowing across eastern Patagonia. The great volume of meltwater probably also cut channels through the Primera and Segunda Angosturas (fig. 11).

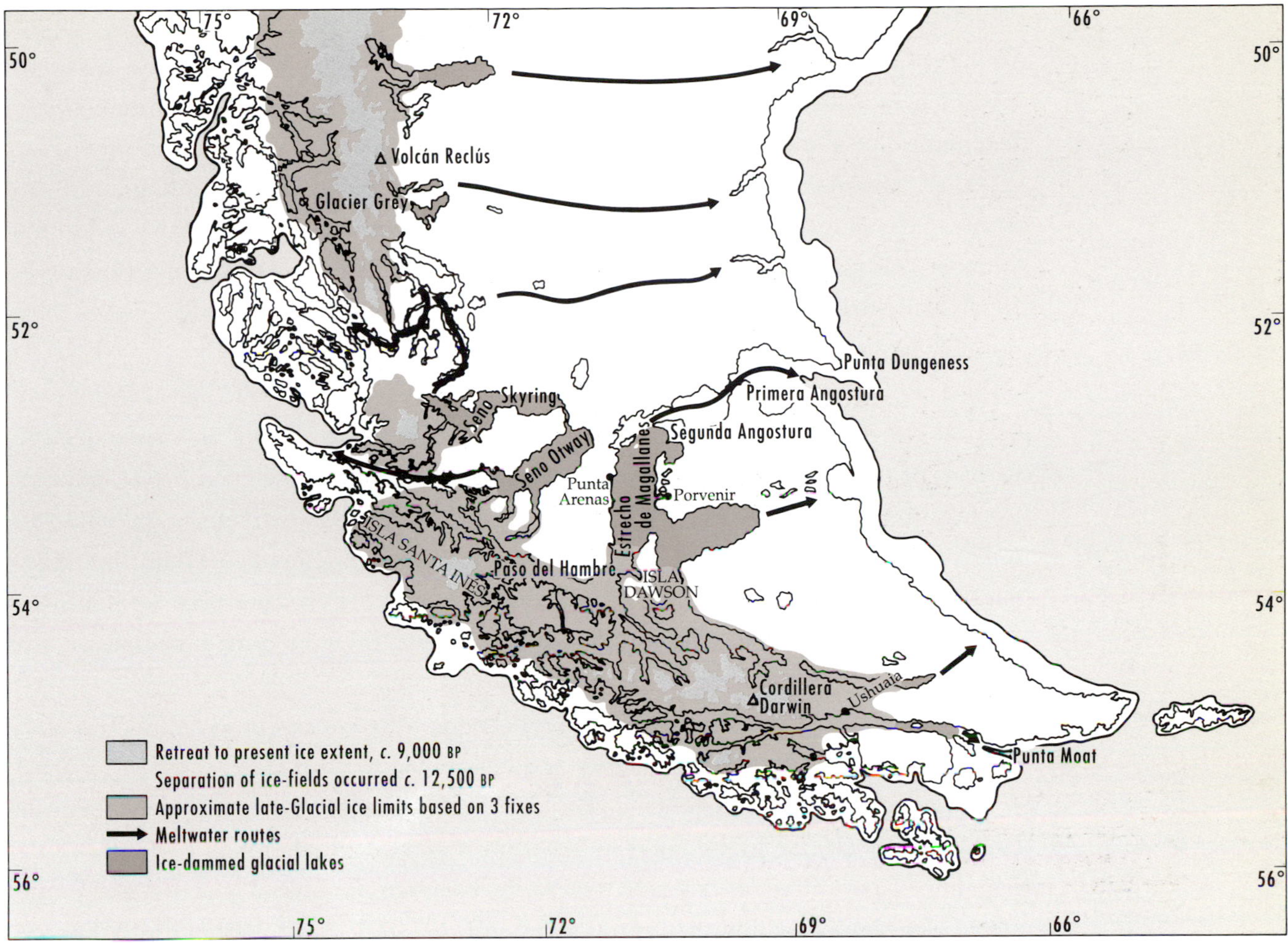

Fig 12 Late-glacial ice limit, *c.* 12,000–10,000 BP.

The last major Patagonian glacier advance occurred at *c.* 14,500 BP.[11] In the Chilean Lakes Region the glaciers terminated only a few kilometres behind their earlier Last Glacial Maximum positions, while in the Estrecho de Magallanes the glacier advanced close to Punta Arenas.[12] In the Canal Beagle a large outlet glacier draining eastward from the Darwin ice-fields may have terminated west of Puerto Harberton, perhaps at Gable Island, during this time.[13]

During the last glaciation maximum global sea level was more than 120 m lower than present-day sea level.[14] Therefore, Atlantic water would have been unable to penetrate over the shallow threshold of *c.* 40 m depth between the Primera and Segunda Angosturas and we presume this sector was dry land at the time, apart from a major river of meltwater draining to the Atlantic (fig. 11). Pacific water could only enter the central and western section of the Estrecho de Magallanes through the western channels when they became free of glaciers. The gradual rise in global sea level from about 17,000 BP indicates that a slow but steady melting of the great northern hemisphere ice-sheets was under way,[15] but it was not until *c.* 9,000 BP that it was high enough to penetrate the Segunda Angostura.

The late-glacial interval

After *c.* 14,000 BP in the Chilean Lakes Region and on Isla de Chiloé the large ice lobes withdrew rapidly, their retreat accelerated by calving of icebergs into progressively deepening lakes and ocean waters. The ice had shrunk well into the mountains by 12,000 BP.[16] Similar recession affected the large glaciers in the Seno Skyring and Seno Otway,[17] allowing drainage to flow westward to the Pacific rather than eastward to the Atlantic. This meant a drastic reduction in the size and discharge of streams flowing in the Atlantic-draining meltwater channels, cut when the glaciers had lain at their morainic limits.

The extent to which glaciers retreated during the interval 14,000–12,000 BP is not well known. However, a large eruption of Volcan Reclús at *c.* 12,000 BP[18] spread large deposits of volcanic tephra[19] onto the upper catchments of the Grey and Tyndal glaciers flowing from the south-eastern edge of the South Patagonia ice-field. As quantities of tephra were delivered by the glaciers and meltwaters to deltas being built into pro-glacial lakes in the Lago Nordenskjold area south of the Paine massif, it is known that these glaciers still lay more than 20 km beyond their modern positions at this time.[20]

The same tephra from Volcan Reclús has been identified around the central and eastern sections of Estrecho de Magallanes and is interbedded between peat layers buried beneath glaciolacustrine sediments. The peat layers suggest that prior to *c.* 12,000 BP the Magellan glacier lobe had receded from the western channels of Estrecho de Magallanes, permitting drainage to the Pacific of a large pro-glacial lake that had previously been ponded within the central section of the Strait and in Bahía Inútil. During this time much of the area between the Primera and Segunda Angosturas may have been dry and apart from the deeper and enclosed hollows no major meltwater river would have flowed through the Segunda and Primera Angosturas. This, then, may have presented the first 'window of opportunity' for humans to pass on foot from the continental mainland onto Isla Grande de Tierra del Fuego via the connecting land-bridge (fig. 13). The land-bridge was subsequently breached again sometime after the Reclús eruption of *c.* 12,000 BP, when a pro-glacial lake and its outlet river formed as the Magellan glacier readvanced into the Estrecho de Magallanes. The ice may have terminated close to Puerto Hambre.[21] Mean annual temperatures are believed to have been about 3°C cooler in the mountains of Central America and throughout the Andes during this interval.[22]

Abandoned lake shorelines at 20–30 m altitude along the western side of the Estrecho de Magallanes and sequences of glaciolacustrine sediments indicate that the glacier advance dammed a large pro-glacial lake within the Strait and Bahía Inútil (see figs 12 and 13). The pro-glacial lake shoreline terminates at a moraine on the northern peninsula of Isla Dawson. This marks the limit of the Magellan glacier and thus the ice-dam at this time. The moraine is believed to post-date the eruption of Volcan Reclús, and so

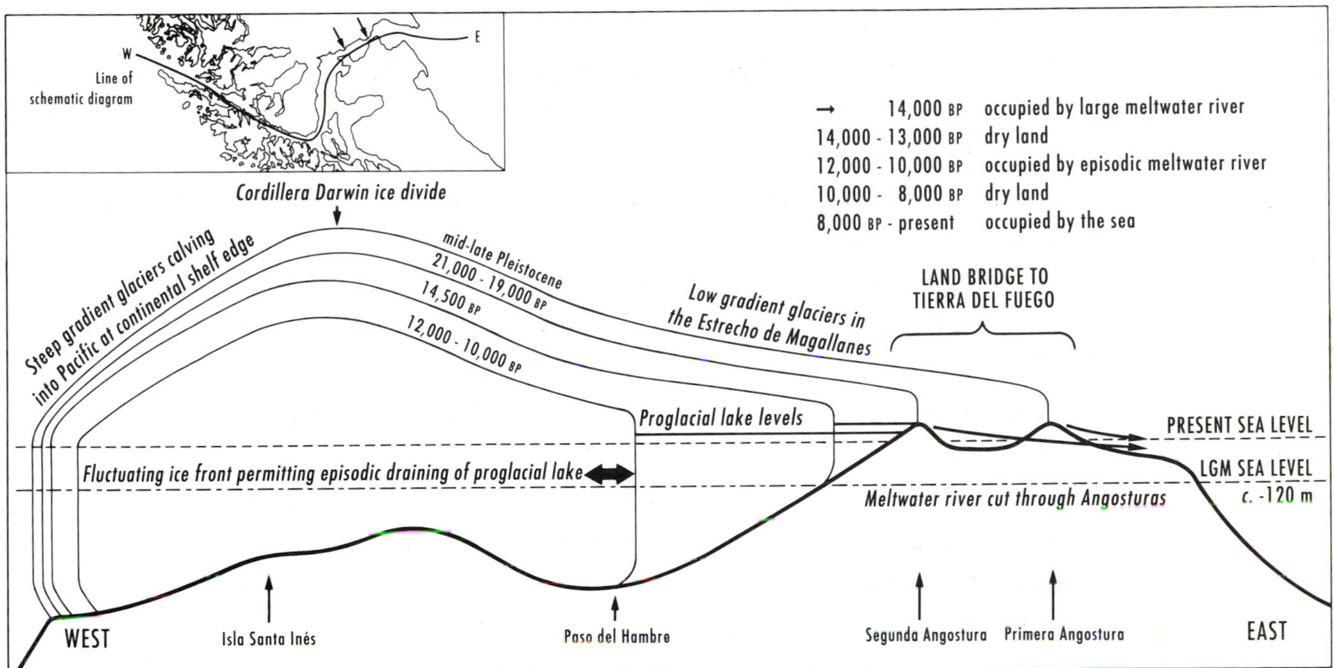

Fig 13 Schematic profile showing the relationship of ice volume in the Estrecho de Magallanes, relative sea levels and the formation of a late-Glacial–early Holocene land-bridge to Tierra del Fuego.

the advance culminated after *c.* 12,000 BP.[23] The extensive pro-glacial lake would have drained through a large meltwater river reoccupying the channel cut through the Angosturas to the Atlantic Ocean, the surface of which still lay many tens of metres below modern sea level.[24] Sedimentary evidence of this lake includes glaciolacustrine clays and silts that were laid down on top of the peat and tephra layers. As a number of interbedded peat and glaciolacustrine layers are present, it seems that the pro-glacial lake periodically drained and refilled, and there is tentative evidence that this occurred at least seven times. Therefore, it is likely that after 12,000 BP there were intervals of tens of years when a land-bridge between mainland Patagonia and Tierra del Fuego came into existence and was free from a large meltwater river. This period represents a second potential 'window of opportunity' during which it may have been possible for humans to disperse southwards by land to Tierra del Fuego (see fig. 13 and chapter 2).

The late-glacial environment

In the same way that fluctuations of the Patagonian ice-fields in response to climatic change can be identified from the sequences of sediments and geomorphology of the landscape, so too it is possible to study changes in the vegetation patterns in response to climatic change. The principal tool is the study of fossil pollen. Pollen is extremely resistant to degradation and is well preserved in lake and peat sediments. The analysis of the fossil pollen content of long sediment cores provides a means of reconstructing vegetation changes at varying spatial and temporal scales.[25] The oldest record of vegetation change, dating from 16,590 BP, was obtained from a peat bog at Puerto Hambre.[26] Further detailed records have been studied from Estancia Esmeralda II on Isla

Dawson,[27] Puerto Harberton on Tierra del Fuego[28] and Caleta Robalo on Isla Navarino.[29] These all consistently show that climatic conditions between *c.* 12,000–10,000 BP in Fuego-Patagonia were colder than present, perhaps 3°–6°C colder. These records are consistent with the evidence for persistent ice-fields in the region until *c.* 10,000 BP. The vegetation cover was dominated by grasses and, in moister areas, sedges and heathland. This treeless vegetation resembles a tundra environment. It is also likely that eastern Fuego-Patagonia was drier than today. The environment of some parts of Fuego-Patagonia at this time therefore appears to have been climatically inhospitable for humans and would have offered impoverished vegetation resources for any early inhabitants (see chapter 2).

The Holocene environment

The final deglaciation of Estrecho de Magallanes and Canal Beagle occurred at *c.* 10,000 BP as Fuego-Patagonia experienced rapid climatic warming at the start of the present Holocene interglacial interval.[30] As glacier ice withdrew from western channels of Estrecho de Magallanes it was now open to the Pacific, like Seno Otway and Seno Skyring, and all major streams entering central and western parts of the Strait would have flowed westward (fig. 14). Although global sea level was steadily rising, due to melting of the great ice-sheets of the northern hemisphere, global sea level at this time was still lower than modern sea level. Therefore, it is likely that the area between the Primera and Segunda Angosturas was still closed to the Atlantic Ocean and this would have presented a third opportunity for overland passage to Tierra del Fuego (see fig. 13).

After *c.* 10,000 BP the Patagonian *Nothofagus* forests expanded outwards from the flanks of the cordillera. The almost uniform character of *Nothofagus* forest in Fuego-Patagonia suggests that there may have been small *refugia* of woodland during the late-glacial interval (12,000–10,000 BP), but these have not yet been identified.[31] Eastward migration of the forest boundary was probably restricted by low precipitation in eastern Fuego-Patagonia which continued to be covered by steppe vegetation. Pollen evidence from Isla Dawson and Lago Fagnano indicates that by *c.* 8,000 BP the forest boundary had shifted tens of kilometres eastward, suggesting that annual precipitation had increased in eastern Fuego-Patagonia at that time.

Within the pollen profiles from Fuego-Patagonia varying proportions of charcoal fragments have been found.[32] Between *c.* 10,000–9,000 BP the concentrations of charcoal fragments appear to reach a peak. Various causes for the charcoal have been suggested, ranging from fires started by Indians to lightning and volcanic eruptions and tephra falls.[33] The volcanoes along the Andean Cordillera are too far away to have started fires in Fuego-Patagonia. Charcoal is not encountered alongside tephra layers which are cold when deposited, having travelled many hundreds of kilometres in the atmosphere. McCulloch[34] suggested that the occurrence of high charcoal concentrations throughout the region between *c.* 10,000–9,000 BP is more likely to have been assisted by the very

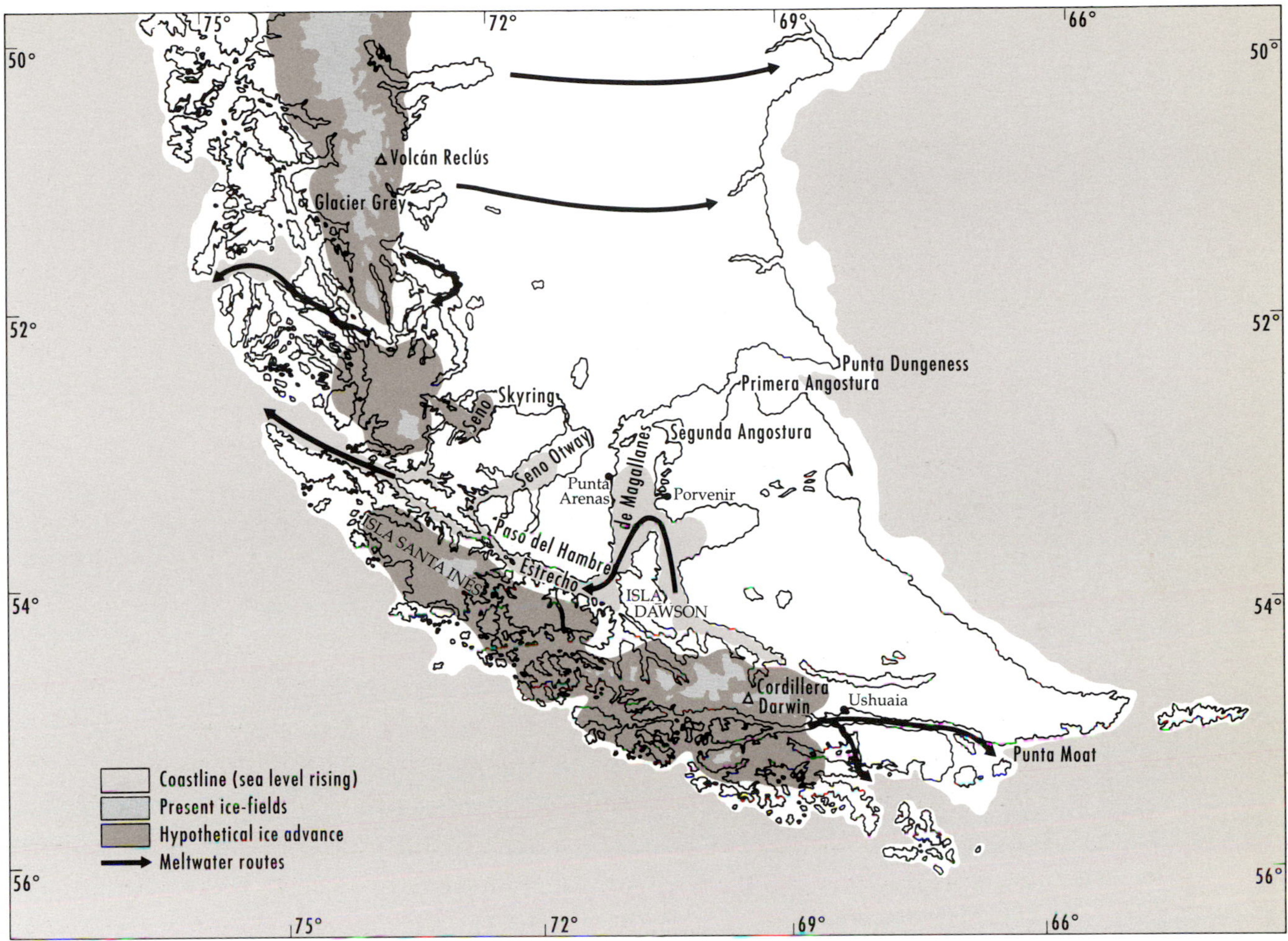

Fig 14 Holocene glacial retreat between *c.* 10,000–8,000 BP.

dry climate experienced at that time. A detailed discussion of the interpretation and implication of charcoal evidence as an indicator of human activity has been made by Heusser,[35] Salemme[36] and Borrero.[37]

The Estrecho de Magallanes was probably a fully fledged marine waterway around 8,000 BP, as the final dissolution of the great ice-sheets in the northern hemisphere returned all their stored water to the oceans. Sea level continued to rise into the mid-Holocene and by *c.* 6,000–5,000 BP it had reached 4–7 m above present-day sea level in Estrecho de Magallanes[38] and Canal Beagle, leading to the inundation of low-lying embayments in the region (fig. 15).[39] After *c.* 5,000 BP sea level fell relative to the land and the inundated areas became dry land again. This produced features such as abandoned shingle ridges and raised beaches 4–8 m above modern-day sea level.

During the late Holocene the eastern forest boundary appears to have withdrawn tens of kilometres westward due to a reduction in effective moisture levels in eastern Fuego-Patagonia. However, within the forest zone the vegetation density and composition appears to be consistent, until the appearance of European settlers and the rapid deforestation along the eastern forest boundary during this century.

Fig 15 View along the Canal Beagle.

Late Pleistocene fauna

Knowledge of the history of Pleistocene vertebrates in Fuego-Patagonia is very limited. The data currently available come from a number of sites. The best known is Cueva del Milodon close to Seno Ultima Esperanza near Puerto Natales.[40] The deposits flooring this huge cave have yielded a late Pleistocene mammalian fauna comprising a medium-sized ground sloth (*Mylodon darwinii*) some three metres long, a native neotropical horse (*Onohippidium saldiasi)*, a large mammal the size of a horse that was endemic to South America (*Macrauchenia* sp.), at least two different camelids and a large cat (*Panthera* sp.) (fig. 16). All of these are now extinct. In addition, there is evidence of guanaco and a variety of birds and rodents which have survived until the present day. Thick deposits of dried dung in the cave provide very tangible evidence that the site was extensively used by ground sloths. Radiocarbon age determinations on samples of exceptionally well-preserved sloth skin and pieces of dung suggest that the sloths were using the cave in the interval between about 13,500 to 10,000 BP.[41]

More recent research has identified *Lama (Vicugna) gracilis* at Los Toldos and Piedra Museo[42] and *Smilodon* sp. at Cueva Lago Sofía 4 (see chapter 2).[43] An association between elements of late Pleistocene fauna and humans is recorded at several sites,

Fig 16 Artist's reconstruction of the landscape around Cueva del Milodon, Puerto Consuelo, Ultima Esperanza, Chile, c. 12,000 BP.

most importantly at Cueva del Medio,[44] Cueva Fell,[45] Piedra Museo,[46] Cueva Lago Sofía 1[47] and Tres Arroyos.[48] The latter is especially significant in showing the presence of these animals on what is today the island of Tierra del Fuego.

This relatively low species diversity assemblage contrasts markedly with the great diversity seen in contemporaneous mammal faunas of comparable high latitudes in the northern hemisphere. The Fuego-Patagonian land mass was probably too small an area to have supported a native high latitude mammal fauna with specific adaptations to periglacial conditions like that found in North America, Asia and Europe. Instead, during the colder phases of the Pleistocene, the region was populated by a small group of hardy generalists, possibly those with a greater tolerance of arid conditions. These presumably originated in the highly integrated and much more diverse megafaunal communities of lands further north. Mammalian distribution is not limited by temperature alone, however, as all mammals are quite efficient homeotherms (warm-blooded). Two of the herbivores, the ground sloth and the native horse, could survive on vegetation of low nutritional value, providing there was plenty of it. Like the modern lion, the large cat might well have been a specialist hunter of the horse, and finds from several sites indicate that it also took young sloth as part of its prey.[49] An adult ground sloth with its thick skin armed with bony nodules and its large, powerful claws is unlikely to have had any natural predators, although the young would certainly have been more vulnerable, particularly when humans arrived on the scene.

The ground sloths show no particular anatomical adaptation to extremes of climate other than the fact that they were rather hairy. However, the survival of almost perfectly preserved pieces of freeze-dried skin and other soft tissues tells us quite a lot about prevailing conditions. Recent study of the DNA content of this material[50] has shown remarkably good preservation of quite long base pair sequences, sufficient to be able to comment on the relationship of the ground sloths to their living cousins, the tree sloths. While the details of this do not concern us here, the very fact that long fragments of DNA survive at this site and nowhere else is of some interest. It suggests that at the time of the death of these animals the prevailing temperatures were sufficiently low (i.e. well below freezing) and the atmosphere dry enough to prevent any significant decomposition, oxidation or bacterial activity. These conditions evidently lasted for a prolonged enough period for the organic materials to become thoroughly desiccated. This fits in rather well with evidence for periglacial conditions during the period of *Mylodon* occupation which has been derived from other sources.

The causes behind the sudden disappearance of this late Pleistocene community and its replacement by a Holocene fauna dominated by native camelids, rodents and small carnivores is currently a topic for much debate. Although the changes in environments recorded worldwide at the Pleistocene/Holocene boundary are dramatic, they are not unique and the Pleistocene megafauna had survived numerous similar changes without mass extinction. The exact nature of the interaction between early human populations in South America and the Pleistocene megafauna may never be known, but there has to be some significance to the approximate coincidence between the arrival of humans and the loss of so many large mammals. Whether they were exterminated directly by hunting pressure or indirectly by destruction of their environment, it seems unlikely in the extreme that the arriving humans played no part at all in this major process of faunal change.

NOTES

1 Three principal time divisions on the geological time-scale are referred to in this volume. The Pleistocene lasted for approximately 1.6 million years. The last 130,000 years of this period are conventionally described as the late Pleistocene and the term Holocene is ascribed to the period from 10,000 BP to the present. All ages presented here are given as radiocarbon years, uncalibrated to the tree-ring or coral records, before present (BP). However, present is taken to be 1950, before atomic weapons research affected the measurement of radiocarbon activity.

2 Pisano Valdes 1977; Moore 1983.

3 Pisano Valdes 1977.

4 Mercer 1976.

5 Singer *et al.* 1997.

6 Rabassa and Clapperton 1990; Porter *et al.* 1992; Meglioli 1992; Rabassa *et al.* 1992.

7 Clapperton *et al.* 1995.

8 Clapperton 1989.

9 Rabassa *et al.* 1992.

10 Lowell *et al.* 1995.

11 Ibid.

12 Clapperton *et al.* 1995; McCulloch and Bentley 1997.

13 Rabassa *et al.* 1992.

14 Fairbanks 1989.

15 Ibid.

16 Heusser 1989.

17 Mercer 1976.

18 McCulloch 1994.

19 The correct collective term for all igneous rock material thrown up into the atmosphere – from large volcanic bombs and pumice to fine dust particles – is tephra. Ash is strictly a carbon deposit produced as a result of fire.

20 Marden 1997.

21 McCulloch and Bentley 1997.

22 Islebe *et al.* 1995; Thompson *et al.* 1995; van der Hammen and Hooghiemstra 1995; Roig *et al.* 1995; Clapperton *et al.* 1997.

23 McCulloch and Bentley 1997.

24 Clapperton 1992.

25 Moore *et al.* 1991.

26 Heusser 1984; Porter *et al.* 1984; McCulloch 1994.

27 McCulloch 1994.

28 Heusser 1989a; Markgraf 1993.

29 Heusser 1989b.

30 Rabassa *et al.* 1986; McCulloch and Bentley 1997.

31 Coronato *et al.* 1997.

32 Heusser 1987, 1995; Markgraf 1993; McCulloch 1994.

33 Heusser 1990; Markgraf 1993.

34 McCulloch 1994.

35 Heusser 1994.

36 Salemme *et al.* 1995, 1996.

37 Borrero 1997b.

38 The timing of the relative sea level rise at *c.* 6,000–5,000 BP in the Estrecho de Magallanes and the Canal Beagle is applicable to all coastal areas that are distal to the central dome of the Cordillera Darwin ice-fields and those centred to the west of Fuego-Patagonia. The authors are aware that sites close to the ice-fields would have been isostatically depressed by some metres (the land surface being pushed downwards under the weight of the ice-fields). After the large glacier lobes had retreated there was a lag of several thousands of years before the land surface recovered its former altitude. Therefore, sites at a similar altitude and proximity to the ice, such as at Puerto Hambre, were significantly lower during the Holocene, when relative sea level was rising, and so the sites were inundated by the sea *c.* 2,000 years earlier than sites further away from the ice-fields. By about 6,000 BP the land surface had isostatically recovered. Therefore, the raised beaches within Fuego-Patagonia, which were caused by a relative sea level lowering, are virtually horizontal. A further complication to the relative sea level chronology is that many areas, mainly south of the strike-slip faulting between the earth's crustal plate boundaries in the Estrecho de Magallanes-Canal Beagle area, have experienced substantial vertical movement, in the order of metres, due to earthquakes along active faults. Nevertheless, it is interesting that the Holocene beach on both sides of Estrecho de Magallanes and on Isla Dawson is horizontal and at the same altitude.

39 Porter *et al.* 1984; Rabassa *et al.* 1986; Morner 1991; Gordillo *et al.* 1992, 1993; Clapperton *et al.* 1995.

40 Nordenskiöld 1900.

41 Borrero *et al.* 1991.

42 Miotti 1993a; Miotti and Salemme 1997.

43 Canto 1991.

44 Nami and Menegaz 1991.

45 Bird 1988.

46 Miotti 1993b.

47 Prieto 1991.

48 Massone 1987b.

49 Borrero 1997b.

50 Höss *et al.* 1996.

2 The Peopling of Patagonia
The First Human Occupation

Luis Alberto Borrero and Colin McEwan

The process of peopling: migration or dispersion?

Fig 17 Principal archaeological sites in Patagonia.

The human colonisation of the uttermost extremity of the Americas has always held a particular fascination for prehistorians. Viewed from a global perspective, this was the last major continental land mass to be settled by human beings. The earliest occupation of Patagonia carries obvious implications for understanding when and how North and South America were peopled. It gives a baseline against which all interpretations of the timing of man's entry into the Americas must be compared, and which all calculations concerning the rate of dispersion of humans throughout both continents must take into account (fig. 17).

For many years the colonisation of the Americas was conceived of as a wave-like succession of migrations, each characterised by distinct cultural traits.[1] Although this idea was quite widely and uncritically accepted by many, for others it appeared to be an over-simplified model. At the root of the arguments lay a fundamental disagreement concerning the time depth involved. Some scholars accepted a human presence in the Americas as early as 20,000 BP (the late Pleistocene),[2] while others proposed that this could date no earlier than 10,000–8,000 BP at most (the Holocene).[3] The debate is still with us today, since archaeologists remain broadly divided between those supporting estimates of at least 40,000 BP for man's initial entry across the Bering Straits into North America,[4] and those who limit this to a temporal rubicon around 11,500 BP.[5]

The idea of a relatively late colonisation of the Americas implies that a correspondingly rapid process of migration took place spanning both continents. The time-scale proposed for this amounts to two thousand years at most. Herein lies a second debate which revolves around the question of how migration is to be understood.[6] The 'late' model demands a hypothetical migration conceived of as a continually advancing 'wave' of colonisation. In its extreme form this hypothesis proposes that people almost literally marched south to people the length and breadth of North and South America.[7] This has always been difficult to take seriously. Waves of migratory peoples are no longer accepted as a valid explanation for the history of the dispersion of anatomically modern humans across the globe. No compelling need is apparent to drive such a

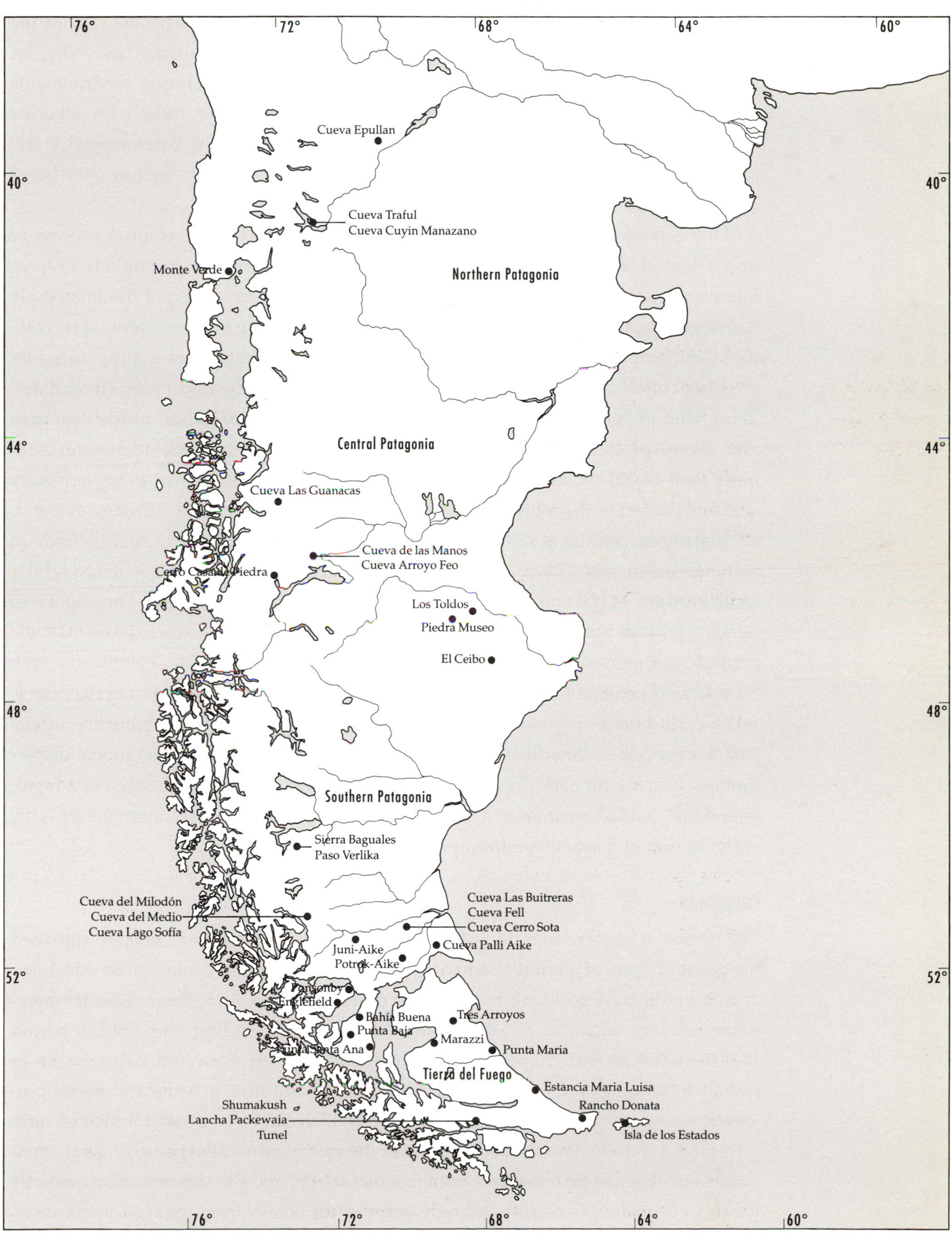

76°
72°
68°
64°
60°
40°
44°
48°
52°
Cueva Epullan
Cueva Traful
Cueva Cuyin Manazano
Monte Verde
Northern Patagonia
Central Patagonia
Cueva Las Guanacas
Cueva de las Manos
Cueva Arroyo Feo
Cerro Casa de Piedra
Los Toldos
Piedra Museo
El Ceibo
Southern Patagonia
Sierra Baguales
Paso Verlika
Cueva del Milodón
Cueva del Medio
Cueva Lago Sofía
Cueva Las Buitreras
Cueva Fell
Cueva Cerro Sota
Cueva Palli Aike
Juni-Aike
Potrok-Aike
Ponsonby
Englefield
Bahía Buena
Punta Baja
Punta Santa Ana
Tres Arroyos
Marazzi
Punta Maria
Tierra del Fuego
Estancia Maria Luisa
Rancho Donata
Isla de los Estados
Shumakush
Lancha Packewaia
Tunel

migration, nor is there any real supporting evidence.[8] In the particular case of the Americas the idea of a 'migratory wave' is charged with inconsistencies. Why, for example, should traits be 'adaptive' in the face of widely differing environments encountered as human populations proceeded south? Moreover, those who advocate the model of recent peopling must confront the evidence of many dates around 11,000 BP for the first human occupation far to the south in Patagonia, as well as elsewhere.[9] These data argue strongly for an initial entry well before 11,500 BP.

Many scholars now support the idea of an earlier and more gradual process of dispersion. However long it took, the peopling of the continent is unlikely to have followed a uniform north to south progression. Human occupation of the immensely varied geography of South America surely proceeded at very different rates, as successful adaptations enabled man to colonise contrasting habitats. This is suppported by the distribution of sites and the temporal span of their associated radiocarbon dates. Those who argue for an earlier and protracted human colonisation of the Americas also face a problem, however, namely the lack of unequivocal evidence for sites older than 14,000–13,000 BP. Much of the data from what are claimed to be very early sites is regarded with ambivalence, if not outright scepticism.[10] Nevertheless, evidence for human occupation is now securely dated to around 12,500 BP at Monte Verde in Llanquihue Province, South-Central Chile.[11] The lack of archaeological evidence further south between 14,000 and 12,000 BP may be explained by the formidable impediment to humans on foot posed by the huge meltwater streams draining towards the Atlantic around this time (see chapter 1).

In its most extreme form the migration theory is untenable. In addressing the dispersal of early human populations throughout the Americas the most plausible model entails a process of slow filling of empty spaces by means of inter-generational dispersion associated with band fission. This obviates the need to invoke the idea of a rapid, intentional displacement toward the south, yet at the same time a southern vector is the natural result of dispersion into empty space.[12]

Patagonia

The retreat of glaciers from their late Pleistocene limits in around 14,000 BP signalled the gradual onset of a milder climatic regime in northern Patagonia. There was, however, a gradient of declining temperature down to Fuego-Patagonia where temperatures were as much as 3°–6°C colder than present during the critical period 13,000–10,000 BP (see chapter 1). An expanded range of flora and fauna began to spread south, followed by the initial human intrusion into a pristine and uncompromising environment with dry, cold conditions which can be compared to that of early post-glacial Europe. Human colonisation of the vast horizontal expanse of nearly continuous treeless steppe must have been tenuous at best, and the archaeological evidence for this occupation is correspondingly scant. Most comes from excavations in caves and rock shelters in Santa Cruz Province, Argentina and Magallanes Province, Chile (fig. 18). There is unequivocal evidence to support the presence of humans by around 11,000–10,000 BP in different habitats, and some hints of an even older occupation.

However, some of the best-known sites where evidence for the earliest human occupation was originally posited, such as Cueva Fell, Palli Aike and Cerro Sota, have recently come under fresh scrutiny and re-evaluation. This is because archaeologists have come to recognise that bones may be deposited in caves by natural agency, especially by predators bringing back parts of their prey. Where human beings are thought to be responsible for the deposition of faunal remains a secure association between human activities and the faunal material must be established. The most recent excavations at cave sites mainly in southern Patagonia (particularly in the Ultima Esperanza area) confirm beyond doubt human occupation by around 11,000 BP.[13] Further supporting evidence also comes from sites south of the Estrecho de Magallanes, such as Tres Arroyos on Tierra del Fuego.[14] Information for northern Patagonia is limited to just a couple of sites and the general lack of archaeological data in the intermediate area between northern and southern Patagonia may be explained simply as the result of lack of field research.

Fig 18 The site of Cueva Lago Sofía. Excavations of the lower levels have revealed some of the earliest evidence for human settlement in Patagonia.

Fig 19 A group of guanaco (*Lama guanicoe*) at Torres del Paine, Chile.

Since the arrival of human beings in Patagonia represented an entirely new element in the ecosystem, the capacity of the colonising hunting and gathering bands to cope with the exigencies of both climate and landscape assumes special interest. In addition

Fig 20 Sea lions (*Otaria flavenscens* and *Arctocephalus australis*) on a rocky promontory in the Canal Beagle.

to the inventory of tools, the associated faunal assemblages excavated at the different archaeological sites will be described. The associations of cultural materials with faunal remains from mammals such as guanaco (fig. 19) and sea lion (fig. 20) provide vital clues to understanding the means of human survival and adaptation.

Archaeological evidence from northern Patagonia

In the Chilean Lakes Region of the western Andes, Monte Verde is an open-air wetland residential site, located beside Chinchihuapi Creek. Excavations have produced convincing evidence for human occupation, with hut foundations, wooden artefacts and ecological evidence preserved under a peat layer dating to around 12,500 years BP. Lithic artefacts include large bifaces made of exotic basalt and quartzite, as well as what archaeologist Tom Dillehay calls 'selectively collected unfractured stones utilized as

grinding stones (...), projectiles (...) and hammerstones'.[15] These were found in close proximity to the hut foundations and shallow clay-lined pits. Abundant vegetal remains have been identified at the site.[16] Among the most important faunal remains are mastodon (*Cuvieronius sensu casamiquela*) and camelid (*Palaeolama*).[17]

In reviewing the evidence for the earliest human settlement east of the Andes the archaeological data is conveniently dealt with following the hydrographic basins of the major rivers draining west-east across the steppe. Evidence from northern Patagonia comes from three caves in the Limay Basin, two in close proximity to the Andean Cordillera and the other on the steppe. Cueva Traful is situated on the right bank of the Río Traful near its confluence with the Río Limay.[18] The initial occupations are dated around 9,400 and 9,200 BP and well-defined hearths are present. Lithic artefacts are associated with canid, guanaco, rodent and bird remains, although it is not yet clear what precisely is the product of human exploitation. The initial occupations at Cueva Cuyin Manzano, a site located near a small tributary of the Río Traful, are dated to 9,300 BP. End-scrapers are common in the earliest deposits of the cave, together with a few guanaco remains.[19]

Cueva Epullan is located in the steppe on the left bank of the Río Limay.[20] The initial occupations are dated between 9,900 and 7,500 BP and include lithic artefacts made of obsidian and basalt, a hearth and four human burials. Guanaco remains are abundant, together with the presence of small carnivores, small edentates (herbivores with poorly developed dentition) and flightless birds. The lowest deposits of this cave overlie basal rock that bears incisions which the excavators tentatively attribute to human activities. If this proves to be the case, then the incisions must date to at least 9,900 BP.

Archaeological evidence from southern Patagonia

In the Middle Deseado Basin, one of the most famous Patagonian sites, a cave known as Los Toldos 3 is located in the Cañadón de las Cuevas, south of the Río Deseado. It has been cited often as evidence for a very early occupation on the basis of a 12,600 BP radiocarbon date from its lowest level.[21] This has been called into question, however, because dispersed flecks of carbon were used to obtain the dates, and the association of this material with the artefacts is not at all clear. Until this date can be confirmed it should be regarded with caution. The strata contain the remains of extinct horse (*Onohippidium* [*Parahipparion*] *saldiasi*), an extinct camelid (*Lama* [*Vicugna*] *gracilis*) and guanaco (*Lama guanicoe*), in association with unifacial marginally retouched artefacts,[22] most of which are side-scrapers.[23] Above, within a context dated to 8,700 BP, the association of horse, guanaco and retouched tools is repeated. However, there are doubts as to whether the date can safely be applied to all the material in the deposit. In the upper strata *Rhea* sp. and triangular projectile points are also present. Other sites in the vicinity have produced finds that may have comparable antiquity of around 10,000 BP.[24]

Fig 21 Images of 'negative hands' painted on the wall of the rock shelter Cueva de las Manos, Río Pinturas, Argentina.

El Ceibo 7 lies about 150 km south of Los Toldos, in the central plateau. A similar assemblage to that found at the base of Los Toldos has been recovered from the lowest levels of this site, but no radiocarbon dates are available. Bones of horse, extinct camelid, puma (*Felis concolor*) and probably guanaco are associated.[25]

The site of Piedra Museo is located in the lower plateau south of the Río Deseado. Here a bifacial tool fragment within the formal range of the Cueva Fell projectile points has been excavated. This is associated with both end-scrapers and side-scrapers, as well as with guanaco, horse, extinct camelid and flightless birds (*Pterocnemia pennata* and *Rhea americana*).[26] One radiocarbon date on camelid bone dates the deposit to 10,400 BP.[27]

In the upper part of the Deseado Basin the site of Cueva de las Manos is found at the base of a stepped cliff overlooking the Río Pinturas. This site is world-famous for its beautiful wall paintings (fig. 21), bearing among other images the negatives of hundreds of hands. An association of slabs with paintings and radiocarbon-dated deposits suggest that people were painting the walls of the cave by around 8,000 BP (see chapter 3). There is evidence for previous use of the cave around 9,300 BP. Triangular projectile points, a bola stone and bones of extant fauna, mainly guanaco but also including puma, fox (*Pseudalopex culpaeus*) and birds, have all been recovered.[28]

The Arroyo Feo site is located in a narrow ravine, very close to the high plateaux, a location that may have been favoured because of its easy access to the guanaco's favoured habitat. The artefacts from the earliest occupations display many similarities with those from the lowest deposits at Los Toldos and El Ceibo and include side-scrapers and other tools probably used for processing guanaco.[29] The assemblage is securely dated to between 9,400 and 8,400 BP.[30]

Near the middle course of the Río Gallegos the site of Las Buitreras is found in a basalt south-facing cliff. An assemblage of stone flakes deposited in association with the remains of *Mylodon listai* and guanaco have been excavated from the lowest levels. The guanaco is only represented by splinters and small fragments. Mandibular bones of an extinct fox (*Dusicyon avus*) and two horse molars have also been found.[31] There is nothing to suggest that horse or fox are directly related to human subsistence at Las Buitreras. Even the case for the exploitation of ground sloth is not as strong as originally supposed. Presumed cut marks on the bone are somewhat dubious and there is no way of securely relating the ground sloth bones with the human occupation. No radiocarbon dates are available. An archaeological context well above the levels bearing megafaunal remains is dated to 7,600 BP.[32]

Cueva Fell is a site located on the right bank of the Río Chico (fig. 22), some 50 km south of Las Buitreras. This was the first site to be systematically studied by modern archaeological methods in Patagonia, and its excavation by Junius Bird in the 1930s represents a landmark in the history of Patagonian archaeology.[33] Bird defined a now

Fig 22 View of Cueva Fell during excavations there by Junius Bird in 1969–70.

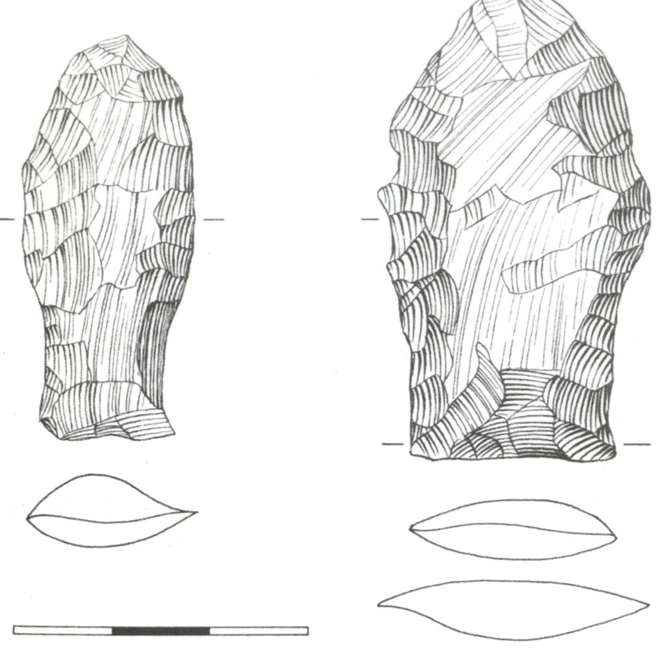

Fig 23 'Fishtail' projectile points from level I, Cueva Fell.

classic sequence, in which he divided the site's history of occupation into five principal periods. These periods are often still used uncritically by researchers, although in many respects the scheme he devised has outlived its usefulness. Bird's periodisation was based on typological classification of artefacts derived mainly from sites in the vicinity of Palli Aike where Cueva Fell is located. It is now recognised that the utility of his scheme is restricted to this localised area and cannot be freely extrapolated further afield.

The lower deposits of Cueva Fell have revealed an association between cultural artefacts and ground sloth, horse, guanaco and bird bones.[34] The artefacts include the well-known 'fishtail' projectile points or, more accurately, Cueva Fell points (fig. 23).[35] These points are abundant, suggesting that the intensity of activity and/or the frequency of repeated occupations at Cueva Fell was far greater than that recorded at other early sites. Nevertheless, it is very unlikely that humans alone contributed to the formation of the deposits. A recent study of the bones deposited at the American Museum of Natural History (AMNH), New York, revealed cut marks on horse bones, but also carnivore-inflicted punctures on horse, *Lama* sp. and ground sloth bones (fig. 24).[36] In addition, a high percentage of hawks, falcons and terrestrial carnivores indicates that some of the deposits at Cueva

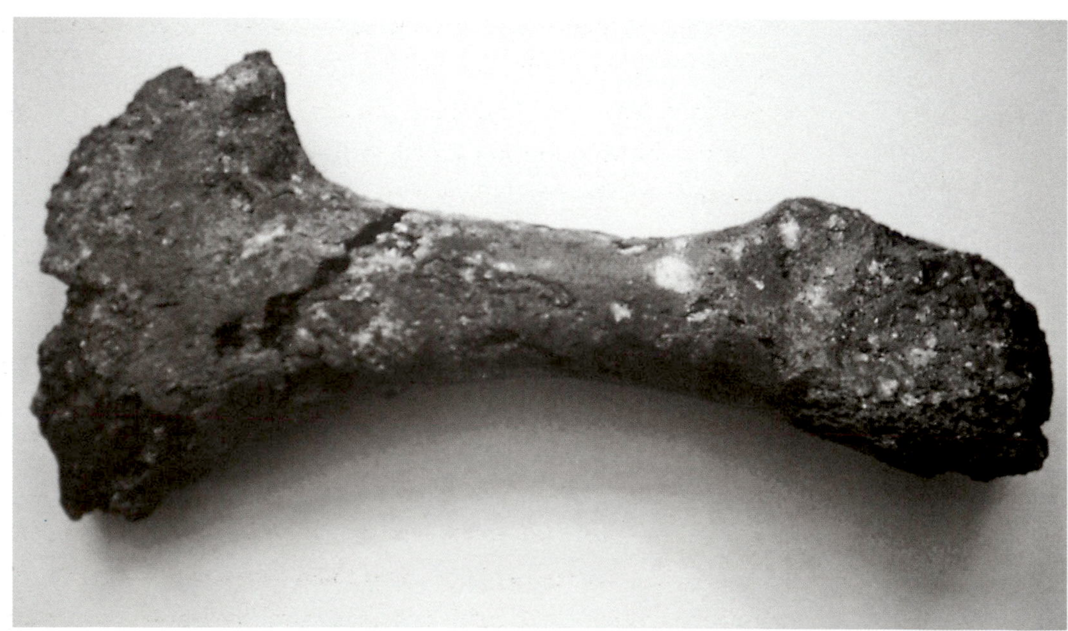

Fig 24 Mineralised fossil horse bone from the lower levels of Cueva Fell showing puncture marks made by a large carnivorous predator, probably an extinct panther.

Fell may be attributed to the activities of these predators rather than exclusively human activity. While the evidence for human occupation at Cueva Fell is clear, it is probably unwise to infer that all the faunal material found in the cave is the result of human action.[37]

Palli Aike is a cave site located within the caldera of an extinct volcano. Some human bones have been found in the cave, as well as many artefacts. The remains of at least seven ground sloths as well as horse bones were recovered at the base of the deposit, which Junius Bird completely removed in the 1930s.[38] There is therefore nothing left for other archaeologists to compare and evaluate his interpretations. A single radiocarbon reading of 8,600 BP should be considered as a minimum age. The sample comprised fragments of sloth, horse and guanaco bones recovered both above as well as within a layer of volcanic ash, so it is not at all clear what in fact has been dated.[39] Studies of the collections from this site at the AMNH have identified trampling marks on the ground sloth bones. Most of the bones seem to form almost complete animals rather than having been dragged in piecemeal by predators. Nevertheless, the presence of cultural artefacts indicates that human agency may have played some role in the formation of the deposit, difficult though it is at present to specify the scope or duration of such activity.

The importance of separating human from natural agency at sites in the Río Chico Basin is highlighted by the case of Cerro Sota. This cave was originally thought by Bird to be an early site in which twelve individuals were buried in association with guanaco, ground sloth and horse. Horse hair from *Onohippidium saldiasi* has been identified[40] and this has been taken to indicate a late Pleistocene date.[41] More recent redating of the human bones indicates, however, that they are only in the order of 3,900 BP.[42] It is quite clear then that in many cases the mere physical proximity of cultural artefacts to megafaunal remains does not necessarily mean that the two are contemporaneous. This further serves to emphasise the hazards of relying on unexamined assumptions to make speculative inferences about human adaptive strategies.

Cueva del Milodon is located in the Cerro Benitez area, not far from Seno Ultima Esperanza on the Pacific coast (fig. 25). Finds within the cave of the dung, hide and bones of the extinct ground sloth have made this site world-famous. The deposits are dated between 13,500 and 10,500 BP.[43] Cueva del Milodon has long been accepted as a setting in which humans and ground sloth interacted, but new evidence precludes this interpretation.[44] No evidence of cut marks have yet been found on sloth bones, neither have artefacts been recovered in clear and unequivocal association with sloth. The earliest cultural deposit in the cave is dated to around 8,000 BP, and this is firmly associated with guanaco bones.

The site of Cueva del Medio, located one kilometre from Cueva del Milodon has established a clear association between human artefacts and hearths with ground sloth, horse and guanaco bones. A total of fourteen radiocarbon dates range between 12,300 and

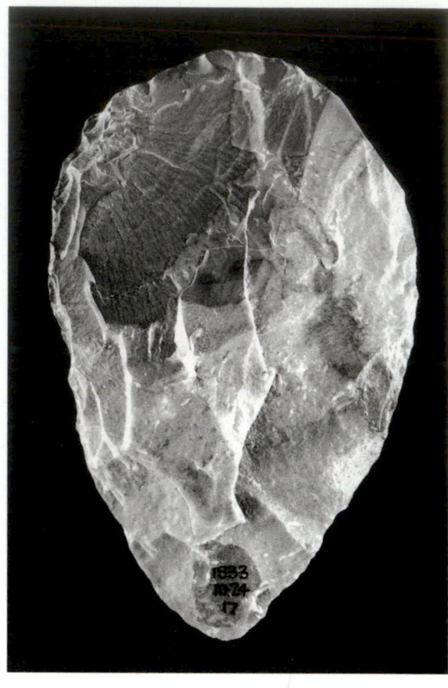

Fig 25 *above left* View from within Cueva del Milodon, southern Chile, Patagonia. The mouth of this great cavern is some 30 m high.

Fig 26 *above right* Later example of a bifacial tool from Bahía Gregory, Estrecho de Magallanes, Tierra del Fuego. Length 11.7 cm.

9,500 BP.[45] A cautionary note is that a single date of 12,300 BP from a hearth has later been repeatedly dated to around 10,500 BP, leading the investigators to reject the older date. Artefacts include Cueva Fell projectile points, end-scrapers, knives and side-scrapers.[46]

Some five kilometres from Cueva del Medio and Cueva del Milodon the site of Cueva Lago Sofía 1 also contains hearths and artefacts, mainly side-scrapers, one knife and one bifacial artefact (for a comparable but probably later example see fig. 26).[47] Faunal remains include guanaco, horse and ground sloth dating to around 11,000 BP.

Archaeological evidence from Tierra del Fuego

Two key sites underpin our present understanding of the very earliest human attempts to colonise Tierra del Fuego. The site of Marazzi, lying in the lee of a huge erratic boulder not far from the Estrecho de Magallanes, was excavated by a French team in the 1950s.[48] A single radiocarbon assay of 9,500 BP is available, dating an array of predominantly unifacial tools and guanaco bones.

The site of Tres Arroyos, a small cave located some 20 km inland from the Atlantic coast, is radiocarbon-dated to between 11,800 and 10,200 BP by three samples. One bifacially retouched fragment of a tool and a number of marginally retouched tools have been found together with guanaco and horse bones.[49] An extinct fox (*Canis* [*Dusicyon*] *avus*) is present and ground sloth ossicles have also been recovered.[50]

On the basis of the faunal remains recovered from these and other sites on Tierra del Fuego certain species exploited by early populations north of the Estrecho de Magallanes appear to be absent. These include ñandú (*Pterocnemia pennata*), huemul (*Hippocamelus bisulcus*), puma (*Felis concolor*) and zorro gris (*Pseudalopex griseus*). As things stand, we are not able to say with certainty whether or not any of these species were ever present on Tierra del Fuego. Even supposing some of them were on the island we do not yet know whether or not they were hunted, and if they were, whether they were hunted to extinction.

The extinction of the megafauna

The timing and possible causes of the extinction of the late Pleistocene megafauna has long been a central issue in Patagonian archaeology. Based on uncritical use of radiocarbon dates derived from deposits that contain the bones of Pleistocene megafauna, it has been suggested that horse and an extinct camelid (*Lama* [*Vicugna*] *gracilis*) survived up to the early Holocene[51] and that ground sloth[52] and other species[53] survived up to mid-Holocene times (see fig. 16).

These suggestions are now difficult to accept. Archaeologists have come to recognise that site formation processes must be taken into account before purported associations between megafauna and radiocarbon dates can be given credence.[54] Only where the bones of megafauna are dated directly can we have any confidence in the results. The admixture that can occur long after the initial deposition of faunal material in a cave inevitably renders indirect dating of associated materials suspect.

At present, acceptable chronological evidence for the extinction of megafauna is mostly restricted to ground sloth, with only scanty evidence for horse or mastodon. This reassessment casts serious doubt on what has long been the accepted sequence of extinctions.[55] The fact is that the final date of extinction for most Pleistocene species in Fuego-Patagonia is as yet unknown. Considering that the literature is full of references to the Holocene survival of different taxa, especially horse,[56] a fundamental conceptual reorganisation of the data is called for.

It is ironic that the most widely cited evidence for Holocene survival of megafauna concerns the ground sloth,[57] which in fact is the only taxa for which a number of direct dates support a late Pleistocene extinction. The dates of disappearance for most of the rest of the taxa are poorly known. For example, it has been claimed that horse is present in a deposit dated 8,700 BP at Los Toldos in the Middle Deseado Basin, but here again it is the deposit that has been dated, not the bone. The available evidence does not constitute proof for the presence of horses during the early Holocene in the Deseado Basin.[58] Horse and *Lama gracilis*, together with guanaco, are present in the older levels of sites in the Middle Deseado Basin and central plateau, including Los Toldos, but again the distinction between the strata and the faunal remains found in them is not always clear and some admixture might explain the apparent presence of the horse bone in the Holocene deposit.

The evidence from the Ultima Esperanza region and elsewhere indicates that extinctions occurred over a longer period than is usually accepted during the Pleistocene-Holocene transition (around 10,000 BP). Mastodon and panther (*Panthera* [*onca*] *mesembrina*) probably disappeared by 12,000 BP, while other species are still well represented somewhat later. Foxes (*Dusicyon avus*), which are now extinct, may have survived until the late Holocene.

The longer time-scale proposed for megafaunal extinctions in Fuego-Patagonia implies that more than one causal factor was entailed and that this is far from being a single 'event'. An oversimplified model that divides ecosystems into those with and those without Pleistocene megafauna is no longer tenable.[59]

Conclusions

Until a few years ago the supposed associations of cultural artefacts and faunal remains excavated at Los Toldos and Cueva Fell were usually cited as the best proof for the initial human colonisation of Patagonia. However, as the discussion above has made clear, long-standing interpretations must now be critically re-evaluated.

The initial dispersion of human populations into Patagonia around 11,000 BP is nevertheless firmly established at other sites. An even earlier presence is not out of the question, as the evidence from Monte Verde makes clear, but in southern Patagonia this has yet to be demonstrated unequivocally.

There are important differences in the range of faunal remains recovered from various sites in Fuego-Patagonia. In the Upper Deseado Basin only evidence for guanaco has been found. This contrasts with territory south of the central plateau, for the ground sloth is present at all the older sites in Río Gallegos, Río Chico, Ultima Esperanza and on Tierra del Fuego. However, the sloth has not been reported in archaeological assemblages north of the Santa Cruz Basin, except at Piedra Museo.[60] There are indications of hunting or scavenging of the animal at Cueva del Medio and Lago Sofía, although clear evidence of this is elusive. The main prey is usually guanaco, while the importance of fossil horse has yet to be determined.

Insofar as the stone tools and weapons are concerned there are many similarities between the earlier assemblages.[61] Most tools are opportunistically made from locally available rocks. No significant changes in the proportions of different classes of artefacts are indicated for the earlier periods.[62] Cueva Fell projectile points appear to be slightly older than the triangular forms, but their presence is not easily linked to the type of prey that was hunted.

Guanaco hunting using bifacial weapons provided the mainstay of the earliest human adaptation to Patagonia. More remote areas such as the Upper Deseado Basin were probably explored rather later and this may explain the almost exclusive reliance on guanaco. There are hints of opportunistic exploitation of the megafauna, but this is very likely to have been a swiftly dwindling resource.

Recent research now shows that crossing to Tierra del Fuego was possible at different times during a broad period spanning the late Pleistocene to early Holocene transition (14,000–8,000 BP) (see chapter 1). Climatic conditions in Fuego-Patagonia for the earlier part of this period were harsh, with temperatures perhaps 3°–6°C colder than today.

Despite a demanding physical environment the first bands of hunter-gatherers made their way by land onto the northern part of Isla Grande de Tierra del Fuego around 11,000 BP. From about 8,000 BP onwards the straits were progressively inundated and the island populations would have been isolated until a canoe technology developed sufficiently to permit navigation of the inland waterways (see chapters 3 and 4).

NOTES

1 Menghin 1952; Palavecino 1971.
2 Menghin 1952; Cigliano 1962; Schobinger 1969.
3 Imbelloni 1947.
4 Bryan 1978; Schobinger 1987; Meltzer *et al.* 1994; Parenti *et al.* 1996; Guidon *et al.* 1996.
5 Haynes 1969, 1987; Guidon *et al.* 1996.
6 Clark 1994.
7 Martin 1973.
8 Gamble 1994.
9 Borrero 1996; Dillehay *et al.* 1992.
10 Lynch 1990.
11 Dillehay 1989, 1997.
12 Borrero 1989b.
13 Nami 1987; Prieto 1991.
14 Massone 1987.
15 Dillehay 1989: 15.
16 Ramirez 1989.
17 Casamiquela and Dillehay 1989.
18 Crivelli *et al.* 1993.
19 Ceballos 1982.
20 Crivelli *et al.* 1996.
21 Cardich *et al.* 1973.
22 Cardich and Miotti 1983.
23 Cardich and Flegenheimer 1978.
24 Menghin 1952; Cardich *et al.* 1993/94.
25 Cardich *et al.* 1981/82: 173–209.
26 Miotti 1992.
27 Miotti 1993a, 1996; an as yet unpublished date of 12,890 BP is also reported from this site: L. Miotti, pers. comm. to J. Rabassa, 1997.
28 Gradin *et al.* 1976, 1979.
29 Gradin *et al.* 1987: 122.
30 Gradin *et al.* 1979; Silveira 1979; Aguerre 1981/82; Alonso *et al.* 1984.
31 Caviglia 1976.
32 Sanguinetti 1976.
33 Bird 1988.
34 Humphrey *et al.* 1993.
35 Bird 1969; Mayer Oakes 1986.
36 Borrero and Martin 1996.
37 Saxon 1979.
38 Bird 1938.
39 Bird 1988: 107.
40 By Whitford (Bird 1988: 209).
41 Turner 1992; Soto Heim 1994.
42 Hedges *et al.* 1992.
43 Borrero *et al.* 1988.
44 Borrero *et al.* 1991.
45 Nami and Nakamura 1995.
46 Nami 1987; Nami and Menegaz 1991.
47 Prieto 1991.
48 Laming-Emperaire *et al.* 1972.
49 Jackson 1987; Massone 1987; Mengoni Goñalons 1987.
50 Prieto, pers. comm.
51 Saxon 1976; Borrero 1977.
52 Ochsenius 1985b.
53 Cardich *et al.* 1973; Miotti 1993b.
54 Schiffer 1987.
55 Graham and Lundelius 1984; Lundelius 1989.
56 E.g. Alberdi and Prado 1992: 278; Menegaz *et al.* 1990: 156.
57 Borrero 1977; Saxon 1976, 1979; Sutcliffe 1985; Ochsenius 1985.
58 Borrero 1997b.
59 See, for example, Lundelius 1989 for one attempt at modelling the process of extinction.
60 Miotti, pers. comm.
61 Nami 1993/94; Borrero and Franco 1995.
62 Yacobaccio and Guraieb 1994.

3 Middle to Late Holocene Adaptations in Patagonia

Francisco Mena

Introduction

The southern extremity of South America has always been dominated by hunting-gathering economies. In fact there are few other regions of the world where such adaptations display comparable continuity and diversity. One consequence of this is that Patagonian prehistory cannot be easily subdivided into periods and phases following the traditional chronological framework widely used elsewhere in archaeology.

Another important point is that although the first human settlers coexisted for a time with Pleistocene mammalian fauna that are now extinct, the characterisation of these bands as hunters specialised in the pursuit of big game is misleading. Nor can these adaptations be described as 'archaic' in the usual sense of the term, meaning the incipient development of techniques of food production in the context of a hunting-gathering tradition. In the immense spaces of Patagonia and Tierra del Fuego neither agriculture nor fully fledged pastoralism ever emerged.[1] What is more, we also lack an adequate term to refer to those post-contact hunting and gathering peoples who managed to maintain their way of life up until the late nineteenth century, notwithstanding the irreversible impact of external political and economic influences.

As we shall see below, simple environmental determinism and easy generalisations are inappropriate. Instead, we will focus on the surprising variability and flexibility of the hunting and gathering traditions that developed in Patagonia from about 8,000–500 BP (middle to late Holocene).

Environmental variability and adaptation in Patagonia

The transition from Pleistocene to Holocene conditions varied across the extensive and diverse geography of Patagonia. In contrast to the eastern steppes, which were never covered by ice, relics of the great Pleistocene ice-masses are still found today as ice-caps and glaciers in the Andes. Whereas around latitude 40° to 42° South the glaciers began to retreat towards their present limit from about 14,000 BP, in Tierra del Fuego (53° to 55° South) periglacial steppe vegetation prevailed until around 9,000 BP, when it began to be replaced by rapidly expanding temperate forest (see chapters 1 and 4).[2]

The contraction of the ice-fields and the corresponding climatic amelioration apparent in northern Patagonia in the early Holocene did not entail a simultaneous and widespread transformation of human adaptations throughout Patagonia. On the contrary, far to the south, in Fuego-Patagonia, very cold conditions persisted and humans continued to coexist with mammals typical of the Pleistocene, such as the American horse (*Equus* sp., *Onohippidium saldiasi*), milodón (*Mylodon* sp.) and ancestral camelids (*Macrauchenia*, *Lama gracilis*). They appear only to have pursued these animals on an occasional, opportunistic basis, rather than hunting them systematically.[3] The effects of climate change may have brought about increased competition and reduction of habitats and this, together with possible hunting pressure from human groups, may explain why these species gradually became extinct (see chapter 2).[4]

Fig 27 Solitary guanaco, Torres del Paine, Chile.

From about 8,000 BP onwards (the beginning of the middle Holocene), temperatures rose higher even than today. This 'climatic optimum' was apparently characterised by great seasonal fluctuations and considerable spatial variation in rainfall. Pollen studies in the southern Patagonian Andes have revealed, for example, that between 8,000 to 7,000 BP drier conditions prevailed than in the early Holocene, not so much in terms of absolute rainfall totals as in their pronounced seasonality.[5] Tierra del Fuego experienced relatively dry conditions between 6,000 and 5,000 BP,[6] and it is clear that there was not a homogeneous adaptive response by human populations to this climatic optimum.[7]

In this period hunting bands followed semi-generalised hunting strategies, concentrating on mammals such as the guanaco (*Lama guanicoe*) (fig. 27) complemented by a variety of other, smaller, species (see chapter 2).[8] They fall outside the traditional model of hunters specialising in megafauna and there is a clear trend towards greater diversity in the archaeological record, with tangible evidence of subtle adaptations to changing conditions in different environmental zones.

Lithic traditions in central Patagonia

In the central altiplano of Santa Cruz province a lithic tradition known as the Casapedrense has been dated to between approximately 7,000 and 5,000 BP.[9] This comprises

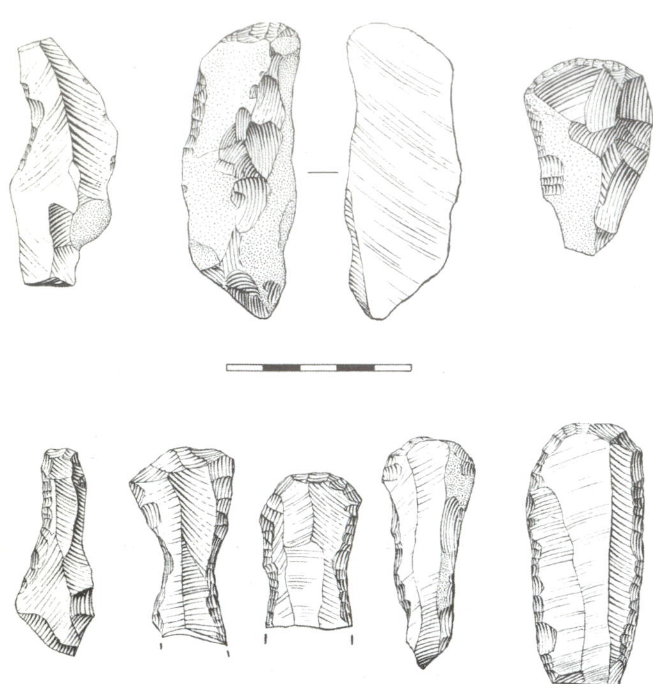

blades, flakes and especially front-scrapers, and is interpreted as evidence of a specialised adaptation to guanaco hunting (fig. 28). The exact nature of this tradition is still much debated because although there are abundant unifacial lithic tools and even occasional bolas, no projectile points have been found. It is a period characterised by new technologies, artistic innovation reflected in the wealth of rock art (fig. 29), and perhaps population growth.

More recent investigations have revealed the presence of a similar tool inventory in later, neighbouring sites.[10] There are also sites on the western fringes of the plains and adjacent mountain valleys that are contemporaneous with Casapedrense sites in the cultural altiplano and that definitely

Fig 28 *opposite above* Lithic tool assemblage typical of the Casapedrense tradition, from excavations at the site of Los Toldos.

have projectile points. Although scarce, these points are quite varied in form.[11] This suggests that in the central meseta (uplands) of Santa Cruz an elaborate lithic technology of blades and flakes developed in the period leading up to about 7,000 BP, along with forms of social organisation tailored to the communal hunting of guanaco on the open steppe by encirclement and the use of bolas (see chapter 10). The effectiveness of this inferred 'specialisation in guanaco' may be explained by a combination of the animals' abundance, together with the advantages of collective hunting and distribution of meat.[12] Collective hunting would have conferred a distinct competitive advantage wherever it was adopted, considering the fact that while the guanaco is an agile and speedy prey, it also follows somewhat predictable group patterns.

The settlement pattern observed in the archaeological record is likely to be the result of brief and repeated occupations at favoured locales by small groups (fig. 30). Casapedrense technology later expanded into the neighbouring cordillera zone, where locally available raw materials were used to manufacture projectile points and spears. These were more effective for hunting species with solitary habits, such as the huemul (*Hippocamelus bisulcus)* and other animals, especially in forested terrain.

Fig 29 *opposite* Painted rock art image showing a female guanaco with her young, Río Ibáñez, Aisén.

Fig 30 *right* Archaeological evidence for a long-standing tradition of guanaco hunting has been excavated at Cueva El Volcán, Río Chico Basin, Santa Cruz.

The absence of projectile points at the steppe meseta sites, just as at those in the cordillera, such as Arroyo Feo[13] and Cueva Las Guanacas,[14] might well be the product of incomplete sampling, given the relatively small areas that have been excavated, or perhaps because these are localities in which the activities practised did not involve the use and discarding of certain specific tools.[15]

Neither the presence of the domestic dog (*Canis familiaris),* nor its possible role in

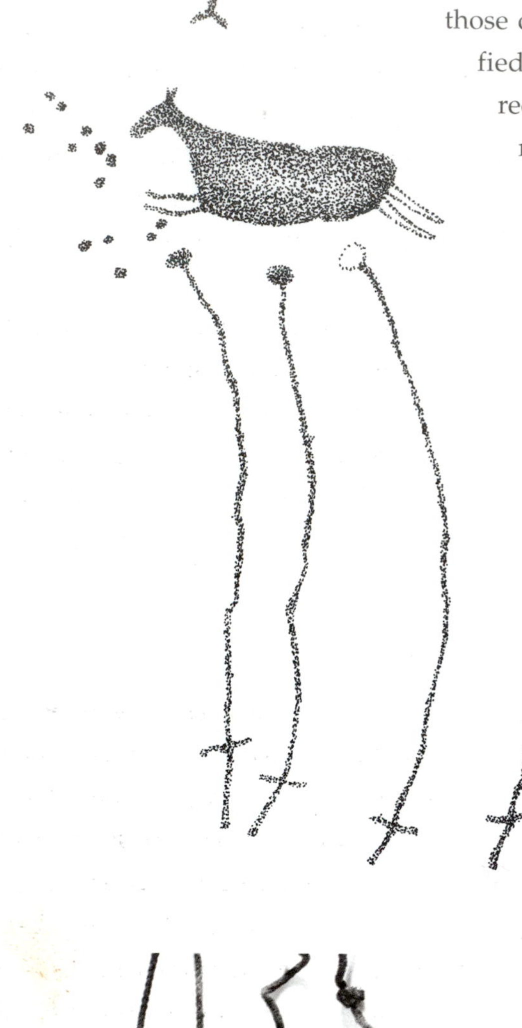

hunting in these societies, is yet clear.[16] Some authors have suggested that finds from Los Toldos 3[17] and from the earliest levels at Cueva Fell[18] are those of dog. However, these and other finds have now been identified as fox (*Dusicyon avus*),[19] which became extinct in relatively recent times. Remains of these extinct foxes have also been found near the Atlantic coast of continental Patagonia.[20]

Many of the technological characteristics of the Casapedrense persisted until around 3,000 BP, and probably much later[21] in the steppe hinterlands extending as far as the Chubut basin in the north and probably down to Ultima Esperanza in the south.[22] The region between the Chubut and Santa Cruz basins therefore comprised a cultural macro-region between 6,000 and 3,000 BP that has been termed the central Patagonian tradition.[23]

The influence of the Andean archaic

Andean 'influences' may help to explain the presence in the lowlands of triangular bifacial points, both in the Pampas and in extreme southern Patagonia,[24] as well as in central Patagonia.[25] More recently, though, the inventory of early Holocene artefacts has grown to include bifacial points not only in the Andean highlands[26] but also throughout wider pampean Patagonia. This bifacial technology was known from very early on in the Patagonian pampas. Its absence in certain contexts, notably in the finds from Level 11 at Los Toldos,[27] could be due to functional variability at such sites,[28] or to periods in which their use declined considerably, thereby reducing their representation in the archaeological record. This appears to be the case with the early Casapedrense in the central mesetas of Santa Cruz already discussed, and the majority of the middle Holocene associations known from southern Patagonia, where bifacial technology was maintained to a greater or lesser degree for a much longer period of time.

On the other hand, it is likely that projectiles were always used less frequently in open country,[29] whereas from very early times there is evidence of the use of bolas in continental Patagonia and on Tierra del Fuego (figs 31 and 32).[30]

Fig 31 *opposite above*
Painted rock art scene showing guanaco, human figure and possible representation of bolas. Cueva de las Manos, Río Pinturas, Santa Cruz, Argentina.

Fig 32 *opposite below*
Bolas used for hunting guanaco, length 2 m. A lighter version with just two stone weights was used for hunting the *Rhea*, a flightless bird native to the Patagonian pampas.

By around 6,000 BP it appears that the systematic exploitation of coastal resources in Patagonia was well under way, although coastal investigations are few and many sites have suffered irreversible destruction by both natural and human action. Sea levels around 6,000 to 5,000 BP reached some four to seven metres above present-day levels, obliterating much evidence for earlier littoral occupations. Coastal settlements in central Patagonia appear around 3,000 BP.[31] It is difficult to evaluate the possibility of much older adaptations along the Atlantic coast due not only to sea level rise, but also to the fact that the artefacts were adapted to specifically maritime functions and lack the diagnostic forms found inland for earlier periods.

The exploitation of coastal resources in southern Patagonia, on the other hand, is documented as far back as 5,000 to 6,000 BP by finds of marine shells in inland sites such as Las Buitreras.[32] This suggests at least ephemeral occupation or seasonal exploitation.[33] This interpretation assumes greater credibility when we consider that it was precisely in the middle Holocene, when the inland occupations reflect great conservatism, that there is the first evidence of the development of a specialised maritime adaptation on the coast.

Maritime adaptation in Fuego-Patagonia

Various finds in the western reaches of Estrecho de Magallanes, Seno Otway and Isla Navarino reveal that a specialised maritime adaptation focusing on littoral resources began to develop around 6,000 BP. This is characterised not only by the intensive exploitation of marine mammals (notably sea lion [*Otaria* and *Arctocephalus*] and coastal birds, especially cormorant and penguins) but also by the development of an elaborate bone-working technology that included multi-barbed harpoons with detachable heads, chisels, wedges and ornaments (fig. 33), and very probably watercraft made of tree bark. The gathering and consumption of shellfish was an important component of this littoral adaptation.[34]

Archaeological finds from the Englefield site[35] have been complemented by those from around the Estrecho de Magallanes[36] and the Canal Beagle which illustrate the spread of this adaptation throughout the labyrinthine channels of the Fuego-Patagonian archipelago. At the Tunel 1 site, a component similar to and contemporaneous with those described above was preceded by what has been interpreted as a brief occupation by a small group of terrestrial hunters at around 7,000 BP. Similar sequences have been recorded at Marazzi and Ponsonby and their technological affinity with Magallanes III complexes from the interior of southern continental Patagonia reinforces the hypothesis that this adaptation had its origin in terrestrial groups during the middle Holocene. Although the distinct complexes are to all appearances quite homogeneous, it is not yet possible to decide whether the transition from terrestrial to maritime adaptations originated in one particular localised area, or whether there were parallel developments on different parts of the coast.

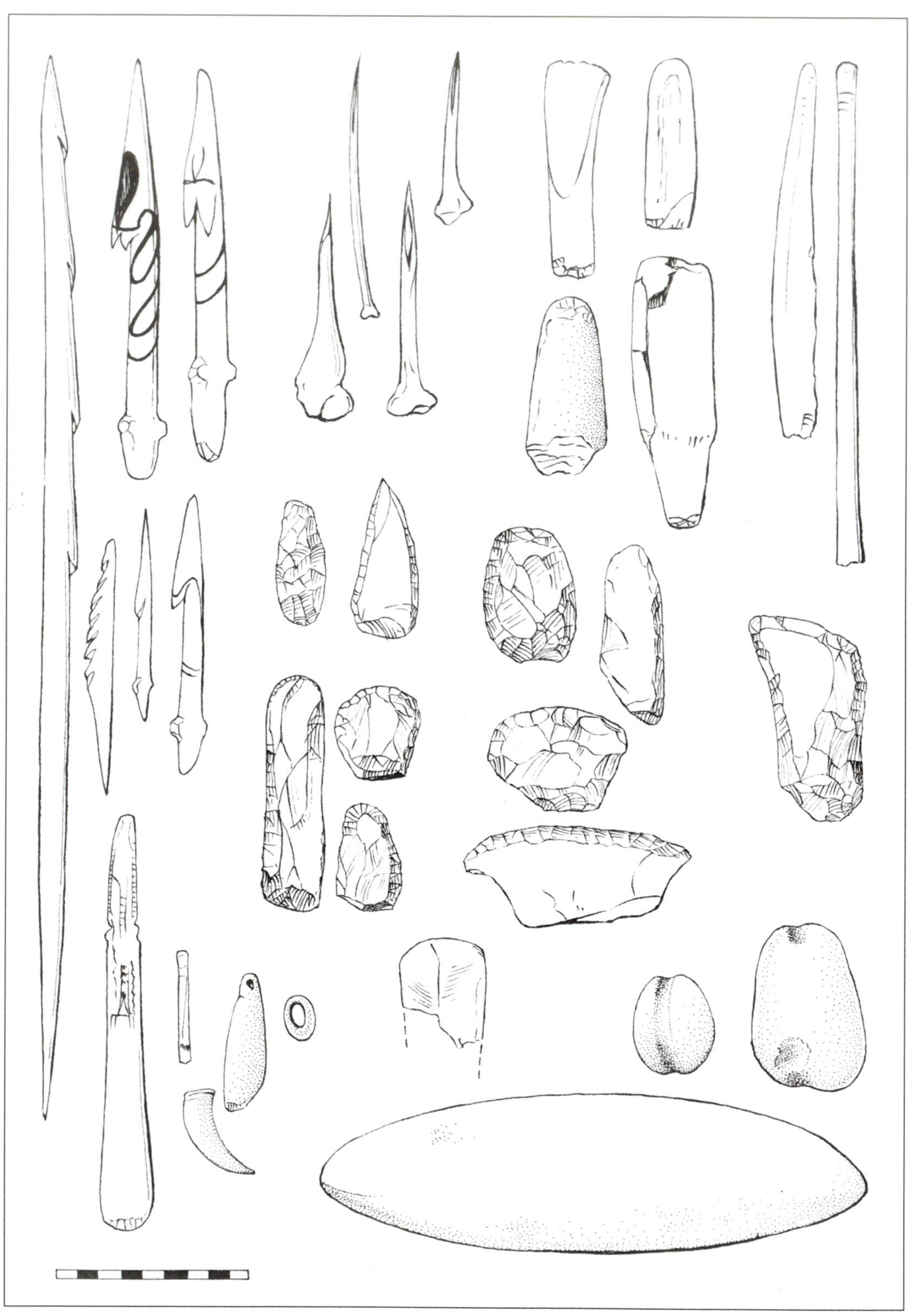

Fig 33 Archaeological assemblage of lithic and bone tools typical of the early maritime adaptation in the Canal Beagle, c. 6,000–4,000 BP.

This confirms what has been observed in other regions of the southern cone where littoral resources were exploited from very early on. It appears that initially this entailed non-specialised seasonal procurement of shellfish, fish and occasionally mammals to complement terrestrial food supplies using simple and flexible hunting and gathering strategies. Over the course of many generations in Fuego-Patagonia the marine adaptation represented a significant shift in the subsistence base along with profound changes in language, social organisation and even the physical constitution of the indigenous settlers.[37] These developments enhanced the mobility of groups throughout the archipelago channels and even included navigation across stretches of open sea such as Estrecho de le Maire. In historical times it earned these peoples the label 'Nomads of the Sea'.[38]

Despite the limited investigations in the western archipelago there is nevertheless no hard evidence to support the notion of a migration from the far north down the entire Pacific archipelago to Fuego-Patagonia, as some have proposed.[39] Other 'external' causal factors evoked to account for the newly evolving marine adaptation include local demographic pressures, sea level rise and the expansion of the *Nothofagus* forest.[40] None of these seem adequate, especially if one considers that population densities on the inland plains and mesetas were always relatively low.[41] Rather, everything points to a gradual development of this maritime way of life along the coasts of Estrecho de Magallanes or the inland bodies of water, including Seno Otway and Skyring, where both marine and terrestrial resources were available along with easy access between the steppe and the coast. This is certainly sufficient to account for the greater number of sites in Patagonia recorded for the later periods.

During the Holocene the eastern sector of the Canal Beagle and Isla Navarino offered a relatively open environment with not only abundant coastal fauna and flora but also access to terrestrial resources, including guanaco. It is here that the highest density of maritime sites with a rich artefactual inventory is found. The marine adaptation is essentially coterminous with the distribution of the temperate forest and was clearly most successful during the later periods in those regions of dense forest with minimal terrestrial resources to the north of Ultima Esperanza and south of Peninsula Brecknock, for example (see chapter 4).[42]

This tradition is remarkably homogeneous throughout its geographical range, but archaeological finds do reveal differences in the lithic inventories of neighbouring groups, such as the presence of obsidian and fine bifacial retouching found at sites in close proximity to Estrecho de Magallanes, compared with the popularity of polished stone in the Canal Beagle. These are perhaps explicable in terms of locally available raw materials and some contact and exchange of such materials between groups in certain areas.

Notable innovations in tools and weapons, including fine obsidian points and a rich bone tool industry, are found among the inland waterways north of the Strait.[43] These diminish in the archaeological record towards the north, where a general impoverishment of the artefactual inventory is apparent, including the loss of incised decoration on bone tools. This seems in part to have been a consequence of the dispersion into, and colonisation of, the remote regions of the outer archipelagos.[44]

During the following millennia distinct patterns emerge in dwellings, body decoration, ritual activity and even language representing the antecedents of the groups known historically as the Yámana and the Kawéskar, to the south and north of the Estrecho de Magallanes respectively. The Yámana, for example, shared many traits in common with this maritime tradition, including basketry and the use of bone (see chapter 4), although they also used the bow and arrow adopted from the Selk'nam.

Some favoured camp-sites suggest sustained periods of occupation and this probably helped to define distinct social entities in the region of Otway-Skyring and the islands of Madre de Dios-Guayaneco and Chonos-Guaitecas.[45] Many such sites are located in situations carefully selected because of their topography and their access to specialised resources. This reflects finely honed patterns of mobility and settlement and each ethnic group's intimate familiarity with its territory. The larger and more frequented camps were located precisely at the juncture of different ecotones offering access to a variety of resources. Other more ephemeral sites are likely to have been used as part of seasonal patterns of mobility and exploitation.

By the nineteenth century the concentration of the Yámana ethnic group in and around the Canal Beagle may have been accelerated by European intrusion into an area that had long been a focus of population exchange and movement. Certain activities may represent something of a departure from earlier patterns. Archaeological sites dating to the last few centuries include a range of specialised sites used to exploit the full spatial distribution of resources, including the organised hunting of guanaco.[46] From about 2,000 BP onwards, at the eastern extremity of Tierra del Fuego, groups with a mixed terrestrial and maritime economy formed the antecedents of those known by historic times as the Haush (see chapter 4).

The late Holocene: stability and adaptive differentiation

Around 4,500 BP the milder conditions that existed during the middle Holocene gave way to a cold phase accompanied by a pronounced glacial readvance.[47] The environmental impact of this climatic event varied according to local rainfall regimes. In the inter-Andean valleys, for example, it appears that there was an expansion of humid forest,[48] while in southern Patagonia and the north of Tierra del Fuego more arid conditions prevailed favouring the spread of the steppe grassland.[49]

This cold spell of variable duration was followed by environmental conditions similar to those of today, including brief and relatively minor fluctuations in temperature that occasionally lasted for longer intervals.[50] The same variability can be observed with respect to rainfall, as revealed by a dry interval dated in northern Patagonia to between 4,000–2,000 BP, contemporaneous with a pluvial episode south of latitude 46° South.[51]

The period between 5,000–2,000 BP is not, however, marked by striking cultural innovations. Some subtle local adaptations can be detected and the territorial affiliations of neighbouring groups are likely to have become more clearly demarcated, but this was a protracted process in the immense reaches of the continental steppe. On the other hand, these incipient ethnic contrasts and distinctions may have been expressed in cultural domains that leave little trace in the archaeological record, such as mythology, ritual life and body decoration.

During the late Holocene there was a clear continuation of traditional subsistence patterns, accompanied by a gradual broadening of their economic and technological range. The use of flake tools persisted in central Patagonia, for example, and the practice of painted rock art in superimposed styles and themes departs little from earlier conventions.[52] On the other hand, an increase in the use of obsidian is apparent, a greater range of the faunal resources are exploited (*Ctenomus, Lagidium, Zaedyus* and larger birds such as geese and flamingo, see fig. 34), and the apparent development of mobile patterns that took advantage of diverse ecological zones[53] (including camps for specialised tasks in the high mesetas) is clearly identified as far back as 2,000 BP in central and northern Patagonia.[54] The adoption by this same date of large triangular points,

Fig 34 Darwin's *Rhea* (*Pterocnemia pennata*), locally called ñandú, near Estrecho de Magallanes.

combined with the presence of grinding instruments, has led to this period being considered as 'transitional' to the historically known ethnic groups.[55] The truth is that these complexes are difficult to define – as their denomination 'proto-patagonian' indicates.

A similar situation is found north of the Río Chubut, aggravated by the inherent limitations of the archaeological record and the lack of investigation carried out at these latitudes. It seems that the lithic flake industries played a less important role here than in the territories further south,[56] although some very large bifacial tools, especially scrapers, are found.

In the Neuquén region the intensive exploitation of rodents and pine-nuts is part of a mobile adaptable strategy that appears to be in place by 3,000 BP,[57] although its antecedents on the flanks of the cordillera may date earlier.[58]

The presence of projectile points indicates links between central Patagonia and the region to the south of the Río Santa Cruz, where generalised and highly mobile subsistence strategies developed. Within the framework of a process of adaptive stabilisation and stylistic differentiation our attention is drawn to the similarities between the continental hunters of the period 4,500–1,000 BP and the contemporary peoples of northern Tierra del Fuego. This, despite the fact that the latter had been relatively isolated following the inundation of the Estrecho de Magallanes around 8,000 BP (see chapter 2).[59] The bow and the arrow appear almost simultaneously in the archaeological record around 500 BP on both sides of the Strait. The projectile points of both traditions show notable formal similarities, although there are subtle technological differences[60] in their production and this has led to the suggestion that there was an active network of exchange across the Strait, perhaps mediated by canoe groups.[61]

While this internal diversification was probably taking place across the whole range of Patagonian cultures, they were nevertheless assuming distinct ethnic and stylistic identities that were later to be expressed in the historically known ethnic groups.

Encounters and exchange

In the archaeological record the last millennium saw pronounced cultural differentiation and interesting technological changes. This perception may in part be a consequence of the greater quantity and quality of archaeological information available for more recent times, but on the whole it would appear that cultural innovation is a product of growing systemic complexity. It is clear, too, that contact with traditions lying beyond the immediate territory of Patagonia also played a significant and even fateful role in these socio-cultural changes. In pre-contact times these influences emanated from more sophisticated polities and empires to the north, and later, following European contact, navigators, missionaries, explorers, colonists, mercantile traders, ranch owners and the military were all involved (see chapter 6).

Although the extreme south of South America is one of the most remote regions of the world, contacts from far afield include the arrival of new populations and the adoption of outside cultural elements. Nevertheless, certain innovations such as bow and arrow technology may have had a local and independent origin in Patagonia, as suggested by evidence from Magallanes[62] and the Fuegian channels.[63] While in the western Andean Cordillera the production of food crops extended as far as 42° South, the extensive eastern plain never sustained indigenous populations with an agricultural subsistence base further than 32° South. Nor did pastoralism develop in more southerly latitudes (see chapter 10).

The arrival of pottery in the Neuquén Cordillera around 1,000 BP is an indicator of

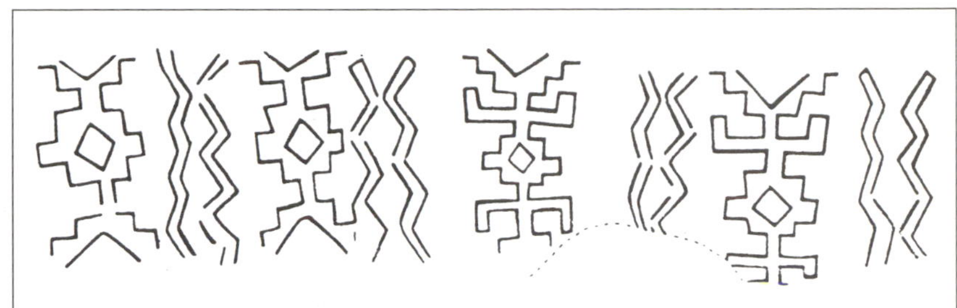

Fig 35 Pottery vessel from northern Argentina, dated *c.* AD 500.

Fig 36 *above right* Certain geometric motifs, such as these found on pottery, resemble some of the geometric patterns found in rock art and on painted cloaks (cf. figs 112, 116 and 118).

Andean contacts.[64] Pottery is found in central Patagonia even earlier,[65] suggesting influences not only of Andean origin, but also from the Tupi-Guaraní tradition of the Río de La Plata hinterland that may have arrived by routes that circumvented north-west Patagonia.[66]

Either or both of these influences may have stimulated the application to pottery of distinctive geometric motifs which have their origins in the hunting traditions of Patagonia (figs 35 and 36). These motifs are widely recorded in the rock art of localities between the Río Negro and the Chubut and were also applied to ceramic decoration and to ceremonial stone axes and are a characteristic trait of the Gununa'Kena, or northern Tehuelche.[67] This style extends as far as 47° South,[68] and further still in the painted cloaks or 'quillangos' of Magallanes (see chapter 10).[69] This without doubt reflects the great mobility of historic hunters in Patagonia, including the massive displacement of populations and frequent long-distance incursions. There are no precise territorial limits for these peoples, and it is advisable to refer in general terms to a southern component (Aónikenk) and a northern component (Gununa'Kena), while recognising the complexity of their spatial relationship in historic times (see fig. 37 and chapter 10).[70]

The introduction of pottery did not affect the subsistence base in which basketry and other materials, such as armadillo shell, were traditionally used as containers and for storage and transport. Some Patagonian hunter-gatherers adopted pottery simply as a ceremonial good or prestige item.[71] Elsewhere pottery vessels may have been incorporated to serve routine domestic functions, and might even have been produced locally. It is likely that pottery vessels were adopted for their utility in cooking meat (since these make better use of smaller game and the fat associated with compact bones such as vertebrae and joints), especially during periods when subsistence resources were restricted, or as a result of population pressure.[72]

Central Patagonian groups adopted ceramics much more selectively, for there are many archaeological sites where pottery is common, while at others it is practically absent.[73] This evidence could be interpreted as the result of the functional or seasonal use of ceramic containers.[74] On the other hand, it might simply be the product of increasing populations and a more intensive use of animal by-products. Although it is not possible to discount the deliberate use of fire in hunting activities from very early times, in recent centuries systematic burning would appear to have developed as a technique of managing grazing resources.[75]

Climatic changes in the late Holocene may have contributed to the differentiation of micro-regional adaptive systems in contrasting areas, such as the arid strip lying immediately east of the central altiplano, and may also have caused the apparent abandonment of some cordillera valleys, such as Río Ibáñez.[76]

The penetration of Mapuche-speaking agriculturists into the western Andean valleys around 1,000 BP was perhaps indirectly responsible for the appearance of pottery in the Neuquén region.[77] Very much later, by the end of the eighteenth century, the Mapuche had almost completely replaced the original inhabitants in all the territory of the sierra and eastern pampas to the north of the Río Negro. Mapuche-speakers practising incipient horticulture and weaving and metallurgical technology extended down to the Río Chubut. They controlled the trade in horses and this, together with the pressures of aggression and conflict in Araucanía, resulted in their influence expanding to the far south of the continent over a period of less than two hundred years. Gradually the Mapuche infiltrated and came to dominate local Patagonian populations, resulting in the admixture of both cultures, despite occasionally violent confrontations in the competition for territory around the Ríos Limay and Chubut.

After the bow, pottery and Mapuche infiltration – and before direct contact with outside colonists – the most striking phenomena in the history of pampean Patagonian cultures during the last few centuries was without doubt the adoption of the horse. This affected all aspects of indigenous lifestyle (technology, economy, mobility and social organisation) and was the central factor in establishing regular trade contacts and commerce with the 'outside' world.

The adoption of the European horse had a variable impact. The Gununa'Kena and the pampean groups became engaged in cattle-herding and trading as a significant economic activity, complemented in certain sectors of the northern pampas by sheep-farming. They incorporated the meat of the female as an essential element in their diet, replacing guanaco skin with horse hides to cover their tents. They also adopted a range of outside weapons and tools, including metal spears and swords and leather shields to mount organised raids, not only against frontier communities but also against the new colonial cities of Bahía Blanca and Buenos Aires. The Aónikenk or southern Tehuelche, in contrast, who adopted the horse as late as the beginning of the eighteenth century, did not substantially change their hunting-gathering patterns, and in many cases simply regarded the horse as a luxury item that was reserved for sacrifice on special occasions. Even here the horse came to occupy a significant role in opening up more extensive systems of exchange that were to change the whole character of the indigenous way of life for ever (see chapter 10).

NOTES

1 However, Bate (1983: 177) draws attention to numerous historical observations concerning the systematic use of guanaco as mascots or decoys, hinting that certain principles of pastoralism were beginning to develop locally.
2 Markgraf and Bradbury 1982.
3 Borrero *et al.* 1988; Borrero 1997a.
4 Markgraf 1985.
5 Markgraf 1984: 251.
6 Markgraf 1983.
7 For example, Bettinger 1980: 237.
8 Mengoni 1986; Aschero 1996; Belardi 1996; Crivelli *et al.* 1996.
9 Menghin 1952; Cardich *et al.* 1973; Cardich 1985; Borrero 1994/95; Cardich *et al.* 1993/94; Cardich and Paunero 1994.
10 Aguerre 1992.
11 Aschero 1982; Alonso *et al.* 1984.
12 Dennell 1987: 83–4; Pagano 1996.
13 Alonso *et al.* 1985.
14 Mena 1983.
15 For example, the skinning and processing of the pelts of newborn guanacos.
16 Cardich *et al.* 1977: 116.
17 Tonni and Politis 1981: 263.
18 Saxon 1979.
19 Caviglia 1986; Jackson, Douglas and Trejo, MS.
20 Miotti and Berman 1988.
21 Mengoni 1987.
22 Prieto, pers. comm.; Perez de Micou *et al.* 1992.
23 Aschero 1987.
24 Orquera 1985.
25 Massone 1981: 106, see also critique by Bate 1982: 189.
26 See Rick 1983; Nuñez and Santoro 1988.
27 Level 11 has been dated to 12,600 BP (Cardich *et al.* 1973). However, as noted in chapter 2, the integrity of this date has been called into question.
28 Compare, for example, Cueva de las Manos, level 6 with points, contemporary with Arroyo Feo 11 without points; Cueva Fell level 10 with points, contemporary with Las Buitreras V without points.
29 Including in 'toldense' levels of Los Toldos 3 and Cueva de las Manos.
30 Laming-Emperaire *et al.* 1972; Orquera and Piana 1987. On Tierra del Fuego they have also been interpreted as possible net weights.
31 See chapter 1 and Gomez-Otero 1994, 1995.
32 Borrero 1989a: 100.
33 Massone 1981: 107.
34 Piana 1984; Orquera and Piana MS; Legoupil 1993/94.
35 Legoupil 1988.
36 Ortíz-Troncoso 1975.
37 Cocilovo and Guichón 1986: 115.
38 *Nomades du Mer* is the title of a book by Emperaire (1963); Horwitz 1993.
39 Bird 1946; Ortíz-Troncoso 1984: 122.
40 Orquera and Piana MS.
41 See, for example, Barth 1948.
42 Laming-Emperaire 1972a.
43 Legoupil 1986: 47; Stern and Prieto 1991.
44 North of the Golfo de Penas crude bifacial points are in evidence, as well as a pattern of cave burial (see, for example, Legoupil 1987; Ocampo and Aspillaga 1984), including the pre-ceramic levels of Chiloé (Díaz and Garretón 1973).
45 Laming-Emperaire 1972a.
46 Orquera and Piana MS.
47 Mercer 1976.
48 Heusser and Streeter 1980: 1347.
49 Markgraf 1983.
50 Mercer 1976.
51 Markgraf 1989: 18–19.
52 Gradín 1983; Aschero *et al.* 1992; Gradín and Aguerre 1994; Borrero 1994/95.
53 Gradín 1980: 190.
54 Gradín 1976; García and Pérez de Micou 1982.
55 Gradín *et al.* 1979.
56 Boschín 1986.
57 Fernández 1988; Orquera 1987: 389.
58 Valdés *et al.* 1982; Crivelli *et al.* 1993.
59 Massone 1984: 133.
60 Nami 1985/86.
61 Bird 1946.
62 Massone, pers. comm.
63 Orquera and Piana 1987: 214.
64 Cardich and Paunero 1994; Borrero 1994/95.
65 Orquera 1987: 371–3; Senatore 1996.
66 Gradín 1978.
67 Menghin 1957.
68 Bate 1970; Gradín *et al.* 1979.
69 Martinic 1976; Prieto this volume.
70 Casamiquela 1969.
71 Pottery is known from as far south as the Estrecho de Magallanes coast, although such finds are likely to be the result of long-distance trade or exchange of these items.
72 Mena 1986.
73 Alonso *et al.* 1984: 284.
74 For example, in the preparation of fat during winter, Goñi, pers. comm.
75 Veblen and Lorenz 1988.
76 Goñi 1988.
77 Canals-Frau 1946.

4 The Origins of Ethnographic Subsistence Patterns in Fuego-Patagonia

Luis Alberto Borrero

Introduction

Fig 37 The approximate distribution of indigenous groups at the time of first contact in the early sixteenth century.

Our present understanding of the cultural antecedents of ethnographic groups recognised in Patagonia and Tierra del Fuego during the early years of European contact begs many questions. How old are the cultural configurations which came to be known as Aónikenk, Selk'nam, Kawéskar and Yámana? Were the natives observed by the first European sailors the direct descendants of the very first prehistoric colonisers of the region? Did the earliest attempts at colonisation succeed or fail over the long term? Is there evidence in the archaeological record of later attempts at colonisation, and did these prove viable? Is there anything to suggest that latecomers may have displaced, or even eliminated, earlier populations? And if descendants of both have survived, is there any means of telling them apart? In attempting to answer these questions the most recent archaeological research is revealing a level of variation at odds with the over-simplified characterisation traditionally applied to these cultures. The new data does not fit comfortably into the standard evolutionary scheme used to account for the ethnographic distribution of the different groups in Patagonia (fig. 37).

To assess the origins of ethnographic subsistence patterns recorded at contact, both archaeological and linguistic data, as well as molecular evidence, provide independent lines of argument which must be compared. These in turn have a bearing on our attempts to understand how the different groups came to occupy the territories observed in historical times. The issue of the continuity or discontinuity of the human populations themselves (biological change) must be carefully distinguished from questions of continuity and modification of their material culture (cultural change). While the information available on the biological characteristics of prehistoric populations in Patagonia is still very limited, there is a growing body of archaeological evidence recovered by survey and excavation which is filling in the picture of cultural variation. Archaeologists rely heavily on stone tools such as scrapers and projectile points to indicate changing patterns of exploitation and adaptation since, with the exception of bone and shell, almost all other perishable organic materials have disappeared. Subtle differences in tool forms can offer adaptative advantages in securing,

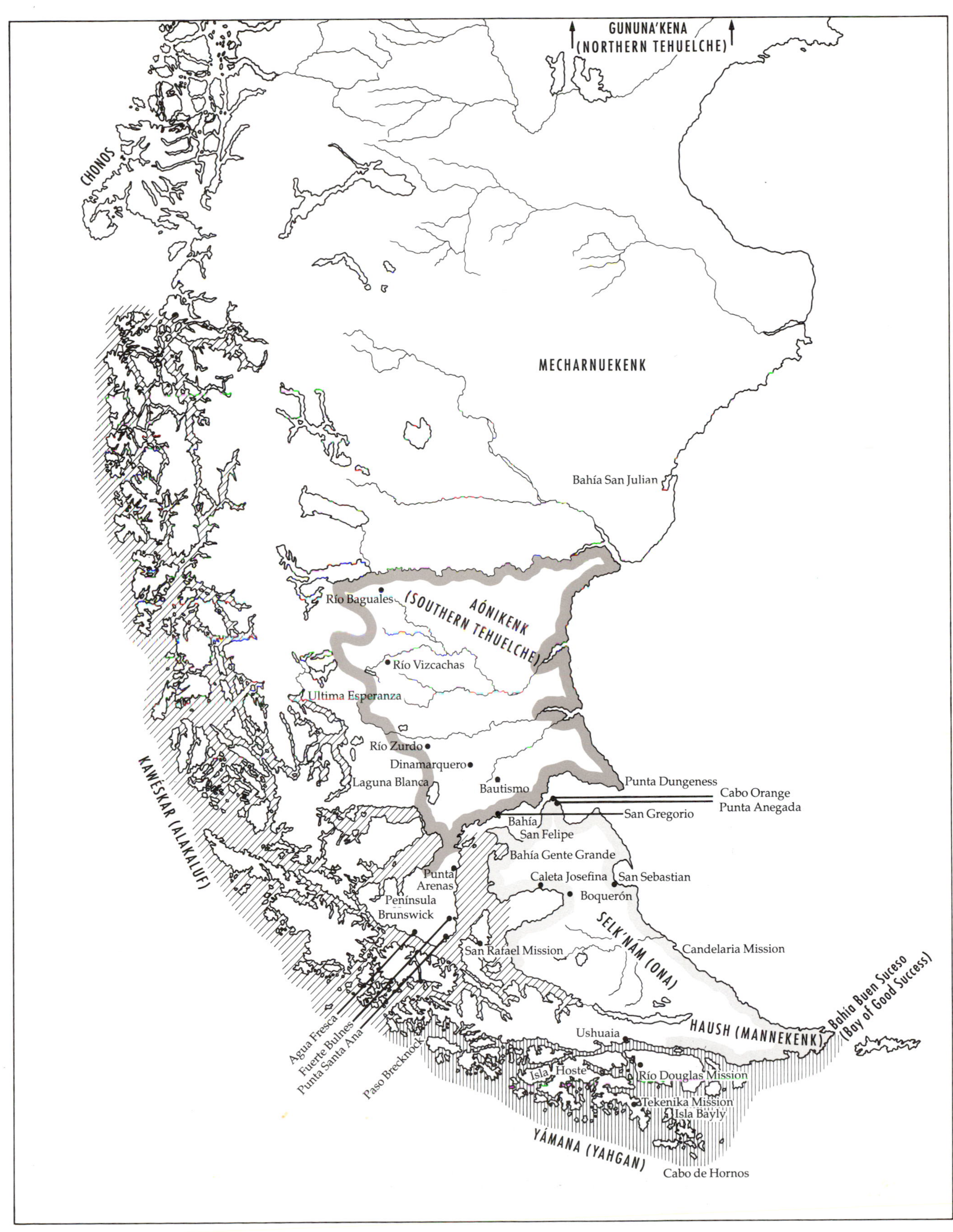
GUNUNA'KENA (NORTHERN TEHUELCHE)
CHONOS
MECHARNUEKENK
Bahía San Julian
Río Baguales
AÓNIKENK (SOUTHERN TEHUELCHE)
Río Vizcachas
Ultima Esperanza
Río Zurdo
Dinamarquero
Laguna Blanca
Bautismo
Punta Dungeness
Cabo Orange
Punta Anegada
San Gregorio
Bahía San Felipe
Bahía Gente Grande
Caleta Josefina
San Sebastian
Boquerón
Punta Arenas
Península Brunswick
KAWÉSKAR (ALAKALUF)
SELK'NAM (ONA)
Candelaria Mission
San Rafael Mission
Bahía Buen Suceso (Bay of Good Success)
HAUSH (MANNEKENK)
Ushuaia
Agua Fresca
Fuerte Bulnes
Punta Santa Ana
Paso Brecknock
Isla Hoste
Río Douglas Mission
Tekenika Mission
Isla Bayly
YÁMANA (YAHGAN)
Cabo de Hornos

then processing, vital subsistence resources. Particular styles of projectile points, such as arrowheads, may have enduring usefulness, so that they become recognised archaeologically as typical culture 'traits'. Nevertheless, the ingenious use of scarce resources to survive in demanding environments introduces a wide range of variability in material culture.

Migration, dispersion or local development?

Fig 38 Yámana canoe with smoke issuing from the fire burning within it, *c.* 1907–8. The standing figure holds a harpoon while another rests on the prow.

The differentiation of Fuego-Patagonian populations may go back as far as 12,000 BP, for by this time humans were already widely distributed in southern South America. We have shown that around 11,000 BP there is good archaeological evidence to indicate that human populations crossed by land from the continent to what is now the Isla Grande de Tierra del Fuego. It is likely that this was the result of a gradual process of dispersion rather than intentional migration (see chapter 2). The earliest settlers were broad spectrum hunter-gatherers who probably survived as small mobile bands foraging for varied resources in an extremely cold and forbidding environment. The final inundation of the Estrecho de Magallanes by the sea around 8,000 BP would have created a formidable barrier isolating human populations on the newly formed island. Perhaps the small sub-populations that were cut off represented only part of the genetic and cultural make-up of the original population.[1] This is known as the 'founder effect' and results in the creation of a large pool of variation for natural selection to act upon.[2] Indeed, differences between the phenotype of human populations from the island compared with those from the continent have been noted.[3] Human remains from the early Holocene have yet to be recovered and so comparative morphological studies are not yet possible. Nevertheless, sufficient independent evidence exists to suggest that the scenario outlined above provided the basis for subsequent divergent evolution.

The alternative is that the early late Pleistocene populations on the island became extinct. Perhaps the resources in the newly formed ecosystems on the island were simply insufficient to support even a sparse human population, especially after the formation of the Strait, when they would effectively have been cut off. This possibility is supported by the paucity of sites dated between 9,000 and 2,500 BP in the north of Tierra del Fuego. After 2,500 BP a striking proliferation of radiocarbon dates attests to the presence of humans almost everywhere in the north of the main island. This contrast supports the hypothesis proposing an initial but ultimately unsuccessful colonisation, followed by a later colonisation and sustained human occupation of the island. In this case the natives that the Europeans met during the contact period would not have been the direct descendants of the earliest colonisers, but rather descendants of the later populations.

If an island population did become isolated on Tierra del Fuego the effect of geographical separation through time would be to create variation in material culture between the two sub-populations north and south of the Strait.[4] For example,

differences in the distribution of key resources, such as mammals, plants and raw materials for making tools and dwellings, would probably have led to divergent patterns in the use of space on the island compared to the southern margins of the continent. Another possible result of isolation might have been to prompt the intensification in the use of traditional subsistence resources, and the exploitation of new ones, with corresponding changes in the material culture. However, even when changes may have taken place in the stature and proportions of humans and in their material culture, a case for population continuity can still be made.

In theory it is possible that the 'rescue effect'[5] was operative for an early population reaching extinction thresholds on the island of Tierra del Fuego, since it was still possible to cross by land between the continental mainland and Tierra del Fuego until 8,000 BP (see chapter 1). If this was the case then the archaeological gap between the early occupations of Tres Arroyos and Marazzi (see chapter 2) and later settlement may simply reflect the lack of archaeological fieldwork. For the time being it seems justified to hypothesise some sort of population continuity.

Later opportunities for colonisation developed as the islands became more thickly forested and the network of channels became navigable in the post-glacial period. About seven thousand years ago the first indications of systematic maritime exploitation are found, which must have entailed the initial experimentation with, and use of, canoes (see fig. 38 and chapter 3). Most scholars interpret these new maritime adaptations entirely as a product of local evolution.[6] An alternative hypothesis posits the long-distance migration of maritime populations down the Pacific archipelago.[7] These peoples would then have superimposed themselves over previous cultural configurations, but as things stand there is little hard archaeological evidence to support such a scenario.

Whether the time depth of the populations on Tierra del Fuego extends directly back as far as 11,000 years BP, or is in fact much younger, the fact remains that the ancestors of the historically known peoples must be sought in the local prehistory rather than in invoking the idea of long-distance migrations of incoming populations.

Historical adaptations

When the first sailors arrived in the Magellanic region they found two fundamentally contrasting adaptations which can be characterised as the 'terrestrial' and 'canoe' cultures. The terrestrial peoples encompassed the Aónikenk of southern Patagonia, the Selk'nam of northern Tierra del Fuego (who focused on the exploitation of guanaco) and the Haush of south-eastern Tierra del Fuego (who complemented guanaco-hunting with the exploitation of coastal resources). According to historical sources, the 'canoe peoples' included the Yámana of the Canal Beagle and Cabo de Hornos, the Kawéskar of the western channels, and the Chonos of the Chonos and Guaitecas archipelagos. Their subsistence was based on maritime resources, relying primarily on marine mammals. This encapsulates the key impressions recorded in the first chronicles and ethnographies. Nevertheless, it is possible that subtle cultural variations went unrecognised during the early years of contact.[8] This is supported by recent archaeological research which highlights discrepancies with the ethnographic picture. These discrepancies include the facts that:

(1) Although birds are not ascribed a central role in the subsistence of the Selk'nam by some ethnographers,[9] abundant bird-remains show up at archaeological sites in what is considered traditional Selk'nam territory.[10]

(2) According to many historical sources, rodents were the critical resource for hunter-gatherers in the north of the island;[11] however, archaeological research indicates that rodent remains resulting from human exploitation are very sparse.

(3) The distribution of shell middens in the Canal Messier in the western archipelagos suggests a greater degree of social interaction for the canoe people than that indicated by historical sources.[12]

(4) There is little detectable difference in the technology of projectile point production between the Selk'nam and the Yámana.[13]

(5) Perhaps surprisingly, the same can be said for Selk'nam and Yámana basket-weaving.[14]

Archaeological research also confirms that there is an underlying similarity in the range of material culture throughout the western and southern channels.[15] To take one example, the so-called 'large Haush harpoon' is not really that different from those produced by the Yámana, as Gusinde readily admits, and this can also be said of other, smaller, harpoons which display a striking morphological similarity.[16]

There are significant differences, then, between the ethnographic descriptions for those groups and what has actually been recovered by archaeological excavation. This points to the need critically to re-evaluate the published ethnographies, for it may well have been the case that the ethnographers were simply dealing with a limited sample of a much broader pattern of human activities. For example, male ethnographers working in Patagonia at the beginning of the twentieth century rarely had access to the female world.[17] Also, the subsistence practices witnessed by ethnographers often occurred within the context of constant encroachment of sheep ranches into traditional indigenous territories.[18] Both factors distort the ethnographical record, which can hardly lay claim to being objective.

When trying to characterise the historical groups in Patagonia and Tierra del Fuego two important factors must be taken into account. One is the fact that indigenous adaptive strategies were changing rapidly at the time of contact. The second is that the recording of ethnographic information has been very uneven. If we were to look at the range of archaeological data as distinct from what is observable ethnographically, we would have to conclude on the basis of present evidence that there were no clear-cut limits between 'cultures'. Instead, we see a continuum ranging from strongly

Fig 39 Yámanas launching a canoe at Río Douglas, Bahía Ponsonby, *c.* 1907–8.

maritime cultures in the islands and channels to the west and the far south, to strongly terrestrial cultures in the steppes in the east and far north.

The linguistic evidence offers an additional independent body of information, for just as we noted a fundamental distinction between the terrestrial and canoe cultures, so, too, the languages spoken by each are very different. Furthermore, dialectical differences can be detected in the Yámana spoken in the Canal Beagle area compared with that spoken on some of the more isolated southern islands. A systematic study of the historical linguistics has yet to be attempted but, insofar as the complex dynamics of language differentiation can be reconstructed with limited information, they will undoubtedly invite comparison with the archaeological data.

The distribution of the maritime cultures is essentially co-terminous with that of the southern beech forest, upon which they relied heavily.[19] This explains why their terri-

tory extended only as far as Isla Isabel on the Estrecho de Magallanes,[20] and down to the southern part of the Peninsula Mitre on the Canal Beagle.[21] Their territory extended as far along the eastern end of Tierra del Fuego as the distribution of forest permitted. This fact underlines the fundamental role of wood and tree bark for these cultures, which they used to fashion items ranging from canoes to buckets (fig. 40).

Canoes were the mainstay of their maritime adaptation. They were not only an indispensable means of transportation, but also formed the focus of family life. Families moved everywhere by canoe, some even carrying fires burning inside them almost per-

Fig 40 *right* Yámana bark buckets. Height 19.7 cm. See fig. 82 for use of bark buckets as bailers.

manently (see fig. 38), and they have been observed consuming mussels on board,[22] although the empty shells were not always thrown back into the sea. As the eighteenth-century traveller John Byron noted, they were sometimes taken back to the shoreline and discarded there,[23] perhaps forming heaps like the one that can be observed beside the canoe in Bahía Ponsonby (fig. 39).

Human mobility in the labyrinthine channel system was problematic because the convoluted topography made direct journeys almost impossible and the weather was often ferocious and unpredictable. Portages made of logs were constructed in places. These cut across islands, giving the groups direct ways of moving through the maze of intricate channels, much to the astonishment of early explorers (fig. 41).[24]

Despite spending a lot of time on the water, the 'canoe people' also constructed huts on land. These were usually confined to a narrow coastal strip and the frames were

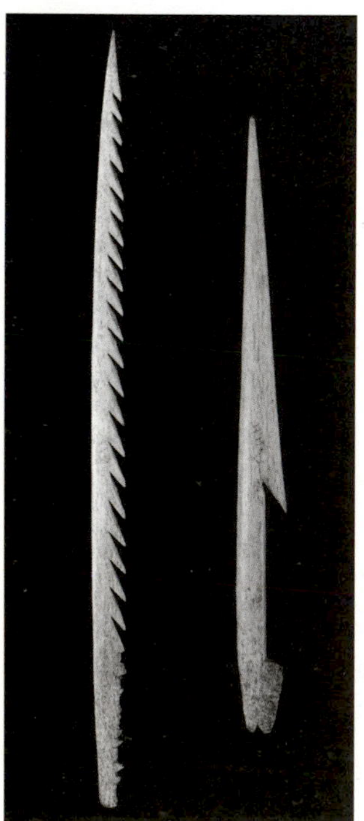

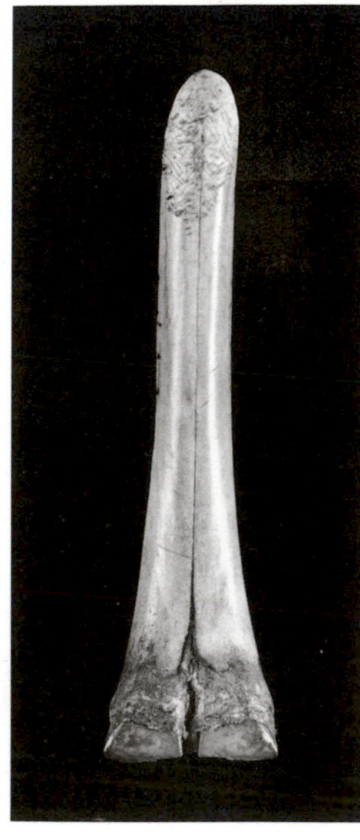

Fig 41 *above* View of part of a portage some 350 m in overall length, Estrecho de Magallanes, 1879.

Fig 42 *far left* Multi-barbed whalebone harpoon and single-barbed harpoon from Tierra del Fuego. Lengths 43.3 cm and 35.7 cm.

Fig 43 *left* Bone wedge used for working wood and bark. The implement is fashioned from the long bone of a guanaco. Probably Selk'nam. Length 16 cm.

Fig 44 *opposite above* Group of Yámana in front of their hut.

Fig 45 *opposite below* Shell scraper bound by a leather thong to a large pebble. Length 19.5 cm.

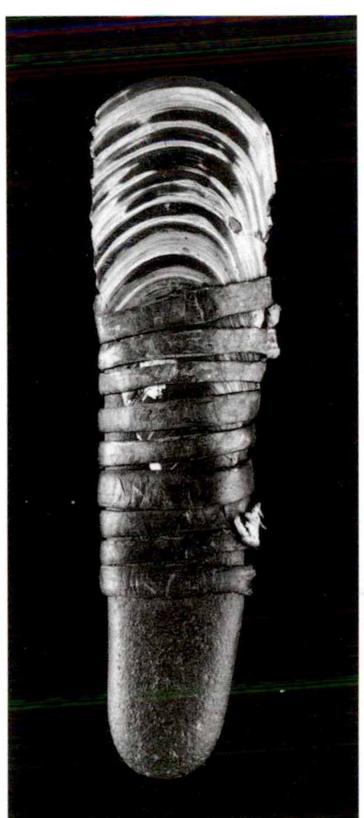

sometimes left to be used again (fig. 44).[25] Tools and weapons made of bone were key elements in this maritime adaptation. Harpoons of different shapes and sizes were fashioned from sea-mammal bone (fig. 42) and used to hunt sea lions and occasionally dolphins (figs 46 and 48). Bone is a logical choice in the channels, where the availability of alternative materials is limited.[26] Bone wedges were also used to extract bark from trees and a variety of cutting tools were made from sea-mammal bone as well as guanaco bone (fig. 43). The lack of other suitable raw materials likewise helps explain the widespread use of shell-knives as cutting tools, made of the larger and more resistant mussels (fig. 45).

Subsistence was heavily dependent on the consumption of sea mammals, supplemented by marine birds, especially shags.[27] Their meat was consumed as well as their eggs. When the opportunity presented itself they hunted otters or pursued huemul or guanaco. The otter was an important prey in the southern channels and together with birds may have been part of the reason for the seasonal exploitation of the more remote archipelagos.[28]

Mussels were regularly gathered at low tide (fig. 50) and the discarded shells formed large and very visible accumulations. Sailors were impressed by these great mussel

Fig 46 *right* Athlinata, a Yámana Indian, making a spear with a hafted, multi-barbed harpoon.

Fig 47 *opposite above left* Athlinata demonstrating how a sling was used. Although slings were simple weapons they were extremely effective for both hunting and combat.

Fig 48 *opposite above right* Athlinata demonstrating how a spear with a hafted, multi-barbed harpoon was used.

Fig 49 *far right* Yámana man kindling a fire.

Fig 50 *right* Yámana women gathering mussels, Bahía Tekenika, Isla Hoste.

Fig 51 Selk'nam group at the eastern end of Lago Fagnano (Lago Kamí), Tierra del Fuego.

heaps and thought that mussels were the principal dietary staple, which was not actually the case. A range of wild plants and herbs helped supplement the diet, especially berries (*Berberis buxifolia*) and wild celery (*Apium australe*).[29]

In striking contrast, the terrestrial hunters occupied the extensive interior hinterlands, forested or not. They invariably moved on foot (fig. 51), horses playing a role only in historical times among the Aónikenk.[30] Minor variations of foot-hunting adaptations are apparent in historical times among different regions of Patagonia and Tierra del

Fig 52 Selk'nam group in front of a guanaco-skin shelter watches intently as a hunter makes an arrow, *c.* 1907–8.

Fuego. The shape and size of their dwellings also varied, with dome-shaped huts being used in Peninsula Mitre,[31] vertical windbreaks in northern Tierra del Fuego (fig. 52) and larger, more elaborate tents in the pampas of the continent (see fig. 80). By historical times conical huts made of large logs seem to have been an important type of dwelling among the Selk'nam, but these probably only developed very late when remnant groups gained access to iron tools and sought refuge in the forest (fig. 53).

Their tools and weapons were made of raw materials obtained from rock outcrops

Fig 53 Tenenésk and his wife in front of a Selk'nam hut.

and the inland forests. Bows and arrows comprised the basic weapons for war and for hunting guanaco (fig. 55). Projectile points were made of stone, a material that, following outside contact, was swiftly replaced by glass (fig. 54). Sometimes these objects were hafted in ways which suggest that they were used as cutting tools.

Bolas were used in the continental pampas to hunt guanaco and ñandú (the flightless bird). This weapon appears in Patagonia at least as early as 4,500 BP, and probably much earlier (see chapter 2) and its importance seems to have increased with time (see chapter 3). When the Aónikenk adopted the horse bolas must have become even more effective when deployed from horseback (see fig. 108).

Rodents were not the important resource that some authors have suggested, but must surely have been consumed.[32] They were trapped in their burrows with the help of

Fig 55 Selk'nam hunter poised to despatch an arrow. He holds the quiver between his teeth.

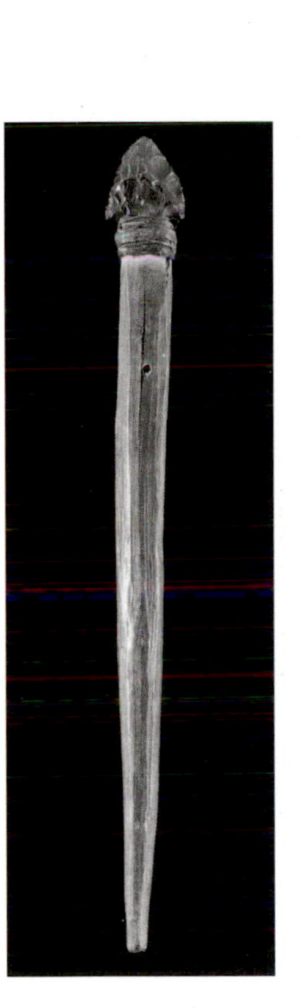

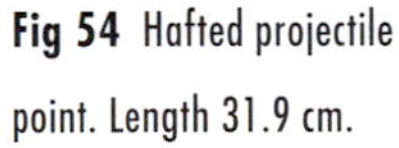

Fig 54 Hafted projectile point. Length 31.9 cm.

wooden sticks. In Tierra del Fuego a variety of traps and snares were used to capture birds, and collective hunting also took place. Birds were apparently less important in Aónikenk subsistence.

Plants played an important role for the Haush and Selk'nam, especially mushrooms (*Cytaria darwini*) and seeds (*Descurainia antarctica*). The preparation of the latter – called *tay* by the Selk'nam – demanded a grinding technology. Well-worn rock mortars are commonly found at sites located in places that were visited repeatedly. The role of plants among the Aónikenk is not well known, although they are reported to have collected a variety of fruits and mushrooms.[33]

The seasonal movement of guanaco herds was crucial in determining the hunting patterns of the Selk'nam on the island, as well as the Aónikenk on the continent.

Fig 56 Selk'nam women on the march, rounding the south-eastern shore of Lago Fagnano (Lago Kamí), Tierra del Fuego, *c.* 1907–8.

Guanaco display marked territorial behaviour and use the same general area all year long. In rugged terrain they migrate within a limited annual range that is rarely larger than 20 km.[34] Thus human groups focusing on guanaco could easily predict the locations where family groups, whether sedentary or migratory, were to be found. They pursued them by trekking to places where they could take full advantage of the topography to ambush the herds.

Just like the canoe people, the terrestrial hunters were never exclusively dependent

on either terrestrial or maritime resources. Even when their economy was centred mostly on terrestrial fauna, maritime resources still played a role (fig. 56). Shellfish were intensively collected, fish speared with barbed harpoons in tidal pools,[35] and beached whales exploited whenever the opportunity presented itself. This happened more frequently than might be imagined.[36]

One consequence of this is that the terrestrial hunters, who repeatedly used favoured haunts near rookeries to hunt sea lions and gather mussels, created archaeological sites consisting predominantly of maritime fauna. The maritime and terrestrial worlds were therefore never completely separated. The best example is that of the Haush, discussed at the end of this chapter. In fact, nowhere was there an immutable boundary between these contrasting cultural adaptations. In places like Admiralty Sound in western Tierra del Fuego, or in the interior seas on the continent, there is clear evidence of contact zones[37] marked by a varied range of archaeological sites.[38]

The antiquity of the ethnographic cultural configurations

European contact brought about important changes to native societies, forcibly modifying many traditional subsistence practices.[39] We must therefore ask whether some historically observed practices are the result of recent contact with Europeans, or whether they accurately reflect long-standing patterns. To solve this puzzle the archaeological, linguistic and ethnographic data available for historical times must be compared carefully with the archaeological evidence for the prehistoric period.

If we accept that historical adaptations were considerably modified in response to changing historical circumstances during the contact period, we can now consider what happened before the arrival of the Europeans. The archaeological record reveals several distinct ways of life, each of them centred on a different suite of resources. Technological studies have identified marked differences in the techniques used in the production of bifacial artefacts on either side of the Strait for approximately the last two thousand years.[40] Other lines of evidence support this pattern of variability. Studies of faunal remains show great diversity in the range of food resources that were exploited, with sea mammals playing a more prominent role in Tierra del Fuego after 6,000 BP.[41] Scant but consistent evidence for hunting ñandú as a source of fat is recorded on the mainland during the same time period.[42] Since ñandú do not appear to have reached the island it is possible that sea mammals instead were hunted in Tierra del Fuego for their fat, among other things, and were important even for terrestrial hunter-gatherers.[43] This increasing emphasis on hunting sea mammals meant that traditional territories grew to encompass the regular exploitation of coastal sites. The sequence of superimposed occupations which can be up to three thousand years long in some places, has produced some quite large sites.

Around 4,000 to 3,000 BP the cultures of Fuego-Patagonia formed a very heterogeneous mixture. More than one multi-generational population was surely involved, since people were distributed almost everywhere, from the outer islands of Cabo de Hornos[44] to the Atlantic coast[45] and the inland waterways and seas on the Pacific side.[46] Nevertheless, there was still much unoccupied territory between these regions. Most of the Patagonian plateaux were apparently used only seasonally, probably for the hunting of young guanaco,[47] and several islands of the western channels were visited only sporadically.[48] In fact, isolation of the canoe people from terrestrial hunters has been proposed as the main explanation for stability in their adaptation and may also account for the divergence in the languages spoken by each.[49]

In continental Patagonia the evidence ranges from sites suggesting a more intensive adaptation to the coast[50] to the incidental use of marine resources by terrestrial hunters,[51] and locations which are clearly the product of a fully terrestrial adaptation. Examples of the latter include the use of land above 1,000 m in the Paso Verlika site in the Sierra Baguales,[52] evidence for exploitation of the huemul in the Río Ibañez region,[53] and the generalised use of lacustrine environments at several sites.[54]

Recent archaeology for the last four thousand years in northern Tierra del Fuego comprises sites with large quantities of guanaco bones, but also includes sea lions at coastal locations. The sites are small, five to ten metres in diameter, except near the coast where huge shell middens have built up close to locations rich in immobile resources, principally mussels. Originally these sites may have begun simply as small heaps (see fig. 39) and grown incrementally in the course of hundreds or even thousands of years. But such impressive shell accumulations are not always long-term habitation sites, for these may or may not have been located close to the coast. In many senses the archaeological record is not a simple and direct product of the ethnographic context in which it was created and we must bear in mind that the formation of a given site could be the result of repeated occupations by different groups for different motives. This is one of many reasons why the archaeological record may not always match what is anyhow an incomplete ethnographic picture.

Differences in the range of prey and hunting technology have in time led to cultural distinctions, some of which have been used to characterise ethnographic groups. But whatever the impressions formed by explorers and sailors in the centuries following contact, we must recognise that these reflect only 'snapshots' amid what was in reality an immensely varied and highly dynamic cultural configuration. By way of example we can offer the long-standing issue of the Haush, foot hunters who nevertheless took systematic advantage of the populous sea lion rookeries of the north of Peninsula Mitre. This group has been referred to by many names, including Haus and Mannekenk,[55] but the application of this label serves merely to gloss over significant ambiguities. Some ethnographic sources[56] suggest that there were few differences between the Haush and the Yámana, while other descriptions[57] clearly suggest Selk'nam affiliations.[58] Human remains recovered in the area can be compared with both the Selk'nam and the Yámana.[59] The archaeological record shows many similarities to that of the Selk'nam, suggesting a comparable adaptation, but with an added emphasis on sea mammals.[60]

These ambiguities make it difficult to classify the inhabitants of south-eastern Tierra del Fuego and it is not really clear at what point in time the label Haush or Mannekenk can be applied. The so-called Haush cultural configuration may in fact be relatively recent, although still pre-dating contact. The more distinctive characteristics, like the dome-shaped hut,[61] or the use of sea lion cloaks,[62] are in place by the time of initial contact in the eighteenth century.[63]

In dealing with this problem, the case of Isla de los Estados, lying across the Estrecho de le Maire that separates it from Peninsula Mitre, immediately comes to mind. Archaeological remains dated to around 2,500 BP have been found on this island which has always been separated by the sea from Tierra del Fuego.[64] Canoes must undoubtedly have been used to cross the Strait and reach the island. Canoe people from the southern channels were surely involved, but no remains have been found that can be unequivocally attributed to them. Instead, the lithic technology is reminiscent of the artefacts commonly attributed to terrestrial peoples from northern Tierra del Fuego.[65]

The observations given above on the ancestors of the Haush also hold true for the ancestors of the other groups encountered in historical times. The elusive image of the ancestors of the Haush, or the affiliation of the inhabitants of Isla de los Estados, merely serve to emphasise the complex dynamics involved in both terrestrial and maritime adaptations. The degree of change implied by the material culture of the inhabitants of Fuego-Patagonia may appear to be great, but it is probably within the normal bounds of material variation for hunting and gathering societies living on islands. It has been suggested that hunter-gatherer adaptations on islands may be more susceptible to external influences due to the reduced range of habitats compared with continents.[66] Recent evidence from the Chonos archipelago illustrates this point.[67] Island populations have few options available in response to direct usurpation of their traditional territories by outsiders and density-dependent adaptations tend to appear faster. Moreover, better opportunities for cultural change arise for smaller populations occupying a new niche[68] and, contrary to much that has been claimed,[69] stability is the exception rather than the rule on islands.

Conclusions

The key theme developed in this chapter is the dynamic relationship between natural and cultural variation. A number of discrepancies have emerged between the archaeological record and ethnographic information recorded in historical times and these paint a more complex picture than that traditionally proposed.

It is clear there were significant variations in subsistence strategies on either side of the Strait after 4,000 BP, each closely tailored to the local distribution of key subsistence resources and their relative importance. Moreover, technological changes beyond those linked to subsistence activities have also been identified. These also indicate that different terrestrial adaptations evolved in late times on either side of the Strait.

Many of the differences in subsistence, settlement strategies and language observed on Isla Grande de Tierra del Fuego and the outlying islands may be a product of isolation. In addition, a completely new maritime way of life makes its appearance around six thousand years ago, or earlier, and this adaptation also exhibits significant variation.[70] This pattern of multi-divergent evolution helps to explain the cultural mosaic found by Europeans in Tierra del Fuego in the sixteenth century. It is not, however, the final word.

NOTES

1 Cocilovo and Guichón 1991.

2 Vayda and Rappaport 1963; see also Rouse 1986: 10.

3 Study of mithocondrial DNA has revealed a lack of the 9 bp COII/tRNA^{Lys} Region V deletion in thirty bone and teeth human samples from the period after 4,000 BP from Patagonia and Tierra del Fuego. Since this deletion is of Asian origin and has been detected in different American groups, its absence suggests either that the original colonising populations might have lacked it, or that it was lost by genetic drift (see Lalueza *et al.* 1993/94). See also Cocilovo 1981; Guichón 1995.

4 See Hammel and Howell 1987: 142.

5 Keegan and Diamond 1987: 58.

6 Ortíz-Troncoso 1975; Orquera and Piana 1983; Hernández 1992; Guichón 1995.

7 Vignati 1927; Chapman 1982.

8 See discussion in Cooper 1917: 5ff.; Mena 1988: 151, and chapter 3, this volume.

9 Gusinde 1982.

10 Lefevre 1989; Savanti 1994.

11 Cooper 1917: 190.

12 Curry 1991.

13 Nami 1985/86.

14 Bird 1946: 68.

15 Legoupil 1985/86; see also Cooper 1917: 29.

16 Gusinde 1982: 227.

17 See, for example, Chapman 1982 and chapter 5, this volume.

18 Borrero 1994.

19 Orquera and Piana 1983.

20 Bird 1980.

21 Vidal 1987.

22 See, for example, Laming-Emperaire 1972b: fig. 8.

23 Byron (1768) records having witnessed this in the Chonos archipelago.

24 See Cooper 1917: 118.

25 Legoupil 1985/86.
26 Herbst *et al.* 1994.
27 Lefevre 1989.
28 See, for example, Legoupil 1993/94.
29 Legoupil 1985/86.
30 Martinic 1995.
31 See Joppien and Smith 1985.
32 Popper 1887.
33 Martinic 1995.
34 Franklin 1982.
35 Gallardo 1910: 203.
36 Borella *et al.* 1996.
37 Gallardo 1910; Casamiquela 1973.
38 Ocampo and Rivas 1996.
39 Dunnell 1991.
40 H.G. Nami, pers. comm. 1988; see Nami 1986 for information on the mainland case, and Kligmann 1991 for a discussion focused on the Canal Beagle.
41 Orquera and Piana 1983; Piana 1984; see also Mena, chapter 3, this volume.
42 See, for example, Caviglia and Figuerero Torres 1976; Massone 1981; Mengoni Goñalons and Silveira 1976.
43 Borrero 1986; Lanata 1996.
44 Legoupil 1993/94.
45 Gómez-Otero 1994.
46 Legoupil 1983.
47 Franco and Borrero 1995.
48 Legoupil 1993/94.
49 Legoupil 1985/86.
50 Prieto 1988.
51 Massone 1979; Bird 1988.
52 Franco 1997.
53 Mena 1991.
54 Goñi 1988; Belardi *et al.* 1992.
55 Cooper 1917.
56 For example, Skottsberg 1913.
57 For example, Lista 1887.
58 Cooper 1917: 51.
59 Cocilovo and Guichón 1985/86.
60 Lanata 1996.
61 Joppien and Smith 1985.
62 Purísima Concepción 1765.
63 Lanata 1997.
64 Horwitz 1993.
65 Horwitz 1990.
66 Ibid.
67 Constantinescu and Aspillaga 1990; Ocampo and Aspillaga 1991.
68 Hammel and Howell 1987: 146.
69 MacArthur and Wilson 1967.
70 Ortíz-Troncoso 1975; Orquera and Piana 1983; Piana 1984; Legoupil 1989; Figuerero Torres and Mengoni Goñalons 1986; Yesner 1991; Horwitz 1993.

5 The Great Ceremonies of the Selk'nam and the Yámana

A Comparative Analysis[1]

Anne Chapman

Introduction

The Selk'nam and the Haush were 'foot people', hunters of land mammals, while the Yámana were 'canoe people', mainly dependent on marine resources. Over the course of thousands of years their forebears had successfully adapted their subsistence patterns to exploit both the pampas grassland and the maritime environment.

The Selk'nam men hunted guanaco, foxes and certain rodents which together comprised their main sources of sustenance, clothing and shelter. They also hunted birds, fished in the rivers and took advantage of the occasional beached whale. Toolmaking was another essential male occupation. The labour of the Selk'nam women involved care of the children, gathering berries, mushrooms, shellfish and birds' eggs, the manufacture of baskets, preparation of hides and sewing skins for clothing. The women, too, were responsible for bearing the heavy loads consisting of all their domestic effects, as well as the infants, from one camp-site to another (fig. 57, and see also fig. 56). The men rarely carried anything except their bows and arrows and the game they had killed, although they did on occasion carry the burdens when the women became exhausted. Women's work was as demanding as it was indispensable for survival although, with the exception of child care, it was not as specialised as the men's tasks, nor did it entail the same degree of training. The male dominance which characterised their economy was expressed in their one great ceremony, known as Hain.

In contrast to the Selk'nam, the labour of the Yámana women was specialised, as well as essential for survival. They were responsible for paddling the canoe and mooring it in the kelp from where they swam ashore, often with a baby on their back. The men did not learn to swim and although they could row they did so rarely, as they were usually occupied in attempting to kill seals, dolphins and the like from the canoe. The navigating tasks of the Yámana women involved serious training and great stamina and was required at nearly all times. The male occupation of hunting was important, though the group could survive on fish, shellfish, eggs, berries and fungi, which the women obtained. Whales were a much sought-after source of food. Those which were sick or dying from wounds inflicted by the orcas (killer whales) were 'finished off' by groups

Fig 57 Selk'nam woman and her child, *c.* 1923.

of men in several or more canoes, who struck at them with harpoons, sometimes for days on end, and occasionally one drifted on shore. Whale-meat and blubber lasted for several months and supplied many families. The seal was sought for food and its oil was used as ointment and its hide for clothing and often for shelter. The otter also provided clothing, though the flesh was rarely consumed. The guanaco was highly regarded as food and clothing, but in Yámana territory it was found only on Isla Navarino and the south coast of the Isla Grande. The men also hunted a variety of birds; the cormorants nesting in the high cliffs were especially difficult to seize. The heavy work of manufacturing the bark canoe also fell to the men. The women aided by sewing together the sections of the bark. This equitable division of labour was manifested in their ceremony called Chiexaus.

The first inhabitants frequented the south shore of Tierra del Fuego and the Canal Beagle some six thousand years ago (see chapter 2). The three groups (including the Haush) had therefore probably been neighbours for a long time before the arrival of the Europeans. By the nineteenth century the Selk'nam and Haush were known to have intermarried with the Yámana along the north shore of the Canal Beagle, and some individuals were bilingual.

Similarities of the two ceremonies

The principal ceremonies of the Selk'nam and the Yámana shared the same objective of initiating adolescent boys or young men into full manhood. Among both groups the ceremonies were the occasion for the periodic gathering of these semi-nomadic people who otherwise spent most of their time in isolated family groups at lonely camp-sites seeking sustenance along the coasts or in the hinterlands of the islands.

The Selk'nam called their initiation ceremony Hain, and the same name was applied to the sacred hut which was the focus of much of the ritual activity.[2] The Selk'nam had adapted elements of their ceremony from the Haush, who had preceded them on Tierra del Fuego by many centuries, if not longer. Both groups had migrated there from Patagonia as hunters. Although their cultural traditions were similar, they were not identical. By the nineteenth century, or perhaps before, the Haush had been confined by the Selk'nam to the eastern extremity of the island.

Colour plate 1a Icebergs on Lago Grey, Torres del Paine, Chile.

The Yámana, for their part, performed two initiation ceremonies, the Chiexaus and the Kina, but here we are mainly concerned with the former because it was their principal traditional ceremony. The initiation rite performed at the beginning of the Chiexaus ceremony featured a spirit called Yetaita, impersonated by one of the male adults, who fought with the initiate. Yetaita is quite similar to the Selk'nam spirit called Shoort (see below). Throughout both lengthy ceremonies the youths (only male in the Hain, both male and female in the Chiexaus) were taught the moral behaviour expected of them, instructed in their respective oral traditions and trained to perform many of the tasks awaiting them as adults. Children, uninitiated youths and the Selk'nam women were all forbidden to enter the sacred huts and were not to be told the 'secret': that the Chiexaus spirit (Yetaita) and the spirits of the Hain appearing during the ceremony were only men disguised as such. Both ceremonies might take place when a beached whale was located, though the Yámana were more dependent on whales as a food source. The ceremonies would end whenever the supply of food was consumed, or when the counsellor or director so determined.

Among the Selk'nam and the Yámana girls also underwent a series of simple rituals when they experienced their first menstrual period. They were confined to their home or to a separate hut for a week or more. Every day they were painted with red clay and designs were applied to their faces; they had to refrain from speaking and were given very little to eat and drink. They were counselled and instructed by the older women concerning their future tasks and roles as diligent wives and mothers. However, these rituals did not form a part of the ceremonies in question.

Colour plate 1b Patagonian landscape near Río Gallegos, Argentina.

Contrasts between the cultures and the two ceremonies

While the similarities between the Hain and the Chiexaus are few and mainly concern their functions or objectives, there are numerous contrasts which reflect the different traditions and provenances of the two groups. The Selk'nam and Haush had come to Tierra del Fuego from the great steppes of Patagonia, while the Yámana undoubtedly had a very long history as a maritime people. Although the patrilocal family (nuclear and extended) comprised the basic unity of these groups, the Selk'nam and Haush were organised into lineages and observed strict rules of exogamy which stipulated the prohibition of marriage within the mother's as well as the father's lineages. Their land was partitioned among the approximately eighty lineages (sixty-nine among the Selk'nam and eleven among the Haush), with designated territorial limits for each lineage. The lineages were grouped in very large territorial units. There were three such units (called *sho'on*, 'sky') among the Selk'nam and an equal number among the Haush. They were called 'sky' because they denoted the cardinal points: the north, south and west for the Selk'nam, and the north, south and east for the Haush. The Selk'nam did not occupy the eastern section of the island and therefore had no territories associated with the east sky. By the

Colour plate 2 *left* Detail of a map of Estrecho de Magallanes by Captain John Narborough showing a group of Indians (probably Kawéskar) on Tierra del Fuego with skin cloaks, baskets and spears, *c.* 1670.

Colour plate 3 *below left* Model canoe made from the bark of the southern beech (*Nothofagus betuloides*) with miniature paddle, woven basket and plaited grass rope. This shows the interior construction consisting of dozens of carefully shaped ribs. Length 91.5 cm.

Colour plate 4 *opposite above* 'Inhabitants of Tierra del Fuego' (probably Haush at Bahía Buen Suceso) by Alexander Buchan, who accompanied Captain Cook on his 1769 voyage. Note the baskets hanging inside and the skins being stretched and dried on frames on the roof and by the right side of the hut.

Colour plate 5 *opposite below* Baskets woven in a tough grass (*Juncus magellanicus*) known to the Yámana as *mápi*. These were used by both the Selk'nam and the Yámana. Height of the tallest 21 cm.

Colour plate 6 Suit of hide armour made from seven layers of horse skin, similar to that in fig. 107. This is said to have been obtained by Captain Philip Parker King in *c.* 1827 from soldiers who had been sent to suppress an Indian rebellion. Length 127 cm, width (with stretched sleeves) 162 cm.

nineteenth century nor did the Haush have any territory in the western part of the island. These four 'skies' were loosely correlated to the spatial location on the island of the eighty territories of the lineages. The main axes of the plan of the ceremonial hut represented this concept of 'skies' (see below).[3]

The Yámana had a less structured system. Their society and territory was divided into five rather loosely defined units, referred to as 'dialectic districts', which were not strictly endogamic, that is, a man would sometimes marry a woman from another district. The individual or nuclear family was the basic economic and social unit. Several related, neighbouring families comprised what is usually called a 'local group', a varying number of which made up each of the five districts.[4] None of these units was significant in the plan of the Chiexaus hut.

At first glance the outstanding contrast between the two ceremonies was that the Hain was devoted exclusively to the initiation of the young men, called *kloketen*, and the social reunion in the ceremonial hut involved only the adult men. On the other hand, both sexes were admitted to the Chiexaus hut: the male and female adolescents to be initiated, called *ushwaala*, and the adult women along with the men. This fundamental distinction reflected the division of labour, and differences in the way in which power was apportioned within each of the two groups. While the Selk'nam and Haush societies were strictly patriarchal, the Yámana society was less so, without however being matriarchal.[5]

The duration of both the Hain and Chiexaus could vary: they usually lasted as long as the food supply allowed, though the former was more adaptable in this regard than the latter. The advantage of an extended ceremony was that it allowed time to train the male adolescents. So it is not surprising that while the Hain usually lasted much longer than the Chiexaus, the latter was performed more often than the former. The Hain ceremony might last an entire year or even longer. The Selk'nam, like the Yámana, profited from a beached whale to celebrate a Hain, but they depended mainly on the guanaco herds and moved about from one site to another, constructing the sacred hut in places where the herds could be hunted nearby. The Chiexaus was reported to last only about two months, until a beached whale had been consumed. Until the beginning of the last epoch of Yámana existence as an autonomous people, in about 1860, whales were very frequently hunted down or located on one or another shoreline. Even in the late nineteenth century the surviving Yámana spoke of having participated many times in a Chiexaus following their initial induction.

The sequence of events or scenes in both ceremonies was flexible, fixed by the director/counsellor, or simply by the desires of the participants. The initiation rite was invariably held at the beginning of the ceremonies, but was not a climax. The Hain had a climax (the death and birth scene, see below) which was sometimes repeated during the same ceremony, but the Chiexaus had no climax at all and the adults re-enacted their *yaka*, often translated as 'games', whenever they were inspired to do so.

The sacred huts of the Hain and the Chiexaus were conceived as a representation of their respective social schemes, though in very different ways. The Hain hut encapsulated the whole of Selk'nam society as a reflection of the cosmos. The four 'skies' (designated by the main posts of the hut) represented the mystic axes of the universe and every adult male who participated in the ceremony had a special place inside the hut, as he had in the cosmos. The Chiexaus hut was a metaphor for the Yámana social scheme. It represented the habitat of their main prey, seals, and its symbolism was focused more on the participants than on the hut itself. The Hain hut was therefore far more 'loaded' with symbolism than the Chiexaus hut.

The Kina

As we have seen, the symbolic attributes of the Hain and Chiexaus are almost diametrically opposed. However, while the Selk'nam had only one initiation ceremony, the Yámana performed another, the Kina, which was carried out as a supplementary initiation for the young males. The basic concept of the Kina and its supporting ideology (i.e. the myth of the matriarchy) had undoubtedly been 'learned' from the Selk'nam. However, the Yámana added many elements to their Kina in the form of scenes performed by some fifty 'spirits'. These were completely absent in the Selk'nam Hain. The Yámana had ample time and opportunity to become familiar with the Hain. However, the Yámana already had their own initiation ceremony and their men were less inclined to lord it over their womenfolk. For these and perhaps other reasons the Kina did not supplant the Chiexaus, neither was the Kina's symbolism simply a copy of that of the Hain, nor was it enacted with the same rigour.[6] The young males were obliged to submit to the Kina initiation after twice having passed the Chiexaus initiation, although why twice should be specified is not clear. By the late nineteenth century a few women were allowed in the Kina hut as participants. Such laxness with the rules of the ceremony was never tolerated among the Selk'nam, in so far as is known.

The Hain hut, its symbols and the participants

The Hain was a large wigwam with a circular base and one entrance facing the east, away from the cleared area where the spirits (actors) performed (fig. 58). Its height and circumference varied according to the length of the tree trunks available, but every attempt would be made to build it as large as possible.[7]

The four principal posts were aligned in a circle at the base of the hut at the cardinal points, called 'skies' (*sho'on*). These posts symbolised the 'centres' (*oishka*) of the 'skies', the 'wombs' (*haiyen*), the places of creation in the universe. Then three additional posts were put up, on the 'periphery' (*shixka*) of the principal posts. Each of the seven posts represented a number of territories and lineages (fig. 59). The three posts were situated between the four central posts, at the north-east, the south-east and the south-west. Why there was no post for the north-west is a question that remains unanswered,

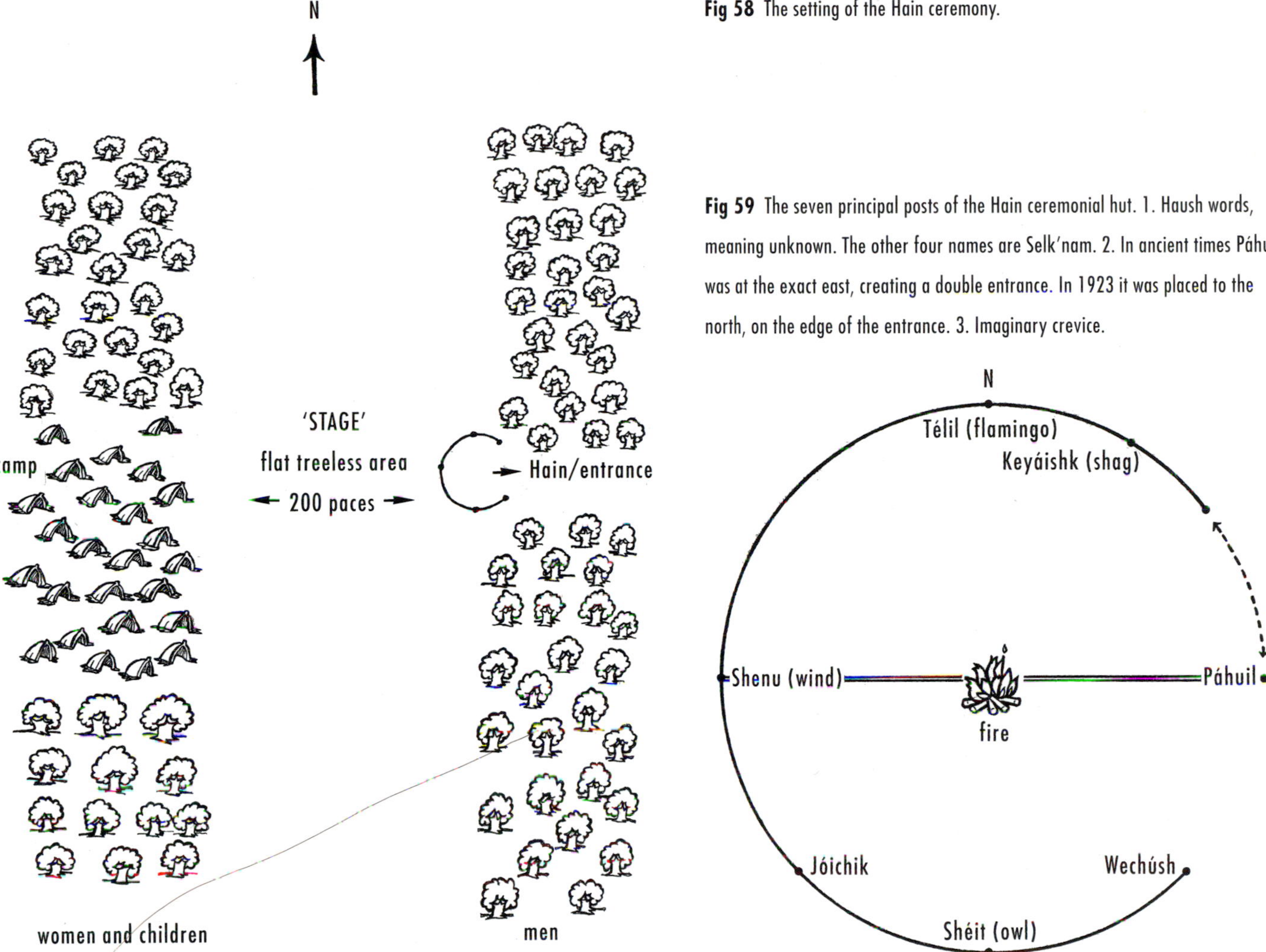

Fig 58 The setting of the Hain ceremony.

Fig 59 The seven principal posts of the Hain ceremonial hut. 1. Haush words, meaning unknown. The other four names are Selk'nam. 2. In ancient times Páhuil was at the exact east, creating a double entrance. In 1923 it was placed to the north, on the edge of the entrance. 3. Imaginary crevice.

except in so far as the number seven had a ritual significance. However, a few territories were assigned to the north-west, the 'peripheral' section which lacked a post, and the men born there stood and sat in this section of the Hain. Each of the eighty (or more) territorial units was assigned either to one of the four principal 'skies' or to an intermediate, peripheral, sky.[8]

The pre-eminent post placed at the entrance to the hut symbolised the supreme significance of the eastern sky . The east and west posts were the first to be set up and were thought of as brothers-in-law. In a physical and symbolic sense they were mutually supportive, as were the north and south posts. As mentioned above, everyone among the Selk'nam and Haush together belonged to one of the four skies (or to a peripheral sky), according to the territory where they were born, which was usually the father's. In 1923 when Gusinde participated in a Hain the Selk'nam had no territory to assign to the east sky, and the Haush had no territories corresponding to the west sky. When the Selk'-nam performed the ceremony without the Haush the east post was occupied by some

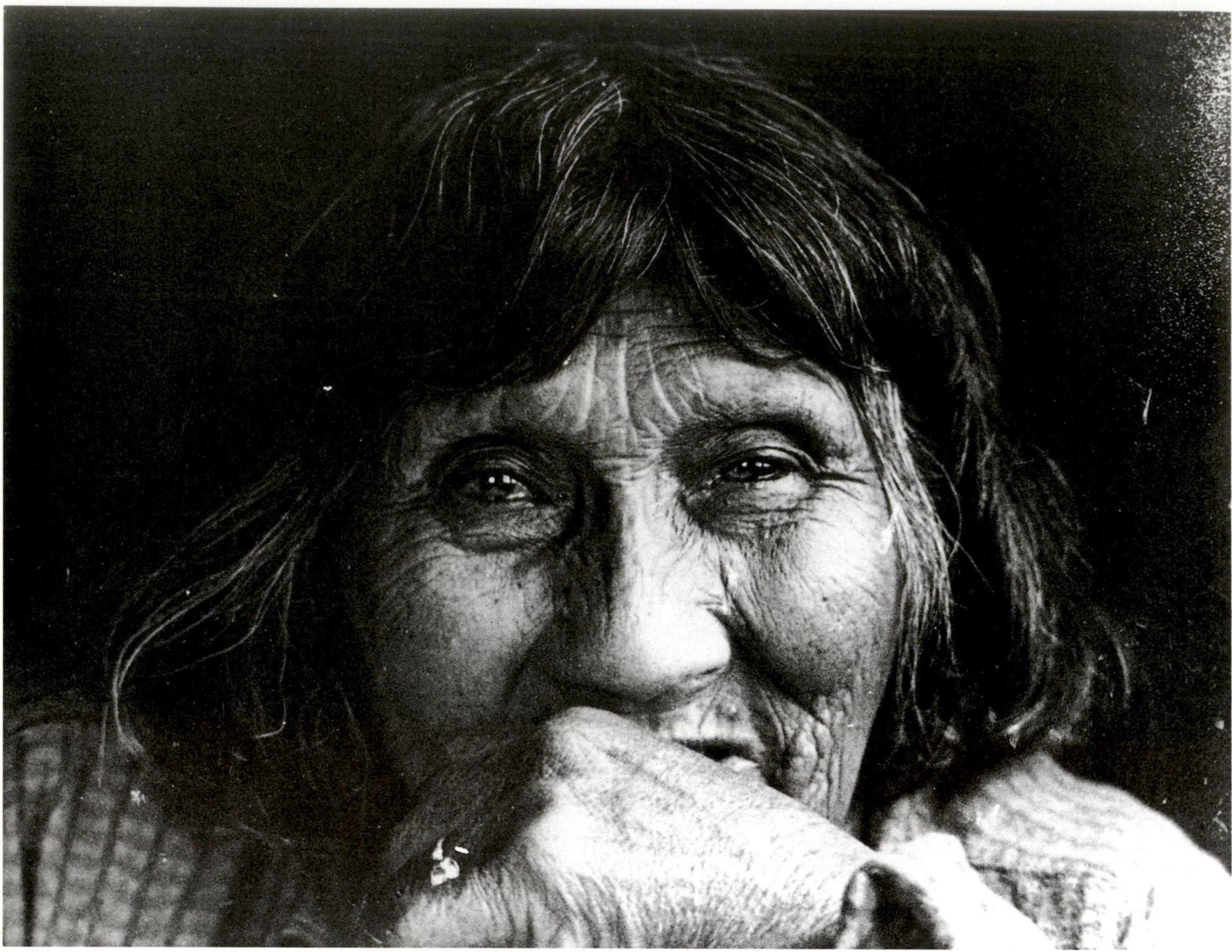

Fig 60 Lola Kiepja in 1966, the year of her death.

men from the north or north-east posts.[9] As skies were the exogamic units (marriage being forbidden between two people who were associated with the same sky), brothers-in-law had to be from different skies.[10]

The four skies were thought of as 'invisible cordilleras of infinity'. The east sky, whose post was named Páhuil (a Haush word) was the most magnificent yet the most treacherous of all. Its great slippery cordillera was surrounded by a sea of boiling water. The magnificent cordillera of the west sky was the centre, or womb, of the wind (Shenu), for whom the west post of the Hain was named. The sun (Krren) was associated with the west sky, and Shenu was his brother. Shenu had assisted his brother Krren, then a powerful shaman, when they attacked the Hain of the matriarchy and its dominant leader, the female shaman Moon (Kreeh). In the beautiful cordillera of the south sky lived Owl (Sheit), for whom the south post was named. His mighty brother Snow (Hosh) also lived there with their sister Moon, once sovereign of the famed matriarchy, who had been defeated by her husband Sun. Finally, the cordillera of the north sky was the home of Sea (Kox) and his sister Rain (Chalu). Here the mystical Flamingo

(Telil) was honoured as the north post of the Hain. The souls (*kaspi*) of humans returned at death to these wombs, the skies, with which each person had been identified during his or her lifetime. In the wombs of the vast outer space the souls were reunited with the eternal forces of the universe.

Fig 61 A man wearing the *tolon* mask.

Fig 62 *above right* A man wearing the *asl* mask.

Each participant formed a part of this complex imaginative edifice. Lola Kiepja (fig. 60), my first Selk'nam informant, once said to me, 'I am Snow [as her territory belonged to the south, the 'womb' of Snow], my mother is Wind [whose territory was classified as the west, where Wind resided], and my husband is Rain [meaning that his territory was considered as being in the realm of the North, that of Rain].'[11]

Two types of mask were used during the Hain ceremony; one, called *tolon*, made of guanaco hide or bark, was conical in form, about seventy centimetres high and usually held on with both hands at ear level (fig. 61). It had long slits for the eyes because the 'actors' often walked or danced sideways. A similar mask, made of bark, was used in the Kina ceremony, but none was used in the Chiexaus. The other type, called *asl*, was simply a guanaco-leather hood stuffed with leaves or dry grass to give it body, pulled down over the head and tied at the back (fig. 62). Small holes were cut out for the eyes and mouth. Lucas Bridges saw a mask of this type which was folded over on the front, thus forming a monstrous drooping nose.[12]

The conical masks were treated with a veneration which puzzled Gusinde. When not

Fig 63 *Kloketens*, or young initiates, who participated in the 1923 Hain ceremony.

in use, these masks were laid carefully against the interior wall of the ceremonial hut and great care was taken that they not topple over. These were not props, they were objects which emanated power and accordingly were handled with much respect. If such a mask were damaged it was thought that its user would fall and injure himself, or even kill himself 'accidentally' during the next performance. If a mask fell off a performer's head, even while he was out of sight of the women, the performer was considered to be in great danger.

The masks were painted, as were the bodies of the spirits. As a general rule the predominance of one colour denoted a specific sky: red for the west, white for the south and black for the north. Certain spirits used a cloud effect produced with a chalk-like powder which signified the west sky. Apparently no one colour was associated with the east sky. The unmasked participants, including the *kloketens*, were also painted with designs (*tari*) which combined with the colours that identified the skies to which they belonged (fig. 63). As each adult man had a place in the system he had the right to paint the symbols of his sky on his body. The counsellors (directors of the Hain) had to correct abuses in the use of these symbols, including those which might be committed by the women, for they too painted themselves frequently during the ceremony and took positions in the camp which corresponded to their respective skies (fig. 64).

The locale of the Hain can be compared to a theatre, and the ceremony to a play. The sacred hut would be the back stage where the 'actors' (the adult males) discussed their roles, donned their disguise and transported their equipment without being seen by the women, the public. I use the term 'actor' in quotation marks because the performers were not just impersonating the spirits in order to control and terrorise the women. The 'actors' were somehow imbued with the supernatural personality of the spirits they were impersonating. The stage would correspond to the level ground, extending from the other side of the hut, some two hundred paces wide (see fig. 58).[13] Here, masked and painted 'actors' played their roles in the different scenes of the spirits, some of whom descended from the heavens while others rose from the entrails of the earth. The seating area of the

Fig 64 Three Selk'nam women painted for the 1923 Hain. Angela Loij, in the centre, is painted with the design (*tari*) of the whale, a symbol of the north sky to which she belonged.

theatre can be imagined as the camp with its huts where the public or audience (the women and children) viewed the performance. The women often came to the edge of the stage to see the spectacle close up and, during certain scenes, they advanced onto the stage and played games with the 'actors'. Like some modern plays the leading 'actor' (Shoort), and others as well, mingled with the public and engaged them in different sorts of 'farces', which at times were intended to frighten and even create panic among them.

Among the audience the mothers of the *kloketens* played a prominent role in the ceremony. The mother of the oldest *kloketen* had special duties, as well as the privilege of wearing the men's headband (fig. 65). During the entire ceremony she was expected to volunteer her time and energy working for the other families in the camp. It was assumed that she was constantly grieving for her lost son, and she was expected to foster this impression. She was responsible for initiating the women's singing twice a day, before dawn and at noon. She was also required to begin the welcoming chant for the Shoort spirit when he emerged from the Hain hut for his daily visits to the camp.

During the Hain the young male Selk'nam was subject to an initiation rite as well as a prolonged learning experience. While being initiated he was called a *kloketen*, but afterwards he would be a *maars*, an adult man. A recalcitrant youth might be obliged to go through the ceremony two or even three times if the elders were not satisfied with his achievements following the first and second Hains. Three Hains might take five years or more, depending on how often the ceremonies were held and how long they lasted, but a man could not marry until he had 'graduated'. It is not without reason that the last generation of Selk'nam spoke of the Hain as a college. In the past a *kloketen* would have been between seventeen and twenty-two years old when he first entered the Hain, as physical stamina, mental alertness and a certain maturity were required of the novice.[14] He had only one supervisor, usually a cousin or an uncle, while in the Chiexaus each initiate was assigned two supervisors, a man and a woman.

Fig 65 A *kloketen* mother.

The *kloketen* was taken on long hunting expeditions with the adult men as training exercises. He was also sent to hunt alone for several days or more. Before he set out the elders warned him that he might run into the dreadful spirit called Shoort. The youth lived off the forest as best he could, hunting in solitude. Meanwhile, one of the men disguised himself as Shoort and set out in pursuit of the novice, surprising him at the moment when he could appear most terrifying. He further frightened the candidate by threatening him, or even striking him, with a burning torch. When the youth returned to camp and told his story the men pretended to be terribly scared, too, with the intention of increasing the candidate's fears. Later he was told, or realised himself, that this Shoort, like the one which had tortured him during the initiation rite, was simply a comrade in disguise. The 'real' Shoort remained in his subterranean abode, probably attentive to just how he was being represented.

Prior to European contact there were four counsellors, or directors, one for each of the four central posts.[15] However, in 1923 when Gusinde participated in a Hain, there were only two. Both were shamans but not prophets. In any event, by then no prophets remained. The counsellors had to know how much liberty might be taken with the age-old tradition. Rather than give orders they persuaded, taught and explained in an effort to prevail upon dissident opinions or projects which might jeopardise the objectives of the ceremony. The wheels of society had to be kept turning, an equilibrium maintained between the forces of the universe and the discrepant centrifugal actions or attitudes of the members of society. In short, the counsellors had to be tactful and convincing diplomats.

The counsellors solicited the collaboration of the *kloketens* for such work as fetching water and firewood and cleaning the hut. Gusinde observed that all such mundane tasks were performed with good humour and without the slightest resentment.

At times the ceremonial hut looked like a communal workshop or a happy get-together. The men would be engaged in making or repairing the hunting weapons, mixing paint materials, preparing feathers for ornaments, making the masks, roasting meat or simply relaxing. Gusinde noticed that the older men spent long hours chatting,

Fig 67 *opposite above* Chiexaus ceremonial hut viewed from the outside.

Fig 68 *opposite below* Chiexaus ceremonial hut viewed from within.

happy to find themselves again among male friends and kin whom they might not have seen since a previous Hain. The women (the public) in the camp were also pleased to meet their seldom-seen kin and friends.

The Chiexaus hut, its symbols and the participants

Gusinde was initiated in the Chiexaus early in 1920, when the ceremony lasted only ten days, the usual duration being about two months. In March 1922, when Gusinde was accompanied by his colleague Wilhelm Koppers, both were initiated, though the ceremony lasted a mere four days.[16] The last Chiexaus was presented during the early years of 1930 on the Chilean shore of Canal Beagle, at Bahía Mejillones reserve on Isla Navarino.

If the locale of the Hain may be compared to a theatre, and the ceremony to a play, that of the Chiexaus, with its communal kitchen, may be thought of as a small-town church and the ceremony a revival meeting (for the adults). But for the Yámana the Chiexaus hut represented a cave (*alain*) at sea level, where the sea lions took shelter. 'Just as these animals gather in their cave, so the Yámana come together in the Great Hut for their games' (figs 67 and 68).[17] It was thirty or more feet long, depending on the number of participants, though sufficiently high so that the occupants could stand up, which they often did while dancing. A large fire was kept burning in the centre of the hut and sometimes two or more fires were lit along the centre aisle. It had an opening at each extreme; the main opening was used by the adults and the smaller one by the *ushwaala*, the initiates. The adults took a seating place wherever they chose along the walls of the hut, which they kept during the entire ceremony (fig. 66). The *ushwaala* were seated near their two mentors or supervisors (*padrinos* in Spanish). The hut had no special orientation and the seating arrangement had no symbolic meaning. The interior was decorated with slabs of wood or the sticks of the structure, which were painted black, red and white in designs of dots and lines. Though the designs may have been only decorative, the three colours again symbolised a cave at sea level: red recalled the rocks covered by kelp, white the froth of the waves and black the mussels.

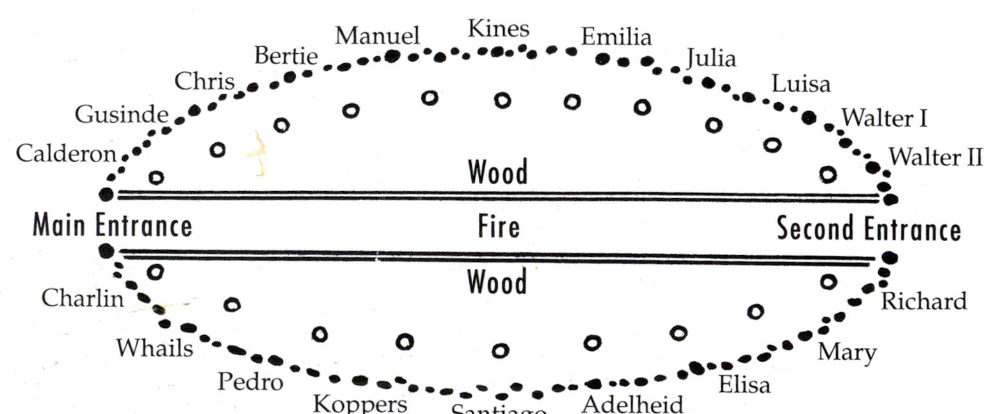

Fig 66 The seating arrangement in the Chiexaus hut of 1922.

An ordinary hut, constructed near the Chiexaus, was used as a kitchen to prepare meals for the adults and adolescents, confined as they were for many weeks to the sacred hut. In 1922 three to five women shared the cooking tasks and returned to the ceremonial hut whenever possible to participate in the activities.

Fig 69 Yámana youth wearing the Chiexaus headband.

Only the adolescent males were subject to the initiation ordeal. The so-called 'evil spirit', Yetaita, like Shoort (the principal spirit of the Hain) emerged from the depths of the earth through the fire to frighten the male *ushwaala*. Yetaita was impersonated by a vigorous man whose body was painted white and decorated with red lines about 5 cm long. In contrast, his face was painted red with white lines drawn in every direction. His hair was tangled and covered with white powder and he wore a sort of cape made of feathers. He was not nearly as disguised as Shoort, who always wore a mask. Unlike the Selk'nam spirit, at least in 1922, Yetaita only fought with the *ushwaala* for ten minutes to frighten him and then revealed his real identity as the culmination of the initiation ritual. It is very likely that this ritual had been performed with much more vigour in the past, as Gusinde's description portrays a very mild sort of initiation which did not involve the torture the Selk'nam youths suffered at the mercy of the Shoort figure. Like the latter, the 'real' Yetaita was said to appear in the forest and frighten the youths if they didn't behave, but Yetaita was never presented in special scenes as was Shoort (see below). Yetaita is the only spirit which resembles a Hain spirit and it, as well as the Chiexaus initiation rite, reads like a watered down version of the corresponding Shoort and the Hain initiation rite.

The other Chiexaus spirits were mostly humans of mythical times who had been transformed into different animals. The adults (women and men) disguised themselves as whales, seals and certain birds and imitated their movements and their chants, snorts and songs. They rarely appeared outside the sacred hut and when they did they were not performing for a public but rather carrying on their assigned roles and performing for themselves, often in a state of trance, possessed by the spirit they were representing. The objective of these scenes, or 'games', was to embody their spiritual ancestors; apparently it was also fun and not exclusively sacred.

All the participants in the Chiexaus wore a headband, or crown, called *hapaxel,* which was formerly made of down and symbolised the foam on the crest of waves (fig. 69). The adults danced, making gentle back-and-forth movements with long painted sticks which they held horizontally and moved in imitation of the oscillation of the sea. 'As the waves constantly enter and leave the caves, those who inhabit the Chiexaus wear their *hapaxel* all the while and several times during the day they imitate the to and fro movement of the waves with the dance stick, dancing at the same time.'[18]

Another important symbol of the Chiexaus were the trees in the nearby forest which were believed to have been people in mythical times and to which the *ushwaala* youths paid special homage when they were sent to gather firewood.

Gusinde was told several times that certain birds (the thrush and cormorant) held

Fig 70 Participants in the Chiexaus of 1920. The Austrian ethnographer Martin Gusinde is seated fourth from the left at the back. The *winefkemas*, representing a predatory bird of the sea, are on the far left and right respectively, holding their strap.

their own Chiexaus. When the *ushwaala* (he or she) were awakened at dawn they sang out *was! was!* as the thrush would, and then broke a branch or stick to reassure the thrush that the *ushwaala* was awake and ready for the tasks of the day.

Although the ceremony was directed by a chief (*jefe* in Spanish) called Ulashtekuwa and an inspector, the most visible authority was Winefkema, who represented a predatory bird of the sea (*Leucophaeus scoresbyi*). Formerly he wore a crown of white albatross feathers, which otherwise only a shaman might wear. He was covered with white paint over which red stripes 2.5 cm or so wide were drawn all around his body at intervals of about 12.5 cm. His face was also painted white with a red stripe reaching on either side from his nostrils to his ears. Winefkema's main attribute was a leather strap twelve to fifteen metres long, also painted white, with red cross stripes (fig. 70). He frequently stood on the roof of the Chiexaus to spy on everyone nearby. He shouted out a loud *ho? ho? ho?* when any uninitiated child approached the sacred hut and ensured that no *ushwaala* escaped from the hut. He would strap a disobedient youth and tie him to the minor entrance of the hut where he would be left without food or drink for half a day or more. The Winefkema, usually with his several helpers, might forcibly recruit the adolescents assigned to the Chiexaus to be initiated. If one resisted he and his helpers would swing the strap around him and drag him to the hut. If a girl assigned to be initiated resisted being taken to the sacred hut she would be treated more gently. A cloth (in former times a seal skin) would be thrown over her head and she would be escorted or dragged to the hut. All the *ushwaala* entered the hut, voluntarily or not, with their heads covered.[19]

The Hain ceremony: its two principal spirits

The scenes of the Hain, with the exception of the initiation rite, were entirely absent from the Chiexaus ceremony. The two principal spirits as well as the 'baby' of one of these, will be briefly presented in the following paragraphs. These spirits personify the intensely dramatic leitmotif of the ceremony: the struggle of the heroic male to control the dangerous female. This universal theme not only comprises a fundamental contrast with the Chiexaus, it situates the Hain and its mythology on a par with the classical literature and theatre of the Old World. The 'message' and performances of the Chiexaus are less ponderable but more fraternal.

The roles and the characteristics of these two spirits, Shoort and Xalpen, are the kernel, the dynamic nucleus, the main thrust of the spectacle, portraying as they do a misogynist/misanthropist couple. The terrifying daily sojourns of the principal male spirit, Shoort, into the camp to intimidate the women will be described; however, the initiation rite in which this spirit played the torturer and his other scenes will only be mentioned briefly. Shoort also played parts apparently unrelated to his aggressive role. He appeared on stage in eight different disguises, representing the passage of the diurnal time.

He was usually disguised as an owl, which was closely associated with the personage who was transformed into the sun (see below). These and other indicators form the basis for proposing that Shoort is the symbol of the sun which, though implicit in the ceremony, is never overtly declared. I suggest that Shoort epitomises the dauntless male, the great shaman Krren, who became the sun. Krren discovered the secret of women's power, of the female Hain. He led the 'great revolt' during which nearly all the women were massacred. And it was the sun who also led the inauguration of the male Hain and founded the patriarchal society.[20] In everyday language *krren* signifies both the sun and the day, and Shoort probably symbolised both.

I also propose that the only mythological ancestor with which Xalpen may be identified is the vanquished yet implacable matriarch, Kreeh, who was transformed into *kreeh*, the moon.[21] The basis for this hypothesis is, firstly, that Xalpen's husband is Shoort (assuming he represents the sun). Secondly, the texts of the chants sung by the women to pacify Xalpen are almost identical to those which they sang to the Moon to calm her when she was in eclipse. Thirdly, the plan of the Hain hut, whose mistress was Xalpen, is a symmetrical inversion of the moon's heavenly domicile, where she received the shaman's spirits who visited her during an eclipse. Fourthly, both Xalpen and the moon, when in a fit of rage, threaten to kill the men and even to devour them. And, as if to affirm their femininity, both are mothers. The beautiful Tamtam (later transformed into a canary) was the daughter of the moon and the charming K'terrnen, Xalpen's baby.

The Selk'nam women lived in a patriarchal society in which male authority was very real, though not usually manifested through violence. Moreover, the women were not without defence. If a woman was beaten or otherwise mistreated by her husband her lineage was obliged to come to her aid. The women had little access to positions of prestige, such as those of shaman, prophet or sage. They played virtually no role in the preparation of the ceremonies and, above all, they were often humiliated and sometimes beaten during the one great ceremony, the Hain. These and other discrepancies between the sexes appeared on a symbolic level as irreconcilable. The men were the sun, the women the moon. The diurnal forces were posited against the nocturnal forces; warm, life-giving rays against cold, tenebrous beams. But if the lunar forces were so barren, how could it be that women create and nourish life? Although this contradiction remained unresolved, it was circumvented by the scenes in which Xalpen killed the *kloketens* and even the adult men. Thus symbolically men were deemed superior to women because they were sacrificed in order to save society; therefore women owed them absolute allegiance.

Once the ideological premises were accepted, it became imperative that women remain submissive and that they never regain the ascendancy they once enjoyed during the epoch of the primeval (mythological) matriarchy. So long as husbands kept their wives in subservience a revolt could be averted. But if a wife were to be disobedient or insubordinate to her husband, her behaviour might be imitated by other women and the latent moon quality, which exists in all women, might begin to express itself, gain momentum and culminate in a general insurrection in which the women would re-establish the matriarchy. Hence the vital role of Shoort. He had to inspire fear in the women, threaten them daily during the entire ceremony, and often harass and even beat them.

Shoort was the most dynamic and active spirit of the Hain and the one most feared by the women and children; he also tortured the *kloketens* during the initiation rite. Like the dreaded Xalpen, he emerged from his subterranean abode into the Hain hut through the fire in the centre of the hut. He began the ceremony (in two guises) and, weather permitting, was the only one to go daily into the camp and was the last to appear on the final day.

There are more Shoorts than any other Hain spirit. While all appear to be manifestations of the sun symbol, some have different functions and status. But there is a prototype Shoort who is represented by the *k'tétu* (also spelt *ktátu*), a small white owl (*Speotyto cunicularia*). As a mythological being K'tétu had been a powerful shaman. He belonged to the west sky, the sky of the sun, was 'very perfect', handsome and muscular, and played the part of Shoort particularly well during the first men's (mythological) Hain.[22] Later he was transformed into this owl. The Shoort personage of the real Hain was decorated to depict the patterns of the owl's feathers: white bands around the eyes of his mask, white knees and white splotches of paint on his body (fig. 71).

Besides some basic patterns of the K'tétu designs, individual Shoorts were distinguished by a combination of colours and designs on the body and the mask. Lucas

Fig 71 The two Shoorts of the north and left skies.

Fig 72 *above right* Two subordinate Shoorts.

Bridges observed that there was a wide variation in the colouring and pattern of the make-up for this spirit. One arm and the opposite leg might be white or red with spots or stripes of another colour superimposed, to which down could be added. In 1923 Shoort went into the camp wearing the *asl* mask which resembled a pointed cap pulled tightly down over the head and neck. This mask was undoubtedly preferred to the cumbersome conical mask, because this Shoort was in close proximity to the women and at times his movements were very energetic and he had to use both hands.

Besides the eight diurnal Shoorts there were seven principal Shoorts who were associated with the main posts of the Hain and were known by the names of these posts. It was they who meted out the punishment to the women during their daily visits to the camp. There were also an equal number (if not more) of subordinate Shoorts, the helpers and messengers of the principal Shoorts (fig. 72). They came on stage singly or in twos or threes and occasionally went into the camp. Gusinde observed that the subordinate Shoorts were less graceful than the principal ones. Given the quantity of Shoorts which appear in any one Hain celebration, the same men would play more than one of these roles.

Shoort's movements were stereotyped. As Shoort was made of rock the 'actors' had hard, muscular bodies and while performing they gave no sign of breathing. Shoort moved with very small steps, leaping suddenly and stopping abruptly, his body trembling like the *k'tétu* owl. And, like the owl, he jerked his head from side to side while advancing. When he wore the *asl* mask his hands were folded into fists, the upper parts of which were turned to the front. His arms were arched. When he emerged from the Hain and upon re-entering it he lifted both arms, still arched, holding his fists upwards as if flexing his biceps. Like the other spirits he was speechless. His movements were stiff and decisive, as if to fascinate or to create panic in the observers. Great training and aptitude were required of the latter Shoort. This was perhaps the most difficult of all the Hain roles, for the 'actor' could not lapse among the women and children. Any gesture which revealed the real identity of the performer would betray the 'secret'. A child once recognised a Shoort 'actor' by his manner of walking.

Handsome men who played the Shoort roles exceptionally well were long remembered and the women, especially, appreciated a beautiful Shoort among those who paraded on the stage, but not those who went to the camp daily to mistreat them. The men warned the women when a Shoort was about to begin his daily visit to the camp by chanting *ho? ho? ho?*[23] Thereupon all the women, except the *kloketen* mothers, ran into their huts, covered themselves with guanaco furs and lay motionless, for they had orders not to set eyes upon Shoort while he was in the camp. The *kloketen* mothers stood in front of their huts with their heads shrouded in capes, for they must not look at Shoort either. All the women echoed the *ho? ho? ho?* chant from beneath their capes while he strode among the huts. During these visits a shaman accompanied Shoort, probably to give added weight to his authority. If snow was on the ground the shaman discreetly swept it over Shoort's footprints with his own foot, as spirits do not leave footprints.

The daily visits were a time of anxiety for all the women apart from a favoured few: the wives and in-laws of the shamans. Shoort was invariably in a tyrannical, solemn mood. He came to punish those women whose behaviour had not conformed to the model of subservient wife, or who had not given acceptable renderings of the chants, or had not donated sufficient paint and meat to Xalpen. If a man in the Hain hut was not satisfied with the conduct of his wife he confided in the Shoort who was scheduled to visit the camp. The latter acted on what he had been told, as well as on the woman's reputation, or even his own impulses. He sought out the wayward wife in the camp and may only have frightened her by shaking her hut violently, stirring up her hearth, throwing her belongings outside, or flinging a basket at her as she huddled under a guanaco cape. But at times he stabbed at her with a stick, even beat her and tore down her dwelling. In the latter case he proceeded with great caution, as if he were afraid of the construction. First he touched one of the hides which partially covered the hut or tent, then slowly grasped it and finally jerked it forcefully off the wooden frame, throwing it on the ground. He did this with all the coverings of the dwelling until only the posts remained. Then he seized the posts, one by one, scattering them until the structure was entirely demolished. All the while he was very careful to avoid the water bags, for spilt water could wash off his paint.

If Shoort noticed a woman or an older child peering at him he might strike them with intent to kill. Children also hid under the capes or fled to the edge of the camp to escape Shoort, fearing he might kill them or at least whip them. In 1923 the men secretly removed all the firearms from the camp and hid them in the ceremonial hut for fear that a woman might fire at a Shoort. When Shoort was about to depart from the camp one of the men yelled to the women, 'Get up. Shoort is leaving.'

Then the *kloketen* mothers rushed to the edge of the stage, stopped and sang *ho kreek*[24] (another name for Shoort) repeatedly while moving their forearms up and down to pay him homage as he returned to the Hain. As he approached the Hain he stopped in front of the post with which he (the 'actor') was associated, flexed his biceps, jerked his head from side to side while making his whole body tremble, and took a great leap, head first, toward the entrance on the east side of the Hain, as if he were plunging into the underworld.

Frequently a few men came into the camp, their faces covered with blood, telling the women that they had been wounded by Shoort in retaliation for some female misbehaviour. The women attempted to care for them, without however being allowed to inspect the wound closely. The men in the Hain hut had jabbed their lips, nose or ears with a pointed stick and/or used guanaco blood to produce the blood with which they daubed the 'wounded' men.

On the last day of the Hain Shoort made his final visit to the camp and the director simply announced to the public that the ceremony had come to an end.

Xalpen was the most sinister of all the Hain creations. She was unpredictable, irascible, the ally of no one, not even the women. All the earth spirits, with the exception of a spirit called Halaháches, were at her command. Although she was Shoort's wife all the men, and especially the *kloketens*, were considered to be her husbands. As she was gluttonous (*chiteré*) and cannibalistic she would devour any woman or child who came too close to the ceremonial hut.

Xalpen was rarely shown on stage and sometimes did not appear at all during an entire ceremony. But her presence inside the hut was constantly felt. In 1923 she was displayed only once, on the thirty-first day of the ceremony which lasted fifty days. Xalpen was the only spirit represented by an effigy, but only her upper half, said to be made of rock, was displayed. The frame of the effigy was about six metres long and constructed of long bows tied firmly together with guanaco nerve strings. It was partially stuffed with branches, twigs, leaves and grass and covered with guanaco hides with the fur turned inside. This covering was entirely painted, either with white chalk or with red ochre decorated with long white stripes. Her lower body was flesh and was not shown to the public, nor was her index finger with its long, sharp nail. One man or several men moved the structure from the inside. Lucas Bridges saw 'a Xalpen' led onto the stage by a shaman and noticed that the man inside the structure staggered along slowly, often pausing under its great weight, until he manoeuvered it into position facing the women from a distance. Lola Kiepja told me that she knew of a Xalpen moved by three men inside.

On eight occasions during the 1923 Hain she emerged from under ground, passing through the fire inside the Hain, raging and demanding food. She carried a large leather bag adorned with red-and-white painted stripes. This bag had to be filled with food for her to take back 'home' and feast upon. The women knew the moment of her arrival by the men's repetitive cry of *wa* from within the Hain. As she was invariably hungry, her bag flew out of the Hain onto the stage. Thereupon the women ran toward the Hain bearing baskets full of mushrooms, berries, fish or any other food, for Xalpen accepted anything edible. They ran, chanting *ha? ha? ha?*[25] in a playful mood, to the centre of the stage, as close to the Hain as they dared, and set down the baskets. They returned to the camp, probably pleased that they had fed the monster, for when she had food in her bag she usually calmed down for a while. At times when Xalpen was in a frenzy of hunger a shaman, painted with a black line from ear to ear across his upper lip, his cape with its fur turned inside, would go to the camp accompanied by several other men to demand meat from the women for Xalpen. Angela Loij told me that after they departed the women took positions in the camp at the points of their respective skies and sang in her praise. The unrelenting repetition of this dramatic scene contributed greatly towards sustaining the intensity of the long ceremony.

But the scene of the death and birth was the climax of the ceremony. It took place at night by the light of a huge bonfire on centre stage. Because of Xalpen's indomitable sexual urge and much love-making with the *kloketens* she eventually became pregnant. The birth pains drove her into an uncontrollable frenzy. When her suffering became most intense she threw a bow out of the Hain. This was an ominous sign, for it meant that she was about to kill someone in order to vent her rage caused by the torments of the birth pains. The Hain quaked as never before, as her ghastly screams boomed through its walls and flames sprang through the roof. The Hain trembled as if there were an earthquake, the men from within vigorously shaking its structure. The hollow screams of Xalpen (the men were pounding the floor with rolled-up guanaco hides) were heard from the swaying hut. Then flames flew out of the apex, for the men first set fire to a long pole and then poked it through the apex making it appear as if the hut was on fire. Amid the turmoil Xalpen, using her long, sharp fingernail, disemboweled the *kloketens* one by one. The women heard their terrible *wa* groans as each expired and they intoned the *yo te kó ho li*[26] chant, hoping to appease the murderess who was killing the fathers of her baby. Suddenly all was silent and then the women knew that the baby had been born and that Xalpen had returned with it to the underworld.

The men were overwhelmed with grief for the *kloketens*. A short while later the women, who had gathered on the edge of the stage, saw two elders carrying the corpse of a *kloketen* drenched in blood. One elder supported its head flopped to one side and the other its legs and feet. Its eyes were closed, guanaco blood seeped from its ears and mouth and poured from the disemboweled wound which reached from its neck to its genitals. The procession moved slowly and silently around the stage and returned to the Hain. Soon two other elders emerged carrying another corpse, until all the (dead) *kloketens* were displayed. The women approached them as close as they were allowed, chanting the *hain kojn hórsho* lament. The oldest women stepped forward, waving their capes in an attempt to give breath back to the corpses. Federico, who was *kloketen* in a Hain of 1920, told me, 'I felt really sorry to see the women cry so. They really thought their sons were dead.' A day or so later, when they were all brought back to life by a small shaman spirit named Olem, a real shaman announced to the women, 'All is well. Now you may leave. The *kloketens* are alive again.' Federico commented that the women felt very relieved.[27]

During the fifty-day duration of the Hain in 1923 a less bloody version of the death and birth scene was played twice, which illustrates the theatrical aspect of the Hain. If the Hain were simply a ritual, this scene would logically be enacted only once. As a rite, what would be the need or justification for repeating it? But as theatrical spectacle it was re-enacted because of its highly dramatic content. In this context we can understand the reaction of the women as public. They believed the young *kloketens* had been killed by Xalpen, the first time as well as the following time or times, for they were participating in a drama and not merely observing a ritual. The impact of the ceremony as theatre is crucial to an understanding of the women's supposed ignorance of the 'secret'.

After the *kloketens* had been restored to life a shaman announced to the public, 'Soon you will see something beautiful. Get ready!' The women prepared themselves for the scene by painting their faces with small white dots in lines which radiated from the lower eyelids down onto the cheeks. When they heard soft hand-clapping from the Hain they knew that baby K'terrnen was emerging from the earth and they began singing *héj ká rak?*[28] (fig. 73), the welcoming chant, as they stretched out their arms to draw the baby out of the Hain so that they could rejoice in admiration of 'Xalpen's gift of life'.

The new arrival was impersonated by a slim *kloketen*. The baby could be of either sex; if a girl, the 'actor' pressed his genitals between his legs and bound them there with a string made of guanaco nerve or tendon. Esteban Ichtón said that this role was very difficult to play and that the performer was chosen from among the youths who were *hauwitpin*, perfectly formed. Federico agreed, adding that the actor's body had to be so straight that there was no space between his legs when he was standing and that his chest had to be flat, without prominent nipples.

Fig 73 The baby K'terrnen being presented to the women by the counsellor Tenenésk during the 1923 Hain.

K'terrnen was entirely painted and decorated with parallel rows of down, from the tip of its conical mask to its fingers and toes. The tiny feathers were glued to the infant's body on red and black or mixed-coloured paint. The bright paint colours seen through the soft white down produced a glimmering effect, making the baby seem all the more supernatural. Esteban explained that, as K'terrnen was not adorned on its back, great care was taken to keep its face toward the public. The baby held its body rigid with the arms flat against its sides (careful to sustain its mask) and, as it was made of rock, it did not breathe, but swayed slightly back and forth as it looked straight ahead. Lola Kiepja explained that although the creature was newborn it grew fast but still could scarcely walk, so it had to be supported. This was the task of two respected men, usually shamans, who appeared with their faces adorned with one dot above the nose and one on each cheek. They wore an especially handsome feather headdress and their capes with the fur turned inside. (In their daily lives the Selk'nam always wore their capes with the fur outside.)

The *Wunderkind,* to use Gusinde's term, emerged from the Hain taking very tiny steps, braced on either side by the two elders who gently pushed it sideways, stamping their right heels on the ground as they did. The baby took one little step with the left foot, then an even smaller step with the other foot, then drew it up to the left heel while holding both legs stiffly together. The threesome slowly advanced sideways across the stage, facing the public. Lola used to imitate K'terrnen's gait for me, moving her shoulders slowly to and fro while chanting *héj ká rak*?

If K'terrnen saw a woman in the public who had been the object of complaint by her husband it stopped and took a few steps backwards. Even so, the women continued singing of their admiration and contentment all the while the baby was on stage. When it returned to the Hain, the men greeted it with gentle hand-clapping, while the women shouted: 'It has gone, below! *kau kó? him*'.

Though the Hain was aimed at admonishing the women to remain submissive wives, they did experience moments of real enjoyment, such as during the K'terrnen scene. When all is said and done, did they really believe that Xalpen was an earth monster, that she actually did massacre their beloved sons, that Olum brought them back to life, and that K'terrnen was a grown-up baby? Were they persuaded that the spirits were contriving to punish and humiliate them, and that their very lives were in danger? Was the Hain a religious ceremony whose symbols were a testimony of their faith, or was it a moving play, a theatre, believed for the moment but known to be fiction? Or was it a combination of both? Were the women really duped? Angela Loij confided in me that 'while the men were busy in the Hain' women gathered near the camp but in some out of the way place (fig. 74). Amid much laughter one or two women imitated Shoort, another a *kloketen*. Such mocking of the 'official' Hain strongly suggests that the women knew that Shoort and probably the other spirits were men in disguise, though they, like the men, firmly believed that the spirits really existed.[29]

Fig 74 Group of Yámana women and girls at Bahía Orange, Isla Hoste, in 1882–3.

Outstanding contrasts between the 'canoe people' and the 'foot people' prevailed not only with respect to their adaptations to different environments and their social organisations but also their ceremonial traditions. Assimilation of the Yámana to certain Selk'-nam cultural manifestations should not obscure the authenticity of these two great hunting-gathering traditions.

NOTES

1 Martin Gusinde is the author of the most extensive study of the Indians of Tierra del Fuego, originally published in German in four tomes. These have subsequently been translated into Spanish and published, from 1982 to 1991, as nine volumes (in four tomes) in Buenos Aires by the Centro Argentino de Etnología Americana. The first tome of the translation in Spanish (in two volumes), dedicated to the Selk'nam, though a complete edition, does not include the album of photographs or the map published in the original edition. The second tome (in three volumes) deals with the Yámana. The third tome (in two volumes) concerns the Halakwulup (Kawéskar or Alakaluf), but contains less detailed information than the others, probably because Gusinde's manuscripts were destroyed during the Soviet occupation of Austria in 1945 and he was obliged to rely on his memory and perhaps notes which escaped destruction. The subject of the fourth tome (in two volumes) is the physical anthropology of the three groups. Only the Yámana volume has been translated into English and published in off-set in five parts by the Human Relations Area Files, New Haven, 1961. This is not, however, a complete translation and is not easily accessible. The mythology of the

Selk'nam and Yámana has also been translated into English by Johannes Wilbert. Other important and easily available sources are Thomas Bridges' Yámana-English Dictionary and his son, Lucas Bridges', well-known book, *Uttermost Part of the Earth*. Dr Paul D. J. Hyades, a member of the French expedition to the Cabo de Hornos area in 1882–3, also made an important contribution to knowledge of many aspects of the Yámana culture, though he never witnessed the initiation ceremonies and had no original information on them. The author of this article has spent years working with the last few knowledgeable descendants of the Selk'nam and Yámana concerning their traditional cultures.

2 Gusinde erroneously called it the Kloketen ceremony, which is the term used for a youth while he was undergoing his initiation.

3 Chapman 1982: 20, 50–60. Among the Selk'nam a more extensive kinship unit, which might be called a kindred, was not represented in the Hain hut, as only siblings shared the same kindred.

4 Gusinde 1986, II: 607–10, 763–7.

5 From here on I will refer mainly to the Selk'nam, though often the Haush will be implied. There is less detailed cultural data concerning the latter, but it is known that they celebrated a ceremony very similar to the Hain, from which the Selk'nam probably assimilated many features.

6 The Kina ceremony was presented in 1922 for Gusinde and his colleague W. Koppers (from 6 March to 11 March) for the young male Yáhgans who had never seen it. Gusinde wrote seventy-three pages on the Kina (1986, III: 1286–339), without counting the other references to the ceremony throughout his text. Koppers also described it quite extensively.

7 It should be emphasised again that the Hain ceremony and the symbolic plan of its hut, as described in its last period principally by Lucas Bridges in the early twentieth century and by Gusinde in 1923 (when it was performed over a fifty-day period near Lago Fagnano on the Argentine section of the Isla Grande, Tierra del Fuego), was a blend of both the Selk'nam and the Haush traditions. We have no data on how the Haush 'Hain' was celebrated by the Haush alone, nor is its name known. But the Selk'nam of the southern region, and their neighbours the Haush, often performed the celebration together, as was the case in 1923. Much later information gathered by the author concerning subsequent Hains largely corroborates and supplements the previous data. The last Hain was enacted about 1933.

8 Chapman 1982: 20, 80–6; Gusinde 1931 (translated into Spanish in 1982). The names given to the seven principal posts reflect the dual origin of the ceremony. Three posts had Haush names: Páhuil, Wechush and Joichick, the meanings of which remain unknown. The names of the other four posts are common Selk'nam words: Telil (flamingo), Sheit (owl), Keyaishk (cormorant or shag) and Shenu (wind). The myth of the first masculine Hain relates that these posts were named for the seven great shamans who hewed the posts from rock. The relationship between the posts and their names is not literal. For instance, the posts named for birds were in no real way associated with the living birds.

9 Chapman 1982: 85.

10 The lineages (and their corresponding territories) associated with one of the four principal 'skies' enjoyed greater prestige than those classed as peripheral. This requires more explanation than space here permits.

11 Chapman 1982: 85.

12 Bridges 1935: 36.

13 Gusinde 1931: 832–3.

14 Gusinde 1931: 829, 1031.

15 Echeuline in Chapman 1982: 93.

16 Gusinde was permitted to take notes during the ceremony in 1922 and afterwards interviewed a number of men and women on the subject. He wrote a hundred-and-sixty-seven pages on this ceremony (1986, II: 771–929; III: 1288–92, 1455–60). See also Koppers 1924.

17 Gusinde 1986, II: 803, note 260.

18 Gusinde 1986: 829.

19 Gusinde 1986, II: 799–808, 805–7, 829, 837 note 292, 840, 882.

20 See the corresponding myth in Gusinde as translated in Wilbert 1975, 161–4.

21 For the two principal myths concerning the moon see Gusinde in Wilbert 1975: 147–61.

22 For this myth see Wilbert 1975: 161–5.

23 Chapman 1978, II: chant no. 5.

24 Chapman 1978, II: chant no. 6.

25 Chapman 1978, II: chant no. 8.

26 Chapman 1978, II: chant no. 21.

27 Chapman 1982: 139–40.

28 Chapman 1978, II: chant no. 24.

29 Chapman 1982: 146–56.

6 The Meeting of Two Cultures

Indians and Colonists in the Magellan Region

Mateo Martinic B.

Introduction

The first sightings of strange phantoms floating on the sea like waterfowl must have filled the indigenous inhabitants of southern South America with a mixture of fear and curiosity. Their astonishment probably grew each time they glimpsed the beings aboard these leviathans, speaking loudly in incomprehensible tongues, clothed from head to foot and carrying sticks which spat fire amidst a thunderclap (fig. 75). This is how the European explorers and their ships must have appeared to the Indians during the early years of contact. The stark contrasts between these two different worlds would come to shape the character of all later interaction (fig. 77).

The first historical encounter between Ferdinand Magellan's crew and the Indians

Fig 75 Armed engagement between Dutch mariners and the Selk'nam at Cabo Orange on the southern shore of the Estrecho de Magallanes, Tierra del Fuego. Drawing by van Noort, 1599.

took place in April 1520 in the Bahía San Julian on the east coast of Patagonia. The Indians were a band of Tehuelche. The initial apprehension of the aborigines was most likely followed by a trusting curiosity, answered in kind by the newcomers, resulting in a cordial relationship that was reinforced by the distribution of trinkets. This type of contact was almost the exception to the rule during the first century of sporadic European presence on these southern shores. Violent encounters must have erupted frequently, probably fomented by the Europeans' rough treatment of the natives when

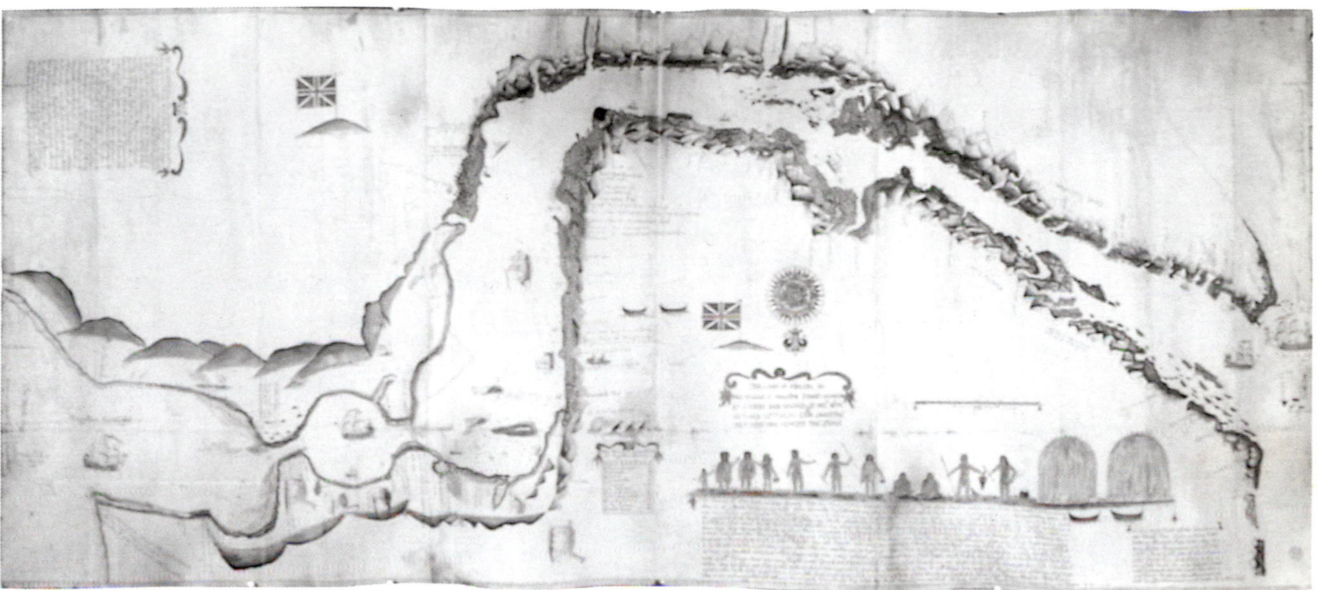

Fig 76 Estrecho de Magallanes as represented on the map made by John Narborough, c. 1670. See colour plate 2 for detail.

their brutal and unjustifiable aggression provoked in turn a defensive reaction. Examples abound, the most notorious being the events triggered by Pedro Sarmiento de Gamboa's men at Bahía Gente Grande, Tierra del Fuego (February 1580) and at Punta Dungeness and San Gregorio on the continental mainland (February and March 1584).[1] If these were only skirmishes, then truly cruel and bloody clashes were instigated by Francis Drake in the Cove of Cuaviguilgua, located in the western reaches of the Estrecho de Magallanes (August 1578), and by Olivier van Noort's crew at Cabo Orange on the northern coast of Tierra del Fuego (November 1599).[2]

However, after such an inauspicious start, the mutual hostilities slowly dissipated. During the seventeenth century European ships (including vessels which voyaged from Chiloé and the central coast of Chile and Peru) seldom sailed to this region and the memory of those bitter incidents probably faded.

In 1670 a scientific expedition led by John Narborough, a British naval captain, entered the Estrecho de Magallanes,[3] inaugurating an era of research in southern South America that would last for two centuries (see fig. 76 and colour plate 2). During this period peaceful relations were established with the various indigenous groups and this permitted the first investigations into their ethnic and cultural traits.

Narborough is credited with providing a promising start to the new relationship with

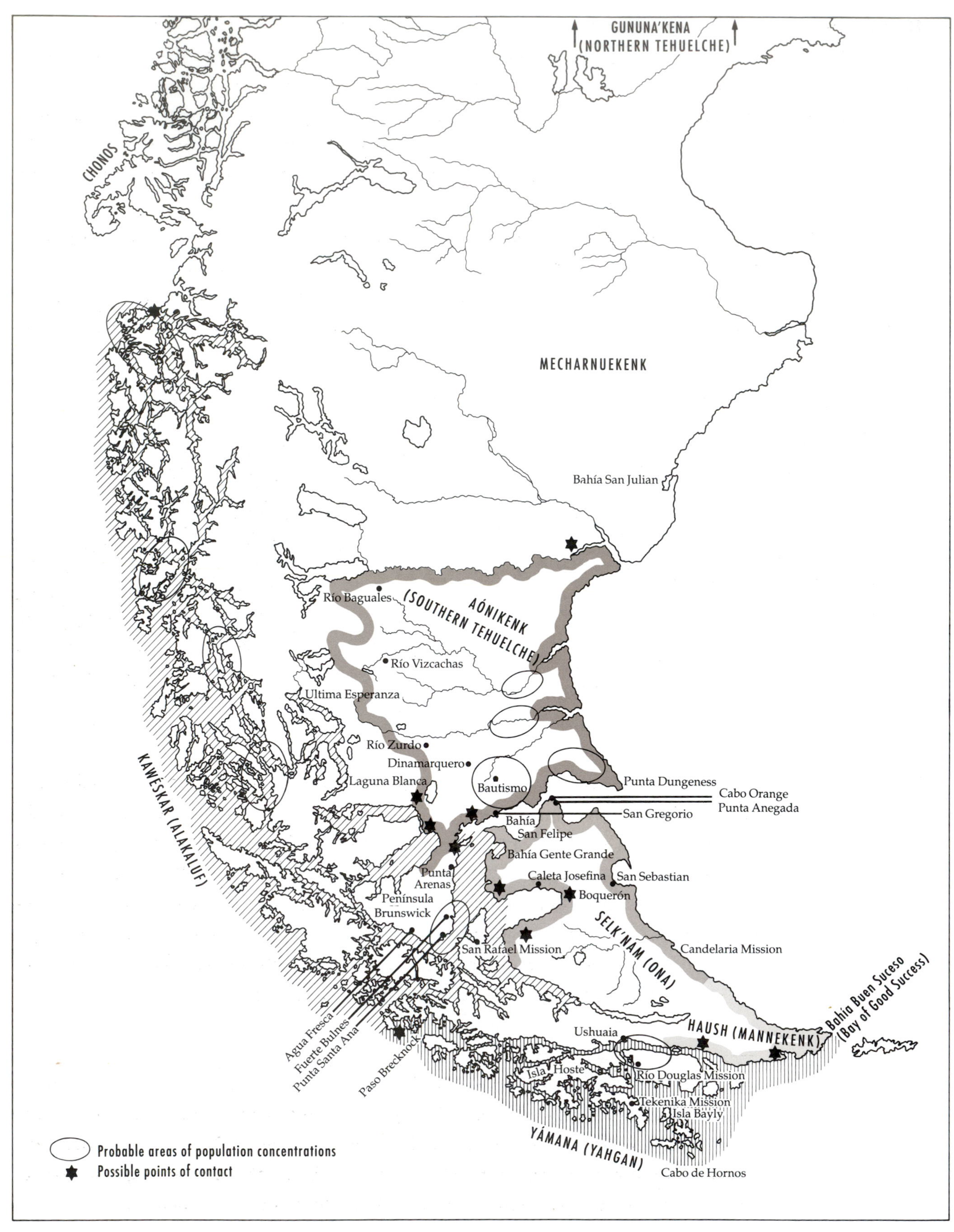

GUNUNA'KENA
(NORTHERN TEHUELCHE)
CHONOS
MECHARNUEKENK
Bahía San Julian
Río Baguales
AÓNIKENK
(SOUTHERN TEHUELCHE)
Río Vizcachas
Ultima Esperanza
Río Zurdo
Dinamarquero
Laguna Blanca
Bautismo
Punta Dungeness
Cabo Orange
Punta Anegada
San Gregorio
Bahía
San Felipe
Bahía Gente Grande
Caleta Josefina
San Sebastian
Boquerón
Punta
Arenas
Península
Brunswick
San Rafael Mission
SELK'NAM (ONA)
Candelaria Mission
KAWÉSKAR (ALAKALUF)
Bahía Buen Suceso
(Bay of Good Success)
HAUSH (MANNEKENK)
Ushuaia
Isla Hoste
Río Douglas Mission
Tekenika Mission
Isla Bayly
Agua Fresca
Fuerte Bulnes
Punta Santa Ana
Paso Brecknock
YÁMANA (YAHGAN)
Cabo de Hornos
Probable areas of population concentrations
Possible points of contact

Fig 77 *opposite* Indigenous territories, population concentrations and principal points of contact during the historical period.

the Indians which was pursued to various degrees by French navigators between the latter part of the seventeenth century and the first quarter of the eighteenth century. These contacts developed further in the 1760s as a consequence of a series of trips to the region made by John Byron,[4] Louis Antoine de Bougainville[5] and Antonio de Córdoba Laso de la Vega.[6] Somewhat later more sustained interaction occurred during the period of hydrographic exploration carried out by Captains Philip Parker King and Robert Fitzroy from 1826 to 1834.[7]

With respect to the Aónikenk, apparently amicable encounters took place mostly along the northern coast of the Strait, especially around Bahía San Gregorio. Initial contacts with the Kawéskar took place on the east coast of Peninsula Brunswick (fig. 78). However, the Europeans also came into contact with both the Kawéskar and the Yámana in

Fig 78 Kawéskar Indians signalling to a steamship in Canal Smyth, *c.* 1880.

the intricate archipelagos of western Patagonia and south and west of Tierra del Fuego, albeit with less frequency and intensity. They had only occasional encounters with the Selk'nam from the sixteenth century up until the end of the ninteenth century. Except for the clashes mentioned above, these meetings were mostly peaceful. While there was violence this was probably provoked by undisciplined crews of wayward vessels during the seventeenth century and subsequently, up to the middle of the eighteenth century, by seal hunters dedicated to the pursuit of marine mammals – rough and violent people, not in the least bit concerned about the indigenous population.[8]

Colonisation of the Magellan Region

Such was the tenor of the relationships between the Indians and the newcomers in the extreme south of South America when, during the fourth decade of the nineteenth century, colonisation began in earnest. Southern continental Patagonia and Tierra del Fuego were originally incorporated into the dominion of the emerging Kingdom of Chile in 1554. In 1843 possession was formally confirmed by the establishment of Fuerte

Bulnes, a small military outpost situated on the summit of Punta Santa Ana (located on the east coast of Peninsula Brunswick), and in 1848 by the founding of Punta Arenas (north of Fuerte Bulnes).[9]

When Fuerte Bulnes was established five nomadic Indian tribes inhabited this extensive domain encompassing Chilean and Argentinian territory. The Aónikenk, or Southern Tehuelche, lived in the eastern part of continental Patagonia, east of the forests; the Selk'nam and the Haush – all terrestrial hunters – occupied the northern, central and south-eastern regions of Tierra del Fuego. The Kawéskar and Yámana were canoe tribes. The Kawéskar dominated the Patagonian archipelagos, the western part of the Estrecho de Magallanes and the adjacent Fuegian archipelagos. The Yámana resided in the southern Fuegian archipelago.

Population estimates for these ethnic groups vary considerably for this period. It is likely that there were approximately 1,000 Aónikenk, 3,000–4,000 Selk'nam and Haush and an estimated 3,000 Indians in each of the canoe groups. In 1843, when a handful of settlers founded Fuerte Bulnes, some 10,000–11,000 Indians lived scattered over this vast domain. The establishment of the fort marked the beginning of a permanent presence of colonists in the region and a new phase in the relations between the two cultures. To fully understand how the changing relations between the colonists and the Indians evolved, they must be separated both ethnically and chronologically. Since the two Chilean settlements were established in eastern Patagonia, the home of the Aónikenk, contact first began with this tribe for purely geographic reasons and lasted until their virtual disappearance from Chilean soil by the early 1900s.

Fuerte Bulnes was scarcely established when the first interaction with native Patagonians began. The latter came in peace, a custom confirmed by two centuries of experience. Nevertheless, they were received with suspicion because the settlers knew little or nothing of their ways of life or customs. The Chilean government sought a harmonious relationship with the Indians and imparted precise instructions along these lines to the leader of the expedition and the region's first governor.

After the colonists' initial fear of the Aónikenk lessened, an active exchange began. The Indians visited the settlers frequently and the latter began to penetrate into the areas where the Indians had their encampments. This was primarily a trading relationship, with the colonists offering goods such as food, trinkets, metals, utensils and tools in exchange for guanaco meat, hides from wild animals and leather garments (capes or 'quillangos') (see chapter 10). Thus mutual commercial interests solidified the tentative beginnings of the contact. In 1844 this symbiosis was ratified through a rare treaty of friendship and commerce by Governor Pedro Silva and Chief Santos Centurión.

A tragic mutiny led by the malevolent Lieutenant Miguel José Cambiazo in 1851 served not only to devastate Punta Arenas but to involve the Indians in the bloodshed and rupture trust. With the restoration of the colony in 1852 Governor Bernardo

Fig 79 Aónikenk and colonists trading at Punta Arenas, c. 1880.

Philippi set about trying to re-establish ties with the Indians, which he considered essential for consolidating the colonists' presence. However, this effort succumbed to the simmering resentment of the Indians, who remained outraged over the incident with Cambiazo. As a result the colonial authorities decided to prohibit settlers from having contact with the Indians. In 1855 ties were once again renewed and a more equitable relationship was gradually re-established. In time this became extremely important for the colonists. In fact, until 1870 trade with the Indians was the principal economic activity carried out in Punta Arenas (fig. 79). A bond of friendship evolved between the two groups which remained unmarred by aggressive acts and grew so strong that not even the dispute between Chile and Argentina in the 1860s over possession of Patagonia, in which the Indians became involved, could affect it.

During the 1870s Punta Arenas prospered under Governor Oscar Viel. Likewise, exchange between the Indians and the settlers intensified, especially in commercial terms. The treks traditionally made by the Indians to Punta Arenas proved to be inadequate to meet demand so the colonial traders and hunters began frequenting Aónikenk territory. There was a close relationship during this period which remained particularly strong throughout the decade. Paradoxically, this would eventually contribute to the decline of the Aónikenk population, as will be seen later.[10]

With the introduction of sheep-ranching in 1877–8 colonists began to encroach upon pasture land which belonged to the Aónikenk near the northern coast of the Strait. The continuing search for fresh grazing expanded inland to incorporate supposedly 'unclaimed' territories where the Aónikenk had hunted and roamed since time immemorial. By 1885–90 the ranchers controlled the areas of Dinamarquero and

Fig 80 Group of Tehuelche, *c.* 1837–40.

Bautismo and the plains in the Blanca Lagoon basin, traditional Indian hunting-grounds, as well as other areas in Argentina. In all of these areas sheep-herding was expanding rapidly, resulting in continuous pressure on the Indians to relinquish their access to favoured territories and resort instead to less productive areas.

Towards the end of the century the Aónikenk were restricted to the central part of Patagonia next to the international border and to the lands still uninhabited by the colonists in the Vizcachas and Baguales river valleys in Ultima Esperanza. The first area contained a ten-thousand-hectare reservation (the Río Zurdo valley), which was ceded to Chief Mulato by Governor Manuel Señoret in 1893. The Governor hoped that a 'legitimate' domain for these Indians would be respected by the colonists and would serve to bring a halt to their progressive reduction in number.[11]

This measure did not lead to either objective being achieved because the growing demand for grazing land caused some colonists to eye the potential of the reservation for settlement and to initiate hostile acts towards the Indians. In addition, during the early 1900s the Aónikenk suffered a viral epidemic – accidentally introduced by Chief Mulato, who ironically became ill when he went to Santiago to lay claim to his territorial rights before the Governor of Chile. Unfortunately, this disease proved a deathblow to the Río Zurdo Indians. Within the space of a few years the majority of them died and the survivors migrated to Argentine territory (1906).

Around this same time the Sociedad Explotadora de Tierra del Fuego, a company which had acquired most of the potentially useful grazing land in Ultima Esperanza

Fig 81 Aónikenk group under a soldier's supervision.

through public auctions held in 1905, proceeded to occupy its holdings. Consequently, an Aónikenk group traditionally camped near the Río Vizcachas was expelled to Argentina (figs 80 and 81).[12] This episode represented a turning point for the Aónikenk, marking the beginning of cultural mutations and their march towards extinction.[13] These noble Indians vanished forever from Patagonia's vast eastern limits where they had lived freely and ruled as a people, in harmony with their natural environment, through the centuries. A sixty-year relationship with the colonists was thus brought to a close. On the whole this had been characterised by limited harassment and direct violence against the Indians, with the exception of the episode mentioned earlier.

Proceeding in chronological order, the second aboriginal ethnic group with which the colonists came into contact were the Kawéskar dwelling in the western part of the Strait and channels of Patagonia. The term 'contact' is used here because a sustained relationship like that which existed with the Aónikenk was never achieved. Furthermore, over the years, and as a consequence of this contact, the Kawéskar were first punished, then robbed, and finally treated with compassion.

Groups frequenting the waters around the Peninsula Brunswick occasionally displayed aggressive behaviour. They launched several bloody attacks on the colonists as well as on ships navigating the Strait, thereby earning an infamous reputation with the local authorities. As a result Governor Jorge Schythe commented in 1855 that these Indians were barbarians and that building any sort of friendly relationship with them was impossible. His opinion seems to have been corroborated in 1873, when word reached Punta Arenas that the Indians had rustled cattle from the colony's ranch situated at Agua Fresca and had also attacked the ranchers. Government reprisal was swift and drastic. A military search party was despatched which tried to capture the Indians. Instead a skirmish broke out and several Kawéskar were killed. The following year more cattle were stolen. This time, however, the ranchers themselves went after the rustlers, leaving eight Kawéskar dead and taking several children prisoner.

The violence which characterised the initial phase continued into the early part of the present century. While not intentionally fractious these encounters were invariably exacerbated by a vicious cycle which precipitated reciprocal retaliation: aggressive acts by the Indians against the lives and goods of the settlers and punishment, sometimes harsh and always disproportionate, meted out by the colonists.

The second phase of contact evolved with the whalers and sealers towards the end of the 1860s, when this activity intensified in the Magellanic region's wild, western archipelagos. These men were a law unto themselves, rough and disposed to aggressive behaviour by virtue of the very activities in which they were engaged and the miserable conditions in which they worked. Now and then they encountered the Kawéskar. The sporadic contact that resulted was never friendly. The supposedly 'civilised' intruders constantly harassed the Indians, who were provoked into responding in kind. Thus, open violence and vice combined to create deep mistrust and an ever more difficult situation for the Indians. This contributed greatly to their drastic decline in numbers. The demise of the Kawéskar people was delayed only by the 'protection' afforded by often ferocious weather conditions which served to restrict the intrusion of outsiders to a brief and occasional presence.

During the third phase of contact the Indians were treated with compassion. From the 1870s to the 1930s there was frequent contact between the Kawéskar and passengers and crews of passing ships, including war vessels and those involved in hydrographic exploration (fig. 82). Moved by the shocking spectacle of these Indians – nude, stiff with cold, hungry, stinking, crowded in flimsy canoes that seemed on the verge of sinking – the visitors gave them clothes, food and trinkets, or exchanged these for valuable otter skins.

The contact between the newcomers and the Yámana was far more complex and considerably less brutal than that with the Kawéskar, since missionaries were involved. It is well known that Robert Fitzroy's experience with four Canal Beagle Indians in the 1830s served as the foundation for the subsequent, sustained evangelisation of the Indians undertaken by the South American Missionary Society of England (see chapter 8). The mission work was marked by its own tragedies, such as when the Society's founder

Fig 82 Fuegians (probably Kawéskar) bartering with passengers on a passing vessel, *c*. 1878.

Allen Gardiner and his co-workers died from starvation and abandonment, attempting to fulfil their vows (1851), and when other missionaries were slain by Indians (1859).[14]

Finally, in 1870–1, Waite H. Stirling and Thomas Bridges managed to establish a centre for 'civilising' the Indians at Ushuaia, located on the southern coast of Tierra del Fuego. With the disruption caused by the centre's activities, the missionaries moved south and south-west, seeking out the more remote Yámana groups in need of support. Consequently, missionary stations were established at Isla Bayly (Cabo de Hornos, 1888), Tekenika (Isla Hoste, 1892) and Río Douglas (Isla Navarino, 1906), where numerous missionaries worked in pursuit of their Christian and humanitarian ideals (figs 83 and 84). The missions were finally closed in 1917 when the Indians became too few in number and too scattered to make such efforts practical.[15]

During roughly this same period the Yámana had occasional contact with sea lion hunters, mariners and sailors shipwrecked in the course of attempting the perilous Cabo de Hornos passage. The Yámana never suffered the aggressive treatment and violence that the Kawéskar did with the seal hunters. Beginning in the early 1880s, gold prospectors and a handful of settlers sought to establish themselves permanently in the area. Contact was undoubtedly more frequent between the Indians and this latter group, but never reached the same level as that which existed with the missionaries.

Fig 85 *above* Selk'nam hunters in southern Tierra del Fuego, *c.* 1926.

Fig 83 *opposite above* Group of young children with their English 'tutor' at the Tekenika Mission on Isla Hoste, 1892–1906.

Fig 84 *opposite below* View of the Mission at Tekenika, Isla Hoste, with a traditional log dwelling in the foreground.

Chronologically, the last phase of contact involved the Europeans and the Selk'nam. Here, homicidal violence was the rule.[16] In contrast with continental Patagonia, and even the adjacent archipelagos, the hinterlands of Tierra del Fuego lay off the main exploration routes during the seventeenth, eighteenth and nineteenth centuries. When colonisation in southern South America began, Tierra del Fuego was again ignored; settlements sprang up only on the mainland. In effect, the Selk'nam were relatively undisturbed during the first exploratory expeditions made into their traditional territories (fig. 85).[17] The situation changed, however, in 1881, when prospectors began arriving at Boquerón in search of placer gold which had been discovered in the north-western zone of the main island. The prospectors treated the Selk'nam harshly and without compassion, forcibly taking their women, for example. In self-defence the Indians struck back, but inevitably suffered the worst. Their population dwindled – the bitter outcome of an attempt by a small, crude group of invaders to settle this land. Consequently, when colonists established a sheep-ranch at Bahía Gente Grande in 1885, the Selk'nam were not in a receptive mood. Moreover, since the Indians were ignorant of the outsiders' ideas concerning property rights, they began stalking the docile sheep which they perceived as 'white' guanaco and which were particularly easy to capture. They became extremely adept at stealing sheep, an unpardonable crime in the eyes of the colonial ranchers, since they were expensive to acquire and to transport. This provoked retaliatory action that was excessively severe. Word seldom reached Punta Arenas of the rancher-sponsored lynch mobs and killings that secretly took place. As a result, few inhabitants knew about the painful drama that was unfolding in the plains and mountains of the Fuegian north (fig. 86).

The threat to the Selk'nam's homeland grew with the establishment of two new ranches in the regions of Punta Anegada and Bahía Felipe in the early 1890s. This situation intensified in 1894 when the Sociedad Explotadora de Tierra del Fuego took possession of its vast holdings (amounting to more than one million hectares) and created two large estates: Caleta Josefina and San Sebastián. Thus, in less than fifteen years the Selk'nam endured the occupation of practically their entire homeland by foreigners who subsequently became the undisputed owners. It did not take the Indians long to understand that coexistence with the colonists was impossible, whether they were miners or sheep-ranchers, and especially the latter.

Fig 86 Ruthless 'hunting' forays were mounted against the Selk'nam who were armed only with bows and arrows. Tierra del Fuego, *c.* 1900.

For the colonists, too, living together with the natives in peace appeared impractical. With their drive, work ethic and investments they saw themselves as sowers of progress and civilisation in a vast virgin territory. In addition, their efforts were encouraged and supported by the State and their ownership was sanctioned by its laws. The pioneers in Tierra del Fuego viewed the Selk'nam as an obstacle to economic progress to be overcome or eliminated by force. The sheep-ranching companies in Tierra del Fuego defended their estates as well as their sheep at all costs. Indians who rustled sheep or were involved in acts of aggression against the colonists were captured and punished. This escalated into an all-out war which was kept clandestine, since such a reproachable situation would not have been publicly condoned.

Yet despite the attempts made to conceal the ordeal of the Selk'nam, the inhabitants of Punta Arenas eventually learned that a virtual genocide of this tribe was taking place. The ensuing clamour of indignation received international press coverage, sensitising Chile's National Congress and Administration to the issue. Nevertheless, while officially the government intervened to ameliorate the brutality, the atrocities continued in secret. Large groups of Indians were captured and forcibly transferred to the Mission of San Rafael, located on neighbouring Isla Dawson. The mission was opened in 1889 by the Salesians as a refuge for those Indians who fell victim to colonial expansionism.

Fig 87 The Salesian Mission at San Rafael, Isla Dawson.

If this 'relocation' was not openly supported by the government, it was certainly tolerated (fig. 87).

In less than five years, at the end of the century, the Selk'nam had been virtually eliminated from their ancestral home. Those who managed to elude death or relocation scattered in the forests of southern Tierra del Fuego. In effect, genocide consumed the Selk'nam who had called the island their own for thousands of years. These deeds were an affront to the civilised conscience of the period and acts that each member of the community was responsible for, either directly or indirectly.

From the very beginning, a fractious and violent relationship existed between the settlers and the Selk'nam. It was a conflict weighted heavily in favour of the outsiders with their firearms and ruthless ambition. The only sustained relationship between the Selk'nam and the newcomers involved the missionaries, effectively also foreigners and colonists. It was a relationship different from others found in Magellanic territory, the character of which was largely shaped by the English missionaries: humanitarian and generous, but paternalistic and, as such, authoritarian. The missionaries did not treat the Indians as equals, nor did they seek to appreciate and preserve their culture. The

Austrian priest Father Martin Gusinde was an exception to this rule.[18] His personal efforts were extraordinary, in this case more scientific than religious, but were too late to reverse the process.

The Salesians carried out their work as best they knew, but the effect of their efforts was to concentrate the Indians far from their homelands, mixing tribes and altering their traditional customs and subsistence patterns. They sought to 'adapt' the Indians to the dictates of western culture. To some this is seen as a sound and well-intentioned effort, but it was tragically flawed since it simply accelerated their demise.

Consequences of the intercultural encounter

In sum, each of the aboriginal Magellanic cultures experienced its own particular set of relationships with the newcomers.

The protracted and largely peaceful colonist/Aónikenk relationship did not entail genuinely reciprocal cultural exchange, given the Aónikenk's limited and fleeting impact on the colonists; their influence did not amount to much more than the transfer of some nomadic skills and customs to the ranchers and hunters, some artisan skills (to produce tools and leather capes) and some proverbs and legends. The cultural exchange was overwhelmingly unidirectional, from the colonists to the Indians, and resulted in major changes which affected the latter's hunting and fishing tools and customs, relationship with natural resources, social behaviour, health and very survival as a people. Historical documents and recent archaeological findings confirm that, during the nineteenth century at least, the Aónikenk had virtually stopped producing their customary tools from stones and bones. These raw materials were gradually replaced by ceramics, glass and metals introduced by the colonists. Furthermore, they completely abandoned the bow and arrow for hunting after mastering the horse and bola and learning how to use firearms. Similarly, they incorporated new elements into their repertoire of tools, such as files, chisels, hammers, knives, needles and thimbles, for utilitarian as well as decorative purposes.

The colonists' growing demand for feathers, pelts and leather goods eventually surpassed the Indians' traditional supply capacity which was derived primarily from their food needs. To meet this demand the Indians had to increase their hunting and artisan activities, and profit-making made its way into their culture. As hunting increased new demands were placed on the region's ecosystem. Also, more women were required to prepare the additional hides. The technological response to increased hide-preparation was the production of more scrapers. Glass was used as a raw material for manufacturing these instruments because it was easier to work with than stone and at the same time resulted in greater productivity (figs 88 and 114).[19]

Just as the advent of the horse into the culture of the Indians brought about a dramatic change in their society, the introduction of alcohol also had a powerful but deleterious effect.

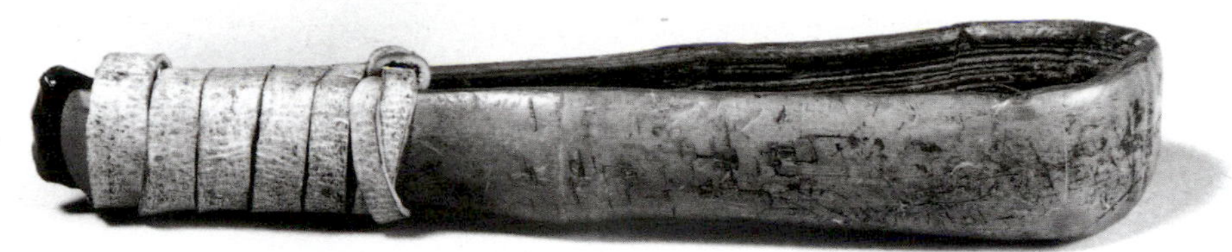

Fig 88 Aónikenk scraper used for preparing hides. The scraper itself is fashioned from glass derived from bottles obtained through contact with travellers and settlers during the historical period. Length 19.5 cm.

Both the Yámana and the Kawéskar's relationship with the colonists contrasted sharply with that of the Aónikenk's, as did the consequences. Contact proved destructive for the Kawéskar. Initially, their camps were raided; later, they were treated with compassion. Essentially, the colonists brought death to the Indians through violence and lethal, contagious diseases which substantially reduced their number. The survivors rapidly lost their spiritual values and customs. The historical case of the Kawéskar is a perfect example of the cultural and physiological impoverishment of an Indian tribe through contact with the colonists and merits further study.

The Yámana tribe had different luck, having been exposed to fewer negative contacts, and was able to affirm and prolong its culture until well into the twentieth century. Only when their number sank below the point of no return, however, did they become progressively more assimilated into western ways, causing the tribe to expire culturally before physically disappearing. A few scattered survivors are all that now remain of these historical, native canoe tribes that once inhabited the southernmost region of the Americas.

The ill-fated Selk'nam were devastated by confrontations with the colonists. In effect, the confrontations were so swift and brutal that in scarcely two decades this ethnic group disappeared almost completely from Tierra del Fuego. The few remaining Selk'nam lived on at the San Rafael Mission and Isla Dawson, the Candelaria Mission and in the forests of southern Tierra del Fuego. In the long term this would prove equally disastrous. At the mission they were assured of sustenance but were prevented from living in accordance with their ancestral customs because the missionaries wanted to fill their time and 'civilise' them by teaching them how to work and by administering religious instruction. Unintentionally, the Salesians adversely affected the Selk'nam by forcing them to adopt a foreign way of life, one which was completely at odds with their former culture and freedom.

Contagious diseases, particularly pulmonary infections, were especially harmful to the Indians. Their immune systems could not cope with the new strains which they invariably contracted through contact and living together with the new settlers. The

Fig 89 Group of Kawéskar women at the Salesian Mission, San Rafael, on Isla Dawson, 1892–1912.

semi-crowding in which they lived aggravated the transmission of epidemic diseases, despite the efforts of the missionaries to teach them hygienic practices. Tragically, during the winter of 1884 half of the Indians at the Protestant Mission of Ushuaia died from pneumonia. But it was tuberculosis which was the most devastating of these diseases, eliminating almost two-thirds of the total Indian population at the Mission between 1896 and 1900.

The efforts of the Salesians to alleviate the agony of the native Indian groups proved futile. In September 1911, when the San Rafael Mission closed, only twenty-five Indians remained out of the one thousand that had entered between 1889 and 1898 (fig. 89).

The dramatic reduction in the population of the Indians was perhaps the most conspicuous consequence of the relationship between the indigenous peoples and the newcomers. By 1910 there were probably fewer than 1,500 Indians in all of southern South America and the irreversible decline of the survivors was by this time inevitable. In scarcely six decades colonisation had succeeded in profoundly altering, and eventually destroying, an ancient order of life and culture.

NOTES
1 Martinic 1983, 1984.
2 Martinic 1977.
3 Martinic and Moore 1982.
4 Byron 1768.
5 Bougainville 1772.
6 Vargas y Ponce 1788.
7 Fitzroy 1839.
8 Martinic 1977.
9 Ibid.
10 Martinic 1979.
11 Ibid.
12 Martinic 1979, 1995.
13 Martinic 1995.
14 Martinic 1973a.
15 Ibid.
16 Martinic 1973b, 1989/90.
17 Pertuisset 1877; Serrano Montaner 1880.
18 Gusinde 1951.
19 Martinic and Prieto 1985/86.

7 The Patagonian 'Giants'

Jean-Paul Duviols

The accounts of giants in Graeco-Roman mythology (Atlas, Antaeus, Typhon), in the Bible (Goliath) and in tales of chivalry all helped shape the imaginative universe of the first European voyagers who travelled great distances to unknown lands. Nevertheless, whole populations of giants occur only rarely in mythology. With the exception of the Cyclops, the phenomenon is generally confined to a particular individual. Once the myth is transposed to America, however, it starts to refer to an ethnic group in its totality – that of the nomadic Tehuelches of the eastern coast of present-day Patagonia. Setting their abnormality aside, the novelty of the New World giants derived essentially from the fact that they were thought to form a homogeneous group, a sort of marginal society. Just like the Amazons, the giants were thought of as real, their existence not at all implausible. It might only take one slightly exaggerated, but not necessarily dishonest, observation to persuade an open-minded traveller to cross the thin line separating the ordinary from the extraordinary. It is difficult to decide at what height a person or a group of people may be considered monstrous. This is probably what lies at the root of the unusually pervasive fascination with the notion of giants which so maintained the curiosity of Europeans over the course of more than three centuries. Another important factor which explains the persistence of such myths is the fact that the giants were 'sighted' several times, at intervals of some years, by sailors of different nationalities, and nearly always in the same cold, desolate regions of the extreme south of the New World. Their geographical location confirmed a widely held theory at the end of the fifteenth century which suggested that people were physically bigger the nearer one got to the North and South Poles. Following this logic, dwarfs would be found in regions close to the equator. Federman doubtless had this in mind when he embarked upon a bold expedition into the Venezuelan forest: 'I took this route in order to see this nation [the Ayamanes], attracted by the reputation of their small size; this was the sole reason I undertook the journey.'[1] After having captured a number of these Indians, the German conqueror verified that, 'The Indians were all small... The biggest measured five spans and some others four, but their bodies were well proportioned.'[2]

Despite everything, the dwarf-people remained less spectacular than the giants, who in the sixteenth-century *milieu* had already become part of a legendary world.

The earliest account to signal their presence on the far side of the Atlantic did not, however, have any impact, since the report in which they are mentioned must have remained relatively confidential. The account is Amerigo Vespucci's, the Florentine who believed he had reached the polar region but who, according to his descriptions of the natural features and the people, can only have been in southern Brazil.[3] He describes a surprising meeting:

> We found a village with about twelve houses where we met only seven tall women. They were all one-and-a-half palms bigger than me... Then thirty-six men arrived and entered the house where we were drinking and they were so tall that even kneeling each one of them was still bigger than me upright. In short, if we refer to their stature and to the proportion of their bodies, they were giants. Each woman was like Penthesilea and all the men like Antaeus.[4]

Islands, especially, are places traditionally predisposed to the extraordinary or the fantastical.[5] So, on a different voyage, Vespucci met other giants: 'I call this island the island of giants, because of their height... They were taller than a tall man. They must have been as tall as Francesco d'Albizi, but better proportioned... They carried great bows and arrows, as well as clubs'(fig. 90).[6]

These references to the presence of giants in the New World seem to have been ignored. The 'news' about them was not widely disseminated until the publication of a text which enjoyed extraordinary success in Europe and which was at the root of a long and at times impassioned debate. Still, the image of men 'taller when kneeling than a European' could have had the same impact as that conjured up by Pigafetta, who speaks of individuals 'so tall that the tallest among us reached only their waists':

> One day, when no one was expecting it, we saw a giant, completely naked, by the sea. He danced and jumped and danced and, singing, spread sand and dust over his head... He was so tall that the tallest among us reached only to his waist. He was truly well built.
>
> The captain [Magellan] gave him something to eat and drink, then he showed him several objects, among them a steel mirror. When the giant saw his reflection he got a great fright and jumped backwards, knocking three or four of us to the ground...
>
> When the giants have a stomach-ache, instead of taking medicine they put a two-foot-long arrow down their throats and vomit green bile mixed with blood. The reason why they throw up this green substance is that they sometimes eat thistles. When they have a headache they cut themselves across the forehead, and even on the arms and legs, to draw blood from several parts of their bodies.[7]

The account of this extraordinary meeting has an important place in the American part of Pigafetta's narrative. The scene is livelier and more detailed than in Vespucci and consequently more likely to capture the reader's imagination. Finally, and above all

Fig 90 One of the earliest representations of Río de La Plata and its inhabitants, including island 'giants'. The vessels are probably those of Amerigo Vespucci's expedition.

else, what immortalised this meeting between Europeans and the Tehuelches is the fact that Magellan gave these giants a name, which from then on would designate an ethnic group and later an entire region of South America:

> The Captain named these kind of people *Pataghoni*. They have no houses, but huts, like the Egyptians. They live on raw meat and eat a kind of sweet root which they call *capac*. The two giants we had on board ship ate their way through a large basket of biscuits, and ate rats without first skinning them. They used to drink a half-bucket of water at once.[8]

The origin of the name Patagon has long been disputed. It is quite probable that the term harks back to a tale of chivalry fashionable at the beginning of the century. However, an idea still prevalent today is that Patagon means, in Spanish, 'a man with big feet', but this is inaccurate. If we look at the article by Maria Rosa de Malkiel,[9] which was initially refuted but later supported by Marcel Bataillon,[10] it looks as though the origin of the term can be found in one of the fantastical characters in the Spanish chivalric tale *Primaleón*. In fact, the story tells of an island where there lives not only a giant named Patagón but a whole population of 'wild men', who:

> live like animals and are very fierce and wild and eat raw meat, which they obtain by

> hunting in the mountains. They are like savages and are dressed only in the skins of animals they have killed. They are so monstrous that it is fascinating to observe them. But this is nothing compared with a man who now lives among them and is called Patagón. They say that this Patagón was born of an animal that lives in the mountains and is the most monstrous being on earth; he is very intelligent, however, and loves women very much. He looks like a dog, with big ears that reach down to his shoulders and with very long, pointed teeth which stick like carved fangs out of his mouth. His feet look like a stag's and he runs so fast that nobody can keep up with him.[11]

It is this Patagón, 'big and very strong of body', that the hero Primaleón decides to fight. It would seem that the character of Patagón combines elements of the myth of a Cynocephalus, referred to above, with that of the formidable giant. Pigafetta's narrative reveals reminiscences of this passage (the Patagonians eat raw meat, they are fast runners and their feet are protected with deer skin), even though the connection between the two texts is difficult to establish.

From then on all navigators who sail along the coast of South America and traverse the Estrecho de Magallanes hope to meet these giant Patagonians. A series of contradicting testimonies will follow, forming a kind of international dossier on the veracity or otherwise of the myth. The tribes which were glimpsed or encountered were many and their movements did not readily permit them to be accurately located. The Tehuelche, whose average size was about 1.80 m,[12] were frequently confused with the 'canoe Indians', who lived on Tierra del Fuego and the adjacent archipelagos and whose size was not exceptional. Here is not the place to repeat the long list of voyages that can be found in Corneille de Pauw,[13] Buffon,[14] and above all Alcide d'Orbigny,[15] but simply to recall certain typical accounts of this strangely distorted vision, and their accompanying interpretations.

Cosmographers, compilers and historians have all helped embellish these tales of giants, which aroused both fear and fantasy: 'The people are as big as giants and a man has been seen there who was two times bigger than the biggest man in Europe, and his footprint was found and it was bigger than two of our feet and had well-cut shoes measuring twenty-four inches long.'[16]

The Spanish colonisers had no more concrete knowledge than other European nations of these southern regions, despite their doomed attempt to establish themselves in the Estrecho de Magallanes. Argensola, narrating the testimony of Pedro Sarmiento de Gamboa,[17] gave new impetus to the legend:

> The Indian captured by our people was a giant among giants, and the story goes that he resembled a Cyclops. Other versions say that they were taller than three and a half yards and proportionately big and strong...
>
> The giants fled away into the countryside so swiftly that they were soon out of musket range, and seeing them one had to say they sped almost as fast as a bullet.[18]

The legend thrived throughout the sixteenth century. The Europeans were convinced of the existence of a nation of giants at the very tip of South America. Here, André Thevet makes a contribution as a 'learned' traveller. This was all the more important because in his particular case he relied on direct testimony. Referring to a perilous foray up the Río de La Plata – far from the territories frequented by the Tehuelches – Thevet, whose view was doubtless more influenced by his readings than his observations, revels in a detailed description of these extraordinary 'savages' to whom he almost fell victim: 'And the savages of this country are of such horrifying and vast stature that the smallest among them is ten feet tall, others eleven, and some almost twelve feet, possessing strength as well as height, and so fleet of foot that they can run more quickly and as fast as a deer.'[19]

Having kept one of the giants on his boat, Cordelier describes with the authority of one who has seen with his own eyes how 'he ate a whole basket of biscuits for his meal and drank as much as a horse, emptying a bucket of water in one go. Although only forty years old, he was eleven feet five inches tall, since in this country men only reach maturity at sixty; forty is still very young and it is quite normal for them to live to be one hundred and twenty.'[20]

Carried away by his imagination, André Thevet gives renewed force to the legend by mixing it with another mythical tradition for which the New World was the preferred setting, that of prolonged youth and extraordinary longevity. To give even more weight to his extraordinary descriptions, Thevet relies heavily on another testimony which tallies with his own:

> One of those who travelled with Magellan was a pilot for King Henry of England, who told me that when they were on the shore of this island, one of these giants wanted to enter one of their boats by force, screaming and shouting with a voice so loud that you would have thought it was the roaring of a bull or an elephant rather than the voice of a man.
>
> Hearing such a fearful noise from this colossus more than thirty children, all eight feet tall, arrived and forced the Christians, who saw that the great oafs might take the vessels by force, to fire four or five shots from their canon, without stone or ball, simply to frighten them.[21]

However, not all travellers saw in these sturdy Indians the fabled giants, and some even dared say so, all the more willingly since such observations cast doubt on the word of the Spanish:

> These men be of no such stature as the Spaniardes report, being but of the height of English men: for I haue seene men in *England* taller than I could see any of them. But peraduenture the Spaniard did not thinke that any English men would haue come thither so soone to haue disproued them in this and diuerse others of their notorious lies: wherefore they presumed more boldly to abuse the world.[22]

On the other hand, accounts by the Dutch sailors who travelled a lot in the region of the Strait at the end of the sixteenth and the early seventeenth centuries helped fuel the

Fig 91 An engraving depicting 'giants' combining the physique of the 'savage' with facial features clearly deriving inspiration from Dutch models. The canoe with a fire burning within and a multi-barbed harpoon are faithfully represented.

legend. Seebald de Weert fought these huge people and he reckoned them to be as high as ten or eleven feet tall. After this titanic confrontation (figs 91 and 92),[23] the Dutch, who had lost some men in the battle, stressed all the more the 'primitive brutality' of the Tehuelches rather than their size:

> If they did not so much actually find these men cruel, or acting as brute beasts, they nevertheless witnessed the results of their brutality on the Dutch corpses which had been buried in this place and which they then dragged out of their graves and inhumanely disfigured... Among other things, they cut a great slash in the surgeon's cheek and squashed his head with a club, thrust an arrow in his side as far as his heart, cut his parts and pulled him thus into the water, from where we recovered him and put him in the ground again.[24]

Olivier van Noort, who only caught a glimpse of them at Port Desire, doesn't hesitate to call them man-eaters:

> These Patagonians were tall and had a terrible stare, long hair and painted faces...
>
> There is another race, further inland, called Tiremenen, that live in a place called Coin. They are as big as giants, ten or eleven feet tall, and come into conflict with other groups, who they reproach for eating ostriches, apparently a better meat than other kinds, but we guess that they all eat human flesh.[25]

Knivet and Jane, who authored the report of the Englishman Cavendish's second voyage, also gave an exaggerated account of the Patagonians glimpsed at Port Desire:

Fig 92 Engraving by Theodore de Bry illustrating a literary passage which describes an attack by Dutch mariners on the 'long haired giants' at Bahía Verde, Estrecho de Magallanes.

> The coast of Port Desire is inhabited by giants fifteen to sixteen palms high. I have myself measured the footprint of one of them on the riverbank, which was four times longer than one of ours. I have also measured the corpses of two men recently buried by the river, which were fourteen spans long. Three of our men, who were later taken by the Spanish on the coast of Brazil, assured me that one day on the other side of the coast they had to sail out to sea because the giants started throwing great blocks of stone of astonishing size from the beach right at their boat. In Brazil I saw one of these giants which Alonso Díaz had captured at Port Saint Julien: he was just a boy but was already thirteen spans tall. These people go about naked and have long hair; the one I saw in Brazil was healthy-looking and well proportioned for his height. I can say nothing about his habits, not having spent any time with him, but the Portuguese tell me that he is no better than the other cannibals along the coast of La Plata.[26]

It is interesting to note that the Spanish sailors who cruised these waters some years later were a lot more reasonable in their observations, reducing the giants to more accurate proportions. In fact, they were content to stress that they 'were taller by a whole head than we Europeans'.[27]

After that the Patagonians seem to have been forgotten and the rare accounts of sailors in the seventeenth century are rather negative. The Englishman John Narborough denies that their height is extraordinary, the Dutchman Jacques l'Hermite finds them well proportioned, no more. It is highly likely that these travellers had encountered the inhabitants of Tierra del Fuego, the Yámana, Selk'nam or Kawéskar. The same applies to Froger who, during the expedition commanded by M. de Gennes, makes ironic comments about the Indians found at Puerto Hambre: 'These are the Patagonians which some writers told us were eight to ten feet tall, and about whom they exaggerated so much, having them drink buckets of wine. They seem to us extremely sober and the tallest of them is not even six feet high.'[28]

However, a reputedly educated and serious French traveller, Amédée Frézier, gives renewed life to the legend although his testimony is based purely upon second-hand information, and not on personal observation. Finding himself on the island of Chiloé on the Pacific Coast he writes:

> Further inland there exists another nation of giants called the Caucahues. As they are friends of the Chonos, they sometimes come with them to the Spanish houses in Chiloé. D. Pedro Molina, who was governor of this island, and several other witnesses of the place, have told me that they were almost four *vares* high, in other words, nine to ten feet; these are the ones called Patagons, who live on the eastern coast of the deserted lands mentioned in the ancient reports, which were counted to be fables, because in the Estrecho de Magallanes there are Indians who have been seen who are actually no taller than other men.[29]

The myth of the giants of America has clearly had its ups and downs! Just as it was beginning to fade, a new, very detailed account brought the Patagonians back into fashion in the second half of the eighteenth century. This was by Commodore John Byron, whose report was widely circulated and revived a debate that had been begun long before (fig. 93):

> Immediately on our landing they came about us to the number of two hundred or more, looking at us with evident expressions of surprise, and smiling, as it should seem, at the great disproportion of our stature.
>
> After many amicable signs, which appeared equally agreeable to both parties, our Commodore, who had the foresight to take with him on shore a great number of trinkets, such as strings of beads, ribbons, and the like, in order to convince them of our amicable disposition, distributed them with great freedom, giving to each of them some, as far as they went. The method he made use of to facilitate the distribution of them was by making the Indians sit down on the ground, that he might put the strings of beads, etc., round their necks; and such was their extraordinary size, that in this situation they were almost as high as the Commodore when standing.
>
> ...Their middle stature seemed to be about eight feet; their extreme nine and upwards; though we did not measure them by any standard, and have reason to believe them to be rather more than less.
>
> Their clothing consisted of the skins of guanacos, or Peruvian sheep, which reached from their shoulders down to their knees; and their hair was long and black, hanging down behind. The faces of the women were painted most extravagantly, and their

Fig 93 'A sailor giving a Patagonian woman some biscuit for her child.' The frontispiece to John Byron's travel epic, *A Voyage Round the World* (1767).

> stature equally surprising with that of the men. We saw some of their infants in their mothers' arms, whose features, considering their age, bore the same proportion.[30]

This famous testimony had all the more impact since the observation was made about a large number of individuals surrounding the visitors, whose friendliness was not without ulterior motives. In fact, the English were not merely content to do a little smuggling or to inspect Spanish ships, as Lord Anson had done previously. They wanted to set themselves up in a place from where they could control the Estrecho de Magallanes and the South Seas. The preface to the French translation, taking an exotic line, denounces the sceptics in a sixty-eight-page introduction:

> The existence of giants on the shores of Patagonia is no longer in doubt, and it is surprising that it was an issue for so long...
>
> The public, always disposed to accept anything new and extraordinary, wanted nothing more than to believe in giants; but philosophers, prejudiced as they are, willingly reject anything new which has a hint of wonder to it without really considering it, and have no desire at all to hear about a new race of men whom they haven't seen, and the sheep-like herd of dim-wits and half-baked philosophers don't dare expose themselves to ridicule by adopting a popular opinion. Wise men were doubtful, but the expedition by the Admiral of the fleet, Byron, puts the lid on all these uncertainties.[31]

The debate between publishers, for whom marvels boosted sales, and intellectuals, who supported critical enquiry, was fed by a succession of testimonies. The editor of the account of Pernetty's voyage skilfully declared himself convinced of the presence of a race of giants in South America, even though the evidence which he printed talked only of big men (fig. 94):

> I know that the majority of travellers that sailed the Estrecho de Magallanes in the seventeenth century saw only people of ordinary stature in Patagonia; they concluded, therefore, that their predecessors had either been lying or had imagined things; the sceptics hastened to adopt an opinion which exempted them from being seen as gullible, and the existence of the giants was soon relegated to the ranks of printed lies.
>
> A giant from Patagonia was never a monster. That the height of the tallest Patagonian is double our own and his body-mass eight times greater, does not cause any physiological dysfunction. When a man of ten feet partners a woman of the same size, a race is created and nature is justified.[32]

Notable among the sceptics were the comte de Buffon and particularly Corneille de Pauw, for whom America could produce nothing extraordinary. It was at this time that Bougainville made his famous circumnavigation of the world. His observations would 'correct' once and for all those made by John Byron:

> These men are of a good size; among those we have seen none was shorter than five feet five or six inches, and none more than five feet nine or ten inches; on the previous voyage people on the *Etoile* saw several who were six feet. What seemed gigantic to me was their great build. . .
>
> . . . I shall finish this piece by saying that we have since found, in the Pacific, a race which is taller than the Patagonians.[33]

An identical testimony is made by his companion, the Prince of Nassau-Siegen, who credits them with 'five feet nine inches, neither more nor less', and exclaims, 'Are these

Fig 94 Anonymous engraving depicting a European exchanging gifts with a 'giant' Patagonian who wears a cloak similar to those made by the Aónikenk.

the giants that earlier voyagers believed they saw and that the English more recently wanted to pass off as such?'[34]

With Corneille de Pauw there is nothing less than a systematic denigration of all things American: he refutes the testimonies of travellers because, paradoxically, he considered them too numerous.[35] He insists, however, that neither Quiros, nor García de Loyasa, nor Camargo, nor Alcazaba, have seen this 'colossal race of Patagonians', anymore than Wood, Anson or Narborough, and he concludes, 'If there really were a population of giants in America, we would have been shown at least some of the living individuals, or their skeletons, in Europe. This is no argument for rational people.'[36]

But according to Juan de Velasco, writing in the early eighteenth century, the skeletons of these giants had been found in Ecuador and constituted exactly that proof unknown to European 'philosophers'. He is not dealing with Patagonians, of course, but what does that matter, for the argument is irrefutable: 'American giants have often been a subject of mockery for the incredulous and particularly for philosophers. They have been unable to deny the physical existence of their skeletons... I dare to assert that these skeletons do exist and I am not the least bit afraid of critical contradiction.'[37]

Just as he had for the Amazons, Juan de Velasco rose to the defence of American 'cultural heritage', even – or rather, especially – when this was challenged by Europeans. He declared that he personally helped uncover more than four thousand skeletons at Ríobamba in 1735, amongst which 'we discovered a whole one, of which the femurs were at least two metres long, and for which the whole body was estimated at more than thirty-two spans, that is, more than eight metres.'[38]

Despite this exorbitant claim, which anyhow remained unknown to most Europeans, the myth of the Patagonian giants lost currency. The scientific approach played its part and Buffon had the wisdom to make a rational survey, reflecting at the same time both exotic exaggeration and systematic scepticism:[39]

> One can see in my work that I have seemed to doubt that this alleged race of giants actually existed. One cannot be careful enough about exaggerating, especially with newly discovered things. Nevertheless, I am very much inclined to believe, along with M. des Brosses, that the differences accorded to the size of the Patagonians by various travellers can only be the result of their not having seen either the people or the country. When everything is taken into account, it turns out that between the lattitudes of 22° and 40° or 45° South there certainly exists a race of people taller and stronger than any other in the universe. These people are not giants but they are all taller, far better built and more substantial than other people.[40]

Thus, by the end of the eighteenth century, this durable myth of giants had finally been laid to rest. These legends, whether they concern mermaids, headless or many-headed monsters, Amazons or Patagonians, were all created by the European imagination and supported by certain timely accounts which were interpreted and amplified in different ways and presented as 'objective' reality. It could be said, in fact, that the Americas was little more than a part of the world which remained partially explored for a long time, and was thus a land of mystery upon which Europeans projected their own imaginations expecting to see something that was literally 'larger than life'.

This essay was first published in French in 1985 by Editions Promodis in Jean-Paul Duviols, *L'Amérique espagnole vue et révée.*

NOTES

1 Federman 1557: 50. The Ayamanes referred to here by Federman were Indian groups who inhabited the mountainous regions of what are now the provinces of Falcón and Lara in Venezuela.

2 Ibid: 51. His curiosity satisfied, Federman rapidly had the dwarfs baptised, then sent them back into their forests regretting, however, that he could not use them as porters. The chief of the Ayamanes presented Federman with his wife, who was four spans tall and who, according to Federman, was disagreeable and would not stop crying since she – along with her companions – considered the Christians to be demons.

3 The land that Vespucci describes is in fact very fertile, and the people are cannibals who may correspond to Tupi-Guarani groups, but not to the Tehuelches of Patagonia.

4 Levillier 1951: 114.

5 In the *Devisement du monde* Marco Polo is certainly talking about giants. They were supposed to live on an island near to that of the Cynocephalae (the many-headed monsters), the island of Zanzibar: 'They are tall and well-built, but not as tall as they are burly. They are so tall that they resemble giants, and so strong that one alone easily carries the load of four ordinary men, and eats as much as five ordinary men.'

6 Levillier 1951: 242. It seems likely that this passage may have inspired the German engraving entitled 'Das sind die new gefunden Menschen'.

7 Pigafetta 1519, quoted in Peillard 1964: 100–5.
8 Ibid: 105–6.
9 Malkiel 1952: 321–3.
10 Bataillon 1962: 27–45.
11 Anon. 1524: chap. CXXXIII, fol. CXLII b.
12 'At present we have at our disposal several valuable series of anthropometrical measurements, both from the last survivors and from the bones of preceding generations. Although everything goes to show that our Choniks represent a handsome type of man, and one of the tallest on earth, one cannot, however, refer to them as giants.

As for the Tehuelches, the average height of three men measured by Lehmann-Nietsche is 1.765 m. Latchman, on the other hand, gives an average height of 1.8 m for the male and 1.68 m for the female Tehuelches... As for Imbelloni, from a group of nineteen men (whom he had measured personally or of whom he had derived the measurements from previous authors), he reached an average height of 1.777 m...' Canals-Frau 1953: 170–1. See also Imbelloni 1949: 57–8.
13 Pauw 1770: vol. II, part 3, section II: 'Des Patagons'.
14 Buffon 1834.
15 Orbigny 1839: vol. II, 26–75.
16 Alfonse 1559.
17 Sarmiento de Gamboa 1768.
18 Argensola 1609. With regard to this, des Brosses (1756) accuses Sarmiento de Gamboa of being, 'a vain man and a liar, and his historian, Argensola, not only adopts fables without hesitation, but freely adds new ones'. It must be noted that Argensola has a tendency to exaggerate when, in referring to Magellan's voyage, he asserts, 'He captured giants who were more than fifteen spans high, that is approaching twelve feet; but they died soon after because they did not have their usual food, which was raw flesh.' (Argensola 1609: vol. I, 35.)
19 Thevet 1575: vol. II, fol. 903 r.
20 Ibid: fol. 906 r. It is highly doubtful whether Thevet himself actually saw the giants which he felt necessary for the embellishment of his work. Whilst he proved himself to be reasonable when dealing with the Amazons, he admits to having let himself be taken advantage of. He appears to have remained convinced of the existence of these fantastical beings of such inordinate size, but his credulity is difficult to accept, however. The fear he must have experienced when, being unwell, he was nearly buried alive by the savages (see fol. 904), must account for much of this frenzied description, which is reminiscent of tales of chivalry.
21 Ibid: fol. 903 r.
22 Drake 1854: 278.
23 Cf. Barent 1703.
24 Barent 1703: vol. I, 568.
25 Brosses 1756: vol. I, 296, 299.
26 Ibid: 232.
27 García de Nodal 1621.
28 Froger 1715: 101, 102.
29 Frezier 1716: 78–9.
30 Byron 1767a: 44–6.
31 Byron 1767b.
32 Pernetty 1769. Pernetty does not mention the Patagonians in his account of the voyage. The evidence given was that of Duclos-Guyot and de Chesnard de la Giraudais, who wrote that, 'Having examined the Patagonians at their leisure, they found them to be of great height, the shortest being at least five feet seven inches tall'. It should be noted that among the sailors on the expedition there was 'an officer, M. de la Ronde de Saint-Simon, who embarked at the Malvinas, was born in Canada and is five feet ten inches tall and with a proportionate physique.'
33 Bougainville 1771: chap. VIII, 'Entrevue avec les Patagons'.
34 Nassau-Siegen: fol. 144.
35 'In my opinion nothing reveals the sterility of a subject more than an abundance of details; and verbosity and diffusion are the common faults of all travel narratives', Pauw 1770: vol. II, part 3, 281. Carlos Quesada, writing about de Pauw's thesis, adroitly summarises his ambiguity and his contradictions when he states, 'on the one hand he claims to be taking an anthropological and an historical approach, but on the other he systematically tries to assert the superiority of European civilisation over the life of the savages. By eliminating all the data that contradicts his opinions, he deprives himself of the means indispensable for achieving a distinguished study.' Quesada 1982: part 2, 99.
36 Pauw 1770: vol. II, part 3, 326. Cf. the controversy between Pernetty and de Pauw in Gerbi 1960: 74ff.
37 Velasco 1927: 184.
38 Ibid: 186. It referred to 'a field of giants', i.e., a cemetery of mammoths like that near Bogota in Colombia described by Humboldt.
39 As Michèle Duchet rightly points out, 'More distinguished and more open than that of de Pauw, Buffon's anthropology serves as a foundation for a theory of civilisation. Whilst de Pauw attributes not only the degeneration of the Americans but also the deterioration of the Creoles to the extremes of the climate, Buffon strongly links the idea of a brutal natural environment with that of a man remaining in a state of savagery.' Duchet 1971: 213–14.
40 Buffon 1834: XII, 398–9.

8 Travelling the Other Way
Travel Narratives and Truth Claims

Gillian Beer

All narratives take the reader or listener on a journey, and many of them tell the story of a journey too. Narratives are organised to move through time, to transport the reader, and to bring us home again, augmented by the experience and by the knowledge we have acquired. This narrative motion is enacted as much in non-fictional accounts, like the many records of nineteenth-century surveying voyages, as it is in the *Odyssey*, or *Gulliver's Travels*. The differences begin when we examine the freight the reader gains by the expedition.

Almost all accounts of travels offer wonders, as well as a record of hardship endured by the narrator and his (usually his) companions. When Othello woos Desdemona he does so with his 'travellor's history' which is also a 'travaillous history': the ear does not discriminate between hardship and travel; their identity is part of the pleasure of the story told and part of its verification. The travel narrative, published or recounted, is a record of survival: the narrator is *here* to tell it in retrospect even as the reader sets out on the journey. That double motion offers reassurance: the experiences undergone, the knowledge gained, the treasure or the specimens preserved, are all trophies for the returning traveller and are proferred also to the reader. Material specimens and treasures are to be had only by proxy, but knowledge is more portable and may become part of the reader's own experience by reading the book. The publication of the 'history' affirms the traveller's re-entry into his initial culture, one presented as shared with the reader. After a spell as alien, the narrator is again homely, caught into current society's processes of exchange and affirmation.

These are some of the implicit assurances offered by travel narrative. But the question of its claim to truth is always ambiguous: travellers' tales are notorious for their self-serving exaggeration. The reader cannot check the authenticity of the monsters described, the adventures lived through. Confusions between actual and imagined voyages are frequent. Some writers, like Daniel Defoe (1661–1731), ransacked the accounts of others and adopted the plain style of authentic record, the careful downplaying of crisis, to such effect that his account of *A New Voyage Round the World By a Course Never Sailed Before* (London, 1725) was accepted as a true record for years after his death, to

Fig 95 Group of Yámana in Canal Beagle with HMS *Beagle* in the background.

say nothing of the convincing (but fictional) record of his Captain Singleton's travels in Africa, or Robinson Crusoe's make do and mend on his fortunately fertile island.

The tradition of imaginary voyages is ancient and continuous and natural historians on their travels therefore found themselves writing within rhetorical modes that were both enabling and dangerous to their project: enabling because detailed sensory description was valued in the genre, dangerous because such description was easily melded into fantasy and received as playful exaggeration not controlled observation. Diaries, field notes, samples and specimens, all the local and immediate evidence of encounter and categorisation, therefore became particularly important in vouching for the objectivity of record. Yet at the same time the phenomenological, the personal moment, the record of what is smelt, touched, tasted, seen and heard by the subject, provides other convincing written evidence of the authenticity of what is told. It also translates as pleasure, one of the most compelling persuasive registers that writing can reach.

The question of the personal becomes a key issue: who sees? what is seen? what are the conditions of observation? The personal both vouches for and limits the scope of observation, and its authority. So the persona adopted by the narrator, or the taken-for-granted social contract between narrator and readers, must be exploited to give the widest possible scope and the greatest possible appearance of objectivity and disinterested access. Freiherr Alexander von Humboldt's (1769–1859) *Personal Narrative of Travels to the Equinoctial Regions of the New Continent, during the Years 1799–1804* (trans. H. Williams, 7 vols, London, 1814–29) provided a formidable example for nineteenth-century naturalists. His eminent eye, his range of sensuous descriptions, his human contacts, impelled the reader into an identification that was physical and intellectual, specific and generalising. For Charles Darwin (1809–82), the *Personal Narrative* fuelled his enthusiasm for travel and observation alike and provides a constant point of reference in his description of the *Beagle* voyage: Alcide d'Orbigny is 'second only to Humboldt' (vol. III, p. 110), and the phrase 'Humboldt has observed' recurs frequently (e.g. vol. III, p. 477).[1] Humboldt's presence in citation also indicated the international gentlemanly community of enquirers.

The title-pages of many a travel narrative reveal the strategies of endorsement adopted. Henry Walter Bates (1825–92), Alfred Russel Wallace's friend and collaborator, in his title suggests an all-inclusive cornucopia without too much self-consciousness about categories of knowledge; the whole is sustained, and contained, by his self-description as 'the Naturalist': *The Naturallist on the River Amazon: A Record of Adventures, Habits of Animals, Sketches of Brazilian and Indian Life, and Aspects of Nature under the Equator during eleven years of travel* (2 vols, London, 1869). Bates emphasises the length of his sojourn ('eleven years') and the range of his interests. He includes events ('adventures'); systemising ('habits'); and amateur and contingent observations of other peoples, not claimed as ethnographic studies ('sketches'). He acknowledges different levels and styles of knowledge-acquisition within one person's experience. Though social class is often important in the traveller's self-presentation, it is not so in the Bates example: here, in the late 1860s, his profession ('naturalist') is emphasised.

Earlier, the gentlemanly traveller, such as Louis Antoine, comte de Bougainville (1729–1811), is assumed in his *Voyage autour du monde* (1771) to have a synthesising gaze that can encompass the discrete findings of fieldworkers and accommodate them to his own large vision. The trust of the authorities that send the traveller out is also an imprimatur: the King, the Admiralty, the Royal Society, and, in the period that most concerns me here, the support of the British Association for the Advancement of Science (so we find, for example, in 1831 an account of 'His Majesty's sloop *Chanticleer's* voyage under Commodore Henry Foster, FRS').

Underpinning these social and intellectual claims to authority, and seemingly largely unobserved by initial writer and reader, is a formation we can afford at present to be sharp-eyed about: that of the imperial and colonising enterprise. That process may have a religious function: missionaries going forth to convert individuals and cultures. It may be part of land acquisition and conquest. It may also be part of a concern to map the seas, the sounds, the minerals, the rocks, the rivers, the interiors, the peoples of the place. When that exploration is condensed with a pattern of expectation that assumes a range of development in human societies moving from primitive to civilised, a particularly ample authority can be claimed, since the civilised is assumed to be the place from which the writer starts and to which he returns. The writing is itself civilisation at work on the unruly.

Yet current readers would be self-aggrandising if they believed themselves to be the first to offer sceptical critique of the motivation, outcome and justification of voyages of exploration. Near the end of *Travels into Several Remote Nations of the World, In Four Parts. By Lemuel Gulliver, first a Surgeon, and then a Captain of Several Ships* (London, 1726), Jonathan Swift (1667–1745) has Gulliver muse on the 'distributive justice of princes'. For instance, a crew of pirates are driven by a storm they know not whither, at length a boy discovers land from the topmast, they go on shore to rob and plunder, they see a harmless people, are entertained with kindness, they give the country a new name, they take formal possession of it for the king, they set up a rotten plank or a stone for a memorial, they murder two or three dozen of the natives, bring away a couple more by force as a sample, return home, and get their pardon. Here commences a new dominion acquired with a title *by divine right.*

And Denis Diderot (1713–84) inverts Bougainville's *Voyage autour du monde par la frégate du roi* La Boudeuse, *et la flûte* L'Etoile *en 1766, 1767, 1768 et 1769* (1771) in *Supplément au voyage de Bougainville* (1773) with an imagined Tahitian's telling account of *his* journey to Europe: a voyage in the reverse direction that was by no means fictional only, as Gulliver's reference to 'samples' suggests, and as the account of the two voyages of the *Beagle* later in this essay will make clear.

The voyages with which we are chiefly concerned here were those whose prize was represented as knowledge rather than treasure. The categories are, however, not altogether separate. Although the nineteenth-century journeys that set out from Britain to survey the sea and coasts around the world were not piratical, not part of that unconcerned predation that earlier centuries justified as exploration or discovery, they were nevertheless an expression of the will to control, categorise, occupy and bring home the prize of samples and of strategic information. Natural history and national future were closely interlocked. And natural history was usually a sub-genre in the programme of the enterprise, subordinate to the search for sea-passages or the mapping of feasible routes and harbours.

The prosaic quality of such voyages' enterprise could also become part of the claim to truth-telling. Here, there is to be no surplus adventuring, no high-flown description, but an accurate record of observation and encounter. This level aim assumes that the ship's company has one coherent project and plan in view. But the disturbances manifest in the narrative language describing such voyages undermines that assumption. Fascination with the unfamiliar, fear and loathing, the longing for stable systems of communication, sickness, religious fervour and the physical pleasures of exploration all pressed across and became part of enquiry and left their traces in the writing. And so, particularly, do the peoples encountered.

Natural history and indigenous peoples

> He expressed his regret that so little attention was given to Ethnography, or the natural history of the human race, while the opportunities for observation are every day passing away; and concluded by an appeal in favour of the Aborigines Protection Society.

Among the records of the ninth meeting of the British Association for the Advancement of Science, held at Birmingham in August 1839 (London, 1840, 'Transactions of the Sections', p. 89) occurs this summary of a paper by the ethnographer James Cowles Prichard (1786–1848). It suggests one of the most pressing issues raised by travels and their narratives in the nineteenth century and pursued particularly by Prichard. What are the boundaries of natural history? Are human beings within its scope? Are they one species or several? Are they separate from all other species because created as souls by God? And do all, all savages, have souls? Or are they – here danger lies – a kind of animal? (If they, then we?)

Elsewhere in this same volume, in the 'Synopsis of grants of money at Birmingham' and under the heading 'Zoology and botany', we discover the response to Prichard's appeal:

> For Printing and Circulating a Series of Questions and Suggestions for the use of travellers and others, with a view to procure Information respecting the different races of Men, and more especially of those which are in an uncivilized state: the questions to be drawn up by Dr. Pritchard [*sic*], Dr. Hodgkin, Mr. J. Yates, Mr. Gray, Mr. Darwin [etc.]... £5.00 (p. 27).

The grant is among the smallest given, but it is there. The Aborigines Protection Society seems to be less a humanitarian than a natural historical enterprise, though one of an unusual kind since the subjects observed are also to be the questionnaire's informants (not something that other botanic or zoological subjects such as kelp or Ascidiae, sloths, ant-eaters, or armadillos, can be expected to perform). That double role of being the scrutinised subject and the independent respondent is peculiar to human beings. Over and over again the narratives of voyages demonstrate how the borders of natural history were blurred by human encounter and how evolutionary theory profited from that growing uncertainty about the status of the human in knowledge and in nature. The zoological and the linguistic appear side by side as parallel kinds of evidence: so, the surgeon Wilson on the *Beagle*, writes: 'The Fuegian, like a Cetaceous animal which circulates red blood in a cold medium, has in his covering an admirable non-conductor of heat' (vol. II, Appendix 16, p. 143), while Appendix 15 (pp. 135–42) is a vocabulary of Fuegian languages.

A review in the *Gentleman's Magazine* (March 1831), the year that Darwin joined the *Beagle*'s expedition, shows a typical squirm of argument about these matters. The book reviewed is a compendious *Narrative of Discovery and Adventure in Africa, from the earliest ages to the present time: with illustrations of the Geology, Mineralogy, and Zoology. By Professor Jameson, James Wilson, Esq. FRSE and Hugh Murray, Esq. FRSE*. It is not the geology, zoology or mineralogy that fascinates and irritates the reviewer but the peoples encountered. The reviewer is writing within the journal's pro-slavery stance:

> All savages present to us, in certain respects, tricks, habits, and oddities like monkeys; and it is certain that in artificial acquirements they do not reach the elevation of dancing dogs... We are no advocates for the abduction of Africans, because it is robbery, and sometimes consequentially murder ... but [like impressment or conscription it is]... assuredly a means of rendering idle and worthless people useful members of the community. That the African cannot become such useful members at home, is evident from the following tokens of their degrading characteristics as human beings (p. 237).

Whose 'community' is that to be served? The question does not bear answering. The argument presents 'savages' simultaneously as at the very least *like* animals and yet as degraded human beings. The indigenous inhabitant is here, squeamishly though it is put, to be 'improved' only by removal from home and subjection to 'civilized masters'.

Travellers who would have believed themselves heartily against slavery nevertheless commandeered individuals to function as pilots or translators. For example, Robert Fitzroy (1805–65) records a 'boy, whose name, among the sealers, was Bob'. 'Mr. Low had a Fuegian boy on board the *Adeona*, who learned to speak English very tolerably, during eighteen months that he staid on board as a pilot and interpreter' (vol. II, p. 188). Taking local people aboard ship for a time was not altogether unusual: motives varied. One of the most benign was that of Frederick Beechey (1796–1856), as he recounts it in his *Narrative of a Voyage to the Pacific and Bering's Strait, to Co-operate with The Polar Expeditions: performed in His Majesty's Ship* Blossom, *under the command of Captain F.W. Beechey, RN, FRS, etc. in the years 1825, 26, 27, 28* (London, 2 vols, 1831). Beechey came upon a shipwrecked group of Otaheitean islanders who had drifted six hundred miles by canoe from their home. He took on board a family, Tuwarri and his wife and children, and the chief of the group and delivered them back to Chain Island. Tuwarri behaves according to the expectations of natural virtue: he is grateful, regrets parting, and is sorry not to be able to 'send some little token of his gratitude'.

> These feelings, so highly creditable to Tuwarri, were not participated by his wife, who, on the contrary, showed no concern at her departure, expressed neither thanks nor regrets, nor turned to any person to bid him farewell; and while Tuwarri was suppressing his tears, she was laughing at the exposure which she thought she would make going into the boat without an accommodation-ladder (p. 236).

Beechey is mortified by the wife's insouciance and eagerness to be gone. Gratitude had, conveniently, long been assumed to be a natural virtue. He also criticises Tuwarri's lack of curiosity while on board, though he praises his 'strong sense of right and wrong', and he is mildly shocked when Tuwarri 'was not received by his countrymen with the surprise and pleasure which might have been expected; but this may, perhaps, be explained by there being no one on the beach to whom he was particularly attached' (p. 237).

The absence of wonder or surprise was one of the phenomena that most disconcerted Western travellers in their encounters with indigenous people and which they described as most animal-like. Curiosity was so strong a driving force in Western expeditions, and so valued as a disinterested or 'scientific' incentive as opposed to the search for material gain, that the absence of an answering curiosity was felt as rebuff or even insult. Moreover, the reader of the narrative is likely, functionally, to agree with this view unless alerted, since the reading of natural history travel narratives is an intensified form of that zealous curiosity that drives all reading.

Captain P. Parker King (1793–1856), the writer of the first volume of the three-volume set that includes Fitzroy and Darwin's accounts of the *Beagle* voyages, is in the main an astute and sympathetic observer. He describes his first encounter with the Fuegians in January 1827, after visiting the Patagonian Indians, linking the terms 'brutes' and 'want of curiosity':

> They appeared to be a most miserable, squalid race, very inferior, in every respect, to the Patagonians. They did not evince the least uneasiness at Mr. Sholl's presence, or at our ships being close to them; neither did they interfere with him, but remained squatting round their fire while he staid near. This seeming indifference, and total want of curiosity, gave us no favourable opinion of their character as ethical beings; indeed, they appeared to be very little removed from brutes; but our subsequent knowledge of them has convinced us that they are not usually deficient in intellect. This party was perhaps stupified by the unusual size of our ships, for the vessels which frequent this Strait are seldom one hundred tons in burden (p. 24).

King does not quite settle between cowed passivity or, more romantically, dignified remoteness: indeed he makes the point that interpreting the behaviour of other groups is always risky and unreliable. He repeatedly records the degree to which his own group had to correct their initial impressions and emphasises that analogies with either animal or Western behaviour patterns are liable to mislead. As Anthony Pagden puts it in *European Encounters with the New World* (1993), one discovery made by travellers is that 'it is incommensurability itself which is, ultimately, the only certainty' (p. 41).

The need for native interpreters of local languages was therefore pressing. Marshall Sahlins in *Islands of History* (1985) has opened up the ways in which entire cultural systems of reference got disastrously caught across each other in Cook's final encounter with the Hawaiians. Western travellers, whether natural historians or not, soon discovered that the apparently universal repertoire of the body and its gestural systems is dangerously unreliable as a measure of meaning and intent. Language, though limited, is less volatile. With our current emphasis on the indeterminacies of language it is striking to realise the degree to which in travel narrative gesture is treacherous, language (even a few words) a blessedly stable resource and coin.

Beechey, for example, gives an account that is amusing if you are not on the spot, of what happened when he tried to persuade the Gambier islanders to dance, having admired their musical instruments. Beechey, hoping to get the islanders to offer their dances in exchange, gets the marines to 'go through some of their manoeuvres... this, however, had a very different effect from what was intended; for the motions of the marines were misinterpreted, and so alarmed some of his bystanders, that several made off, while others put themselves into an attitude of defence, so that I speedily dismissed the party' (p. 176). Darwin's much later *The Expression of the Emotions in Man and Animals* (1872) may owe much to his puzzling experiences on the *Beagle* and be in part a final attempt to regulate the irregularities he had there encountered.

Darwin and the Fuegians

On board the *Beagle* when Darwin joined the ship's surveying expedition in 1831 as companion to Captain Fitzroy and additional natural historian were seventy-four persons, seventy-three of them men. A girl of twelve or thirteen was the only female aboard. Her own name was 'yok'cushlu', but to discover that one must go to a fragment of a vocabulary on page 135 of the appendix to volume II of the three-volume *Narrative of the Surveying Voyages of His Majesty's Ships* Adventure *and* Beagle. Elsewhere in the text, by both Fitzroy (vol. II) and Darwin (vol. III), she is always called 'Fuegia Basket' as she had been named on the 1830 passage of the *Beagle* to England. She was one of three Fuegians whose return to their homeland was part of the second expedition's purpose and, so far as Captain Fitzroy was concerned, a compelling incentive. The other two were men, 'el'leparu' or 'York Minster', and 'o'run-del'lico' or 'Jemmy Button' (fig. 97). A fourth Fuegian, whose own name is lost but who was hauntingly called 'Boat Memory', had died of smallpox shortly after his arrival in England. It is worth dwelling on the story of the Fuegians' journey to England and return to Tierra del Fuego, and the subsequent return upon return of Darwin and Fitzroy to the same locality to check their whereabouts, welfare and behaviour. Later travellers, such as W. Parker Snow, came on Jemmy Button again twenty years later. The story, pieced together, raises a number of important issues that go into the formation of Darwin's thought. What was the impact of his meeting and acquaintance with these three young people long before he had encountered what he thought of as 'a savage'? And what did Jemmy Button's subsequent history suggest concerning adaptability, survival and cultural diversity and inheritance?

Captain Fitzroy later glosses his reasons for taking the Fuegians to England in different ways. In his letter to the Admiralty (23 May 1831), seeking support for his expedition to return the Fuegians to their own country, he emphasises that 'I hoped to have seen these people become useful as interpreters, and be the means of establishing a friendly disposition towards Englishmen on the part of their countrymen, if not a regular intercourse with them' (Appendix to vol. II, p. 91). That secular and diplomatic explanation is overlaid by a religious one as support comes in from a missionary society who send a young man Matthews to accompany the Fuegians, learn language from them, and then use them as a group from which to promote the conversion of their countrymen. (That goes almost disastrously wrong and Matthews has to be rescued by the returning *Beagle*.) Fitzroy back-projects a lofty humanitarian motive, which he universalises defensively as a 'natural emotion' not capricious behaviour on his part.

Initially, however, it is clear that the various young people were annexed as hostages. Boat Memory and York Minster certainly were so. Fuegia Basket was left behind on board with two other children when women who had been detained escaped by swimming. The other children were returned but Fuegia, showing, Fitzroy asserts, no particular desire to go, was retained. Jemmy Button was conceived as something between hostage and 'interpreter and guide' (vol. II, p. 5). While seeking a boat stolen from the *Beagle* 'accidentally meeting two canoes ... I prevailed on their occupants to put one of the party, a stout boy, into my boat, and in return I gave them beads, buttons, and other trifles' (vol. II, p. 6). Hence the name 'Jemmy Button'.

Fig 96 A Yámana from the Tekenika tribe, Isla Hoste.

This shockingly cavalier appropriation of human beings rings ironically alongside Fitzroy's constant complaints about the Fuegians' pilfering. Yet, that fundamental error acknowledged, Fitzroy cared for the young people. He did not display them. He introduced them to his family and friends. He had them educated and looked after and taught mechanical skills. He disliked them being called 'savages'. Fitzroy claimed, oddly, that even their features improved with education. Describing the physical characteristics of the Yámana (Tekenika) and Kawéskar (Halakwulup), he writes:

> The nose is always narrow between the eyes, and, except in a few curious instances, is hollow, in profile outline, or almost flat. The mouth is coarsely formed (I speak of them in their savage state, and not of those who were in England, whose features were much improved by altered habits, and by education) (vol. II, p. 175) (figs 96 and 97).

Fitzroy's account is riven with contradictions provoked by the gap between his general assertions and his individual reactions: for example, he considers the Tekenika particularly degraded, yet praises Jemmy Button most highly of his charges. During their stay in England Jemmy Button and Fuegia Basket appeared to adapt to their new conditions, though York Minster remained recalcitrant. Jemmy Button relished shoes and gloves; Queen Adelaide gave Fuegia one of her own bonnets. A phrenological examination performed in London unsurprisingly confirmed 'objectively' the judgements already made on their personalities (Appendix 17, pp. 148–9). These are the assurances the reader is offered, apparently bolstered by the 'factual', sample-like, materials of the various appendices freed from narrative process.

Fig 97 The page of comparative portraits that Parker Snow and o'run-del'lico/Jemmy Button looked at together.

Darwin was not present on the first voyage nor implicated in the decision to take the Fuegians away. He joined the ship on which they were to be returned to their native land. He therefore met the Fuegians in their Western demeanour and outfits (fig. 97). Perhaps the degree of shock that Darwin felt when confronted with 'the inhabitants of this savage land', Tierra del Fuego, was because he was habituated to the Westernised young people on board ship; certainly his remarks suggest so: 'I could not have believed how wide was the difference between savage and civilized man. It is greater than between a wild and domesticated animal, in as much as in man there is a greater power of improvement' (vol. III, p. 228). 'Jemmy understood very little of their language, and was, moreover, thoroughly ashamed of his countrymen' (vol. III, p. 230).

Darwin observes that the appalling physical conditions in which the Fuegians live – the cold, the lack of food and heating, the smoke half-blinding them in their wigwams – means that all their energies are engrossed in animal survival:

> It is a common subject of conjecture what pleasure in life some of the less gifted animals can enjoy: how much more reasonably the same question may be asked with respect to these barbarians. At night, five or six human beings, naked and scarcely protected from the wind and rain of this tempestuous climate, sleep on the wet ground coiled up like animals (vol. III, p. 236).

The terms in the surrounding passage swerve, registering a disturbance that will not settle; he calls them 'poor wretches', 'barbarians', 'human beings': 'Viewing such men, one can hardly make oneself believe they are fellow-creatures, and inhabitants of the same world' (p. 235). But in a footnote Darwin argues that their lack of attainment does

Fig 98 Fuegians going to trade in Zapallos with the Patagonians.

not imply inferior capabilities: 'Indeed, from what we saw of the Fuegians, who were taken to England, I should think the case was the reverse' (vol. III, p. 235).

Darwin's encounters with Fuegians in their native place (fig. 98) gave him a way of closing the gap between the human and other primates, a move necessary to the theories he was in the process of reaching. But it came after his experience of Fuegians abroad, since shipboard was a stylised form of England. The individuals, Jemmy, York and Fuegia, seemed to provide evidence of the human capacity for physical adaptation within the individual life-cycle. What was left moot was the question of descent. What would happen to the next generation? Would Jemmy's children be 'improved' by their father's experience? The answer was unexpected and disconcerting, and is much developed in the second, 1845, edition of the *Journal of Researches.*

When Darwin and Fitzroy returned in the February of the succeeding year (1834) they were appalled. A canoe appeared 'with one of the men in it washing the paint off his face':

> This man was poor Jemmy, – now a thin, haggard savage, with long disordered hair, and naked, except a bit of blanket round his waist. We did not recognise him till he was close to us; for he was ashamed of himself, and turned his back to the ship. We had left him plump, fat, clean, and well dressed; – I never saw so complete and grievous a change (2nd edn, p. 227).

The native has gone native

Instead of admiring Jemmy's survival skills Darwin, like Fitzroy, reads this as degradation. Jemmy tells them 'that he did not wish to go back to England'. Darwin is more satisfied when 'we found out the cause of this great change in Jemmy's feelings, in the arrival of his young and nice-looking wife' (p. 227). York Minster and Fuegia Basket have disappeared, York Minster having robbed Jemmy Button. Only distant and indirect tidings are ever heard of Fuegia Basket: a sealer in 1842 'was astonished by a native woman coming on board, who could talk some English. Without doubt this was Fuegia Basket. She lived (I fear the term probably bears a double interpretation) some days on board' (footnote to p. 227).

So the hope of finding interpreters and guides, of sending back missionaries to convert their own people, came to very little. Instead the Fuegians acquired some macaronic skills and learnt to trade with language. Jemmy introduced English terms into the vocabulary of his group. Darwin's sentimental (but wary) hope concerning Jemmy's descendants is mocked by actual events: 'Every one must sincerely hope that Captain Fitzroy's noble hope may be fulfilled, of being rewarded for the many generous sacrifices which he made for these Fuegians, by some ship-wrecked sailor being protected by the descendants of Jemmy Button and his tribe!' (pp. 227–8). It is easy now to see the absurdity of this high-flown hope, for the Fuegians had no reason to see Fitzroy as a benefactor for stealing them from their homeland.

One further travel narrative gives a wry later vignette of transculturation: W. Parker Snow's *A Two Years' Cruise off Tierra del Fuego, the Falkland Islands, Patagonia and the River Plate: A Narrative of Life in the Southern Seas* (London, 1857). Snow met Jemmy Button 'quite naked, having his hair long and matted at the sides, cropped in front, and his eyes affected by smoke'. He still spoke English and on board the ship wanted to put on clothes and requested a 'knife to cut meat'. Jemmy proved himself adept at immediately reframing himself in either context. Snow later comments that Jemmy's tribe was the least to be relied on in any dealings, having learnt a double language and behaviour. 'I had never before fallen in with one who had been transplanted to the highest fields of intellectual knowledge, and then restored to his original and barren state' (vol. II, pp. 36–7).

Snow shows Jemmy his picture in Fitzroy's *Narrative* (fig. 97):

> The portraits of himself and the other Fuegians made him laugh and look sad alternately, as the two characters he was represented in, savage and civilized, came before his eye. Perhaps he was calling to mind his combed hair, washed face, and dandy dress, with the polished boots it is said he so much delighted in: perhaps he was asking himself which, after all, was the best? – the prim and starchy, or the rough and shaggy? Which he thought, he did not choose to say; but which I inferred he thought was gathered from his refusal to go anywhere again with us (vol. II, pp. 37–8).

The Fuegian encounter continued to raise questions for Western travel narrative about cultural choice and helped to undermine assumptions about improvement and authority.

While the rest of the *Beagle*'s company left familiar England, sailed around the world, explored its people, geology, flora and fauna, and returned home, the Fuegians were performing a counter-motion from Tierra del Fuego to England and back. They had not chosen to explore the world or discover its properties. They were taken away from familiar Tierra del Fuego to exotic England by guile or force and then, after many adventures, returned more than two years later to a place not quite that from which they had set out. The two journeys, that of Darwin and that of the Fuegians, share one long lap: for him setting forth, for them returning. The Fuegians could compare England and Tierra del Fuego: Darwin could not yet do so. They could be not only objects of encounter but his informants and authority; and Jemmy Button, at least, we know was so.

It is difficult – impossible – to enter the Fuegians' experience of this story, though certainly as sentimental to imagine that they enjoyed nothing as that they relished everything and were grateful for their kidnap. Telling and knowing are ungrounded by this attempted exchange: what are the natural historical categories for these subjects? The reader can know el'leparu, o'run-del'lico and yok'cushlu, if at all, only under the sign of their Western soubriquets as York Minster, Jemmy Button and Fuegia Basket. Their own narratives were oral, in another tongue, another place. That process of familiarisation and estrangement is repeated in relation to the language of the *Beagle* voyagers themselves. Trying to understand the sensibility expressed by the British sailors in that act of re-naming the Fuegians, re-naming them moreover with those particular nicknames, is likely to make us register our baffled distance from the shipboard community of the 1830s more intensely than does anything in the rest of Fitzroy's urbane or Darwin's ardent prose.

This essay was first published in 1996 by Cambridge University Press in *Cultures of Natural History*, ed. N. Jardine, J. A. Second, E. C. Spary.

NOTES

1 The first form in which the book we now know as *The Voyage of the Beagle* appeared was as vol. III of *Narrative of the Surveying Voyages of His Majesty's Ships* Adventure *and* Beagle, *between the years 1826 and 1836, describing their Examination of the Southern Shores of South America, and the* Beagle's *Circumnavigation of the Globe* (London, 1839). Vol. I was by Captain P. Parker King and covers the earlier expeditions; vol. II is by Captain Robert Fitzroy, captain of the *Beagle*, and his account overlaps temporally with that of vol. III by Charles Darwin. The publisher Henry Colburn produced Darwin's volume as a separate book in the following year as *Journal of Researches into the Natural History and Geology of the Countries visited during the voyage of HMS* Beagle *Round the World*, and in 1845 a second revised and expanded edition appeared.

9 Tierra del Fuego – Land of Fire, Land of Mimicry

Michael Taussig

On 18 December 1832, in his diary of the voyage of the *Beagle*, the twenty-three-year-old naturalist Charles Darwin recorded the mythical scene of 'almost first contact' with the people of Tierra del Fuego.[1] The *Beagle* had sighted Fuegians lighting fires upon seeing the vessel two days earlier, 'whether for the purpose of communicating the news or attracting our attention, we do not know'. Anchoring in the Bahía Buen Suceso he observed more Fuegians (the Haush) – 'perched on a wild peak overhanging the sea and surrounded by woods. As we passed by they all sprang up and waving their cloaks of skins sent forth a loud sonorous shout; this they continued for a long time (fig. 99). These people followed the ship up the harbour, and just before dark we again heard their cry and soon saw their fire at the entrance of the Wigwam which they built for the

Fig 99 Yámana hailing a sailing vessel, Estrecho Murray, Canal Beagle.

Fig 100 Haush encampment on Tierra del Fuego.

night (fig. 100).'[2] Next day Captain Fitzroy sent a boat with a large party of officers to communicate with the Fuegians. 'It was', wrote the young Darwin, 'without a doubt the most curious and interesting spectacle I ever beheld':

> I would not have believed how entire the difference between savage and civilized man is. It is greater than between a wild and domesticated animal, in as much as in man there is greater power of improvement. The chief spokesman was old and appeared to be head of the family; the three others were young and powerful men and about six feet high. From their dress etc etc they resembled the representations of Devils on the Stage, for instance, Der Freischutz. The old man had a white feather cap, from under which, black, long hair hung round his face. The skin is dirty copper colour. Reaching from ear to ear and including the upper lip, there was a broad red coloured band of paint; and parallel and above this, there was a white one; so that the eyebrows and eyelids were even thus coloured. The only garment was a guanaco skin with the hair outside. This was merely thrown over their shoulders, one arm and leg being bare; for any exercise they must be absolutely naked. (118–19)

So much for the spectacle. Then the contact:

> Their very attitudes were abject, and the expression distrustfull, surprised and startled. Having given them some red cloth, which they immediately placed around their necks, we became good friends. This was shown by the old man patting our

> breasts and making something like the same noise which people do when feeding chickens. I walked with the old man and this demonstration was repeated between us several times. At last he gave me three hard slaps on the breast and back at the same time, and making most curious noises. He then bared his bosom for me to return the compliment, which being done, he seemed highly pleased. Their language does not deserve to be called articulate. Capt. Cook says it is like a man trying to clear his throat; to which may be added another very hoarse man trying to shout and a third encouraging a horse with that peculiar noise which is made out of the side of the mouth. (119)

The mouth serves as an organ of language in other ways as well: 'Their chief anxiety was to obtain knives; this they showed by pretending to have blubber in their mouths and cutting instead of tearing it from the body: they called them in a continued plaintive tone cuchilla [Spanish for knife].' (119)

But it is the body in its entirety that serves to articulate this inarticulate language. In his *Journal of Researches*, the young naturalist proceeds, anticipating Walter Benjamin's assumptions about the intimate connection between primitiveness and mimesis by ninety-nine years. They are excellent mimics:

> As often as we coughed or yawned or made any odd motion, they immediately imitated us. Some of the officers began to squint and make monkey like faces; but one of the young Fuegians (whose face was painted black with a white band over his eyes) succeeded in making far more hideous grimaces. They could repeat with perfect correctness each word in any sentence we addressed them, and they remembered such words for some time. Yet we Europeans all know how difficult it is to distinguish apart the sounds in a foreign language. Which of us, for instance, could follow an American Indian through a sentence of more than three words? All savages appear to possess, to an uncommon degree, this power of mimicry. I was told, almost in the same words, of the same ludicrous habit among the Caffres: the Australians, likewise, have long been notorious for being able to imitate and describe the gait of any man, so that he may be recognized.

And he concludes by asking, 'How can this [mimetic] faculty be explained? Is it a consequence of the more practised habits of perception and keener senses, common to all men in a savage state, as compared with those long civilized?'[3]

Perhaps Captain Fitzroy supplies an answer. He was not only engaged in mapping the South American coast and accurately fixing the world's longitudinal reckoning, but was also the activator of a most audacious exercise in mimesis and alterity. He was returning three Fuegians – Jemmy Button, York Minster, and the woman, Fuegia Basket – back to their home from England, where he had presented them to Queen Adelaide two years earlier, to serve now as civilised Christian missionaries instructing their own people (see chapter 8). Before the Admiralty agreed to outfit a vessel, Fitzroy had been ready to complete this mission at his own expense.

In his rendering of the same scene that Darwin describes, Fitzroy provides the reader with a brief introduction, almost an apology. 'Disagreeable, indeed painful, as is even the mental contemplation of a savage', he admits, there is nevertheless great interest in it as well. And he goes on to suggest reasons why this should be so.[4]

It seems to me that this audacious ship's captain, writing in the early nineteenth century, has deftly articulated the key issue of the mimetic faculty in the modern world, namely what makes the mental contemplation of a savage interesting (despite the pain). Moreover, Fitzroy's explanation of *why* looking at the savage is interesting is that such looking is in itself a form of theorising about society and historical process.

The first reason he gives is that one should appreciate that we British were once like the Fuegians, and that is how Caesar found us, painted and in skins. The second reason is that there is something absorbing in observing people displaying childish ignorance of matters familiar to civilised man. And the third reason is the interest occasioned by the Fuegians' healthy, independent state of existence. Of particular interest to what has been called 'the civilising process' is the second reason, this 'something absorbing in observing people displaying childish ignorance of things familiar to civilised man'. Wherein lies the mysterious power of this 'something absorbing'?

Although his description in *The Beagle Record* of the landing on the beach was not as meticulous as Darwin's, Fitzroy chose to draw out one detail that Darwin omitted. First, as with Darwin, there is the contemplation of the spectacle: 'One of these men was just six feet high and stout in proportion: the others were rather shorter: their legs were straight and well formed, not cramped and misshapen like those of the natives who go about in canoes; and their bodies were rounded and smooth.' Then the contact: 'They expressed satisfaction or good will by rubbing or patting their own, and then our bodies; and were highly pleased by the antics of a man belonging to the boat's crew, who danced well and was a good mimic.'[5]

Note here first his optical focus on the Fuegian body, second the actual bodily, sensuous connection between the Fuegians and the sailors, and third the mimicry – but not on the part of the Fuegians, as Darwin so vividly depicted it, but on the part of the sailor. We are thus plunged into a chicken-and-egg problem. Who is mimicking whom, the sailor or the savage? We find the same problem and the same 'trick' of not seeing one's own indulgence in, and stimulation of, mimicry in the 'savage' when it comes to the way that adults in Western societies teach and relate to infants and children. Adults imitate what they take to be baby talk or childish tones of voice and expression and insert themselves in what they take to be the 'child's world', playing with the child, sometimes with the aim of controlling it, or teaching the child by getting it to imitate the adult's imitation – patting the dog this way, not that way, eating this way, not that way, and so forth. In fact the adult is imitating to differing degrees two different things here, one being the child, the other being the dog, the food, language and so forth. Control and education comes about by judicious blending of these two realities, moving one into the other and thereby creating new behaviours and understandings. And what, then, was the adult imitating in the first place – a real reality, as we might like simplistically to describe the issue, such as the child's tone of voice or behaviour? Or instead was the adult imitating the child's mimicry of the adult's mimicry? In which case we seem to be doing something quite strange, going round and round and unable to see that we are doing so, simulating and dissimulating at one and the same time.

Fitzroy's observation about the mimicking prowess of his sailor dancing to the mimicking Fuegians across the colonial divide of first contact is further sharpened by contrast with the account of Mick Leahy, a white Australian gold prospector in the New Guinea highlands a century later, in the early 1930s. First the contact:

> When I took my hat off, those nearest me backed away in terror. One old chap came forward gingerly, with open mouth, and touched me to see if I were real. Then he knelt down and rubbed his hands over my bare legs, possibly to find if they were painted, and grabbed me around the knees and hugged them, rubbing his bushy head against me. His hair was done up in dozens of little plaits and stank terribly of rancid pig grease.[6]

The white men were hungry and wanted to exchange 'gifts' for food with these people who had never before had contact with whites and spoke an unknown language. They 'bought' sugar-cane with glass beads and a pig with a steel axe and decided to camp there the night as their coastal native porters were tired. (In New Guinea no white man could carry a pack.) Then the mimicry:

> We told the [highland] natives of our intention by signs and asked them to come down the next morning and show us the way. This was accomplished by leaning the head on one hand and closing the eyes – gestures of sleeping; pointing to the ground, to indicate this place; then pointing to the east, with a rising gesture – 'sun he come up', and then pointing off down the creek, looking down for a trail and shaking our heads. The natives got it at once, and gave us to understand that they would be on hand. Pantomime serves surprisingly well for conversation when you have to depend on it.[7]

...Whereas Darwin had seen the *natives* as mighty mimics!

The space between

Let us go back to Fitzroy's sailor, for this in a nutshell (in an image of a sailor of Her Majesty's Navy dancing, perhaps a little smile on his mimicking face wet with salt spray and probably hell-bent on drawing out the mimicry of his Fuegian audience) is what I mean by mimesis as a 'space between', a space permeated by the colonial tension of mimesis and alterity, in which it is far from easy to say who is the imitator and who is the imitated, which is copy and which is original. Fitzroy's sailor doing his little dance for the Fuegians makes many of us think again about the exquisite ambivalence we feel at the shock of recognition we receive on reading Darwin: 'All savages appear to possess, to an uncommon degree, this power of mimicry' (figs 101 and 102).

Fig 101 Yámana gesturing from canoe in Woollya Cove, Canal Beagle.

Fitzroy's sailor reminds us of the pleasure, if not the need, the civilised have of such a savage mirror on the edge of the known world, where mimesis as a faculty now burns with the intensity of a mega-category, not only an awe-inspiring concrete imitation of this or that concrete entity but the sheer fact of mimicry itself, mimicry as bound to the savage body as its rightful property. Yet it is the civilised eye that provides this staging, this drawing-out and appreciation of the faculty, a drawing-out that impacts upon and blends into the body of that eye itself, as we in turn see it with Fitzroy's image of the dancing British tar.

In this way mimesis as fact and as epistemic moment can be understood as redolent with the trace of that *space between*, a colonial space *par excellence*, a windswept Fuegian space where mankind bottoms out into fairy-tale metamorphoses with children and animals, so mimesis becomes an enactment not merely *of* an original but *by* an 'original'. Nowhere is this more dramatically played out than on the colonial stage of historic surreality of copy/original reversals as conveyed to us through crucially important snapshots such as Darwin's on the beach at Tierra del Fuego, an image in which civilisation takes measure of its difference through its reflection in primitives. So deeply invested is this scene in Western cultural patrimony, and hence selfhood, that it cannot be shrugged aside or calmly studied from a distance because it enters in all manner of subtle ways into that very Self, into the apparatus

Fig 102 Who is gesturing to whom?

that might attempt the shrugging and, most pertinent of all, into its very philosophy of the senses and of copying the real – all the more baffling on account of the way by which mimesis entertains bewildering reciprocities, mixes them with sentience, with pleasures, with pain, and with the 'ludicrous' and 'odd mixture of surprise and imitation'.

Drawing out the mimetic faculty: the mimesis of mimesis

But we must also admit of a peculiar feature in this when we are assailed time and again by the mighty bodiliness and reciprocal bodiedness of the slap of ('first') contact between sailors and primitives – all that chest-thwacking, bosom-baring, rubbing, patting, walking arm-in-arm, face-pulling, squinting, languaging, dancing, and so forth. And this is more than a substitute for lack of a common verbal language; one can hardly imagine Fitzroy or his sailors acting like this with a group of German peasants or Norwegian fishermen with whom they shared no language.[8]

The very language of representation of this colonial mimesis acquires a crackling, sensuous character, beginning with the minute depiction of skin colour and body-paint, the patting and bearing of breasts – as if the sailors were stripping off, becoming naked like the Fuegians – and then the noises! The noises that in this depiction stand in for language! The clucking noise one makes when feeding chickens. The throat-clearing noise.

The hoarse-man-trying-to-shout noise. The horse-encouraging noise made out of the side of the mouth. (All these animal references!)

So much for sentience, for physicality, for the objectness of the object, for trying to articulate the inarticulatable in which the very language of (Darwin's) articulation strains its utmost to become, like Artaud or Futurist and Dada Bruitism, noise itself, to mime the (Fuegian) mimers, thereby recruiting the animal kingdom – or at least its domesticated sub-kingdom: chickens being clucked into order by what their masters regard as somehow seductive chicken-sounds at mealtimes; horses being cajoled by their masters with what their masters take to be horsey and horse-encouraging sounds. In short, these are the sounds that Englishmen use not merely to imitate animals but to control them, and Darwin, in describing the speech of the Fuegians, whom he catalogues as the lowest grade of man in the world, *compares* their speech to this imitating-controlling habit and vocabulary of 'ours' *vis à vis* animals. Ironically, in order to make this comparison, he *imitates* these sounds – he imitates the imitation in order to better imitate the imitators. And in his imitating we become aware of the sound of sound – of its physical presence in action – and are reminded once again of the two-layered nature of mimesis as sentience and copying.

This double layer is brought out in another striking way when Darwin observes with awe that the Fuegians can imitate the sailor's language 'with perfect correctness' while 'we Europeans all know how difficult it is to distinguish apart the sounds in a foreign language'. So while Darwin (for our sakes, never forget, for the sake of a communicating text, even if it is a diary that only later became a marketing book), mimes the Fuegians' language by its sentience, the Fuegians mime the sailors' language by deadly accurate copying.

But most endearing of all is the competition set up, a competition in miming. The instant they see a sailor, they yield into his shape, his speech, his gait, and of course, his face. 'As soon as we coughed or yawned, or made any odd motion, they immediately imitated us', noted Darwin, such that the sailors, in his description, then begin to squint and pull faces and look awry. In other words, they get into the game too, not only as mimicry of mimicry but, so it seems to me, with a hint of parody as well – parody of sensuous capacity of face-pulling, and parody of mimesis itself. But, says Darwin, our referee in this matter, still they are outdone by the Fuegians mimicking the sailors mimicking the Fuegians.

It's as if the Fuegians can't help themselves, that their mimetic flair is more like an instinctual reflex than a faculty, an instinct for facing the unknown – and I mean *facing*. I mean sentience and copying in the face of strange faces. Note the way they are painted, especially the face, especially the eyes. Note the grimacing of the face that sets off a chain reaction between sailors and Fuegians. And most of all note that there seems to be a tight fit between surprise and mimicry, as Darwin himself noted in his *Journal*: 'After our first feeling of grave astonishment was over, nothing could be more ludicrous than the odd mixture of surprise and imitation which these savages at every moment exhibited' (209). What we find here seems close to shock and subsequent mimetic reaction to it: that odd mixture ... *at every moment exhibited.*

Keener senses, mighty mimicry?

Darwin suggested that the extraordinary degree of development of the mimetic faculty amongst 'savages' might be due to their 'more practised habits of perception and keener senses, common to all men in a savage state, as compared with those long civilized' (206). In his *Journal* he noted on the *Beagle* before reaching Tierra del Fuego that the three Fuegians returning from London (see chapter 8) had remarkable eyesight, even superior to that of British sailors despite the many years the sailors had spent at sea. Only a telescope could pick out what the Fuegians, but nobody else on board, could discern unaided. Yet we are also told that the senses are dulled by living close to nature, as when Darwin remarks that the skill of the Fuegians may be compared to the instinct of animals because it is not improved by experience. He gives the example of their canoes, 'their most ingenious work, poor as it is, has remained the same, as we know from Drake, for the last 250 years', and we detect similar modes of interpretation where he describes how much insensitivity, not acuity, it takes to survive without clothes or shelter in such a bleak environment (216) – and I take it that the bleakness that he refers to here is not merely physical, but inevitably moral and aesthetic as well. Having been absent from the depiction of mimicry, now, as the topic of dullness and fortitude is broached, women suddenly enter and assume the burden of representation, as when Darwin declares in the *Journal* that the Fuegians kill and devour their old women before they kill their dogs, that the lot of women is one of laborious slavery to brutal masters who dash out their children's brains for misdemeanours, or, as in the following touching scene of motherhood amid the cruel elements:

> In another harbour not far distant, a woman, who was suckling a recently-born child, came one day alongside the vessel, and remained there out of mere curiousity, whilst the sleet fell and thawed on her naked bosom, and on the skin of her naked baby! These poor wretches were stunted in their growth, their hideous faces bedaubed with white paint, their skins filthy and greasy, their hair entangled, their voices discordant, and their gestures violent. Viewing such men, one can hardly make oneself believe that they are fellow-creatures, and inhabitants of the same world. (213)

Thus the animality of 'these poor wretches', wrought to extreme by the picture of the women, seems eons distant from the hypersensitivity that primitiveness can also imply. It would therefore seem of dubious, or at least complex, logic to make the commonsensical if somewhat racist assumption, as Darwin does, that the extraordinary miming ability attributed to the Fuegians is a result of their *keener* (note the comparative) senses. And even if the notion of sensory acuity was not complicated in this way, because of dullness existing side by side with keenness, we would have to consider another link in the chain of reasoning here involved, namely that there would seem to be no necessary link between such (alleged) acuity, on the one hand, and wanting or being able to mime and mime well, on the other; having good eyes and ears neither makes one a good mimic nor want to be one.

The 'origins' of mimesis lie in art and politics and not survival

So, in trying to 'explain' the alleged coupling of primitiveness with mighty miming (and the desire to mime), how do we understand this to bear upon an aspect of life that refers not to the individual organism as a biological entity adapted to a demanding environment, but instead refers to social life, particularly the life of the imagination as expressed by the art, ritual and mythology of 'primitive' societies? After all, could the face-painting that so caught Darwin's curiosity be explained as necessary to and part of the materiality of surviving in a cold climate? And wouldn't one be likely to find the analogy of miming precisely in such painting?

If we take a cue from Darwin's pairing of the Fuegians with the Australian aborigines, we see that much later, as the *Beagle* heads for home, he briefly describes in his *Journal* what he calls a 'corrobery or native dance' at Bald Head, Western Australia, in which mimesis is an important feature:

> There was one called the Emu dance, in which each man extended his arm in a bent manner, like the neck of that bird. In another dance, one man imitated the movements of a kangaroo grazing in the woods, whilst a second crawled up, and pretended to spear him. When both tribes mingled in the dance, the ground trembled with the heaviness of their steps, and the air resounded with their wild cries. (451)

Some seventy years later the emu dance also caught the eye of Emile Durkheim. In his book *The Elementary Forms of Religious Life*, he observed that the pioneer ethnographers of the Arunta people of the central desert, Spencer and Gillen, pointed out that in that dance to augment well-being, the Intichiuma of the Emu, 'at a certain moment the actors try to reproduce by their attitude the air and aspect of the bird', and he goes on to underscore what he sees as 'the essentially imitative nature of Arunta rites'.[9] Indeed there are (according to Durkheim's reading of Strehlow),

> scarcely any ceremonies in which some imitating gesture is not pointed out. According to the nature of the animals whose feast is celebrated, they jump after the manner of kangaroos, or imitate the movements they make in eating, the flight of winged ants, the characteristic noise of the bat, the cry of the wild turkey, the hissing of the snake, the croaking of a frog, etc.[10]

And to that marvellous fidelity, we should add that for the initiated men, according to Spencer and Gillen, many months of the year were dedicated to just such mimicry. At the same time, at the close of the nineteenth century when Spencer and Gillen were writing their account of Central Australia, a young man born and bred in Tierra del

Fuego, E. Lucas Bridges, saw the spirit Hachai come out of the lichen-covered rocks (see chapter 5). He was painted all over with red and white patterns. Grey bird's down was stuck over him, and he wore a horned mask with red eye-holes. No horned animal is indigenous to Tierra del Fuego, noted Bridges, yet a hunter of wild cattle would have admired the actor's performance. 'His uncertain advances, his threatening tosses of the head, his snoring and sudden forward thrusts of one horn or the other – all were most realistic. The part he was playing came from legendary myth and had doubtless been enacted by the Selk'nam for countless generations.'[11]

Would not studious application to the ritual practice of myth and magic provide far more of a basis for the mimetic faculty than what the young Darwin called 'the more practical habits of perception and keener senses common to all men in a savage state'? To gauge the intensity of such ritual practice in Tierra del Fuego one has only to consult Bridge's detailed memoir as well as the extensive works of the talented Austrian ethnographer, Martin Gusinde, who worked in that region between 1918 and 1924 (see chapter 5, note 1).[12] Both provide vivid descriptions of the ritual core of Selk'nam society, the lengthy men's initiation known as the Hain occurring in the men's ceremonial house (there was no such house for women)(see chapter 5). Not only is this stupendously 'theatrical' and 'staged', with the women and children providing the 'audience', but it is obvious that in miming the (women-hating) spirits, the men invigorate powers essential for the reproduction of society, especially the power to control what they fear as the sorcery potentially possessed by women – the original fear that, according to myth, led them long ago to most brutally kill all the women and build the men's house in the first place. So important is the ritual power of the theatre of the men's house that Gusinde refers to it as the sovereign power of an invisible state. He thus provides us with the elementary form not only of religion (to invoke the title of Durkheim's classic work) but of the state as well – a performative theory of the state as a mighty theatre of male fantasies, illusions generated by potent male fear of women.

And thus it is apposite to invoke the theme of sacred violence in mimesis. If Frazer directed us to think of the copy as drawing on the power of the copied, and did so from a utilitarian perspective, it is to Georges Bataille's everlasting credit that, in his discussion of the Lascaux cave paintings, he dismisses such a view that sees these paintings as aimed at securing game and argues instead that they are *testimony* to the release of the sacred through the violence of killing and that they follow transgression (in this case, of the taboo against killing).[13] There is no doubt as to the mighty force of sacred violence in the mimetics of the Hain, a force that, following both Frazer and Bataille, we could see as securing its power from enacting the gods as well as from the violence entailed by that enactment. And here we see the most fundamental cleavage in mimesis. For this sacred violence exists in two quite contrary ways. On the one hand the women and children, forming the 'audience', have to pretend – to mime – on pain of death that what they are witness to are real gods and not their kinsmen acting as gods. In this way the public secret essential to mystical authority is preserved. On the other hand is the violence associated with the demasking of the gods that the male initiates are forced to witness in the privacy of the men's house. Through the violence of demasking fused with laughter, the power of the mimetic faculty as a socially constitutive force is thereby transferred from the older to the younger men, the duped becomes one with the dupers, and what Bridges refers to as 'the great secret' fortifies Gusinde's 'invisible state'.

In both instances, male and female, imagined worlds become not only theatricalised but factualised as religious axiom and social custom. Illusions thus serve the cause of belief, if not truth, thanks to the magical series of transfers between theatre and reality held in place by mimetic art and the public secret. Mimesis sutures the real to the really made up – and no society exists otherwise.

Men become not only skilled in mimesis in the sense of simulating Others, which is what impressed Darwin, but become impressed by the power of mimesis to access the sacred and therewith control women's potentially greater power to mime. As simulators, with the forced connivance of women, they reproduce the invisible state in a process wherein acting recreates the authentic. In this vast scheme, women, however, become skilled in the use of the mimetic faculty in a totally different way – with the power not to simulate an Other but instead to dissimulate, to pretend to believe in the Other's simulation...

Colonial violence: the organisation of mimesis, the final solution[14]

To read Gusinde on the late nineteenth-century extermination of the indigenous peoples of Tierra del Fuego (from which these passages are quoted),[15] is to be flung into horror. As in so many other places in the Americas, north and south, at the same time, it is too familiar, yet beyond belief. You feel you are reading some primer on colonial brutality, the ur-event of civilisation and modern state consolidation, face to face with 'savagery' – the savagery imputed to the Other, then mimicked on the body of that Other. The Selk'-nam were presented from the beginning, notes Gusinde, as 'phantoms that threatened European intrusion', and then declared to be 'dangerous obstacles to settlement'. The serious extermination began with the discovery of gold in 1878 and acquired a thorough-going character with the setting-up of sheep-ranches by whites shortly thereafter (see chapter 6). The ranches spread over the lands used by the Indians, who retaliated by killing sheep for food, and a spiral of violence between these unequal forces rapidly developed. Paid hunters were encouraged to wipe out the Indians. Gusinde says they were offered the same price for a pair of Indian ears as the going rate for a puma – one pound sterling. A pregnant woman's ears together with those of the foetus extracted from her womb paid more. Gusinde knew persons who made money shipping skulls to a European museum. Mastiffs were imported from Europe to hunt down Indians; slain sheep were poisoned with strychnine in the hope that the Indians would eat them; and Indian children were innoculated with fatal diseases.

Gusinde lists seven names given to the whites by the Selk'nam at the time of his fieldwork between 1918 and 1924. Two of them refer to the whites' deployment of mimicry in genocide. One meant literally 'clumps of earth with roots extracted from black swampy water'. This referred to the fact that, from the Indians' perspective, the whites always moved in a compact, massed, group, usually dressed in dark clothing so that they were camouflaged. The second name for the whites meant something like helmet of earth/hairy leather hide/clumped earth with grass. In order to frighten and intimidate the Indians, the hunters made simulacra of cavalry, mounting on horseback human-like figures made from earth and grass or from hides. Hence this term for whites: 'figures of earth covered with hairy hides' (154). Could Horkheimer and Adorno have found a better example of the channelling of the mimetic faculty by 'civilisation' so as to simulate an imagined savagery in order to dominate or destroy it? Could they have found a more frightening appellation for civilisation, disguised – 'figures of earth covered with hairy hides'?

Spirit of the mine, spirit of the gift

Together with fire and smoke, the Fuegians' wildness was manifested time and again by their hideous cries abruptly announcing their presence, incessantly demanding white man's stuff. If it is the visual sense and the precise vocal articulation of language that is expressed in Darwin's scheme of representation when he discussed mimicry, it is very much sonorous sound, hollow, noisy, human sound, that is alluded to when presenting trade and barter. In his first paragraph concerning Tierra del Fuego, the *Beagle* entering the Bahía Buen Suceso, Darwin in his *Journal* registers the sonic as a principal scenic element.

A month later, at Ponsonby Sound from where Jemmy Button hailed, the *Beagle*'s boats were again greeted with fire and cries. It was as if in the form of sound, wildness itself erupted from its autochthonous lair:

> Fires were lighted on every point (hence the name of Tierra del Fuego, or the land of fire), both to attract our attention and to spread far and wide the news. Some of the men ran for miles along the shore. I shall never forget how wild and savage one group appeared: suddenly four or five men came to the edge of an overhanging cliff; they were absolutely naked, and their long hair streamed around their faces; they held rugged staffs in their hands, and, springing from the ground, they waved their arms around their heads, and sent forth the most hideous yells. (218)

Captain Fitzroy also described this event in terms of sound and fire. Remarkably so:

> Scarcely had we stowed the boats and embarked, before canoes began to appear in every direction, in each of which was a stentor hailing us at the top of his voice. Faint sounds of deep voices were heard in the distance, and around us echoes to the shouts of our nearer friends began to reverberate, and warned me to hasten away before our movements should become impeded.[16]

Fig 103 Sailing vessel surrounded by Yámana canoes in the vicinity of Isla Navarino.

Fig 104 Distant view of Monte Sarmiento.

It was an impressive scene, a veritable stage framing the sound. The captain continues:

> As we steered out of the cove in which our boats had been sheltered, a striking scene opened: beyond a lake-like expanse of deep blue water, mountains rose abruptly to a great height, and on their icy summits the sun's early rays glittered as if on a mirror. Immediately round us were mountain eminences, and dark cliffy precipices which cast a very deep shadow over the still water beneath them. (106)

When they saw the boats, the Fuegians came in canoes from all directions. 'Hoarse shouts arose, and echoed about by the cliffs, seemed to be a continual cheer' (figs 99, 103 and 104). Soon there were close to forty canoes, each with a column of blue smoke rising from the fire they contained, 'and almost all the men in them shouting at the full power of their deep sonorous voices' (106–7). It appeared like a dream, noted the captain, pleased with the wind, which, filling every sail, allowed him to outpace those fiery, noisy, canoes.

When the scarlet cloth was unfurled, the sound nevertheless continued, its wildness taking on a different tone. 'While in the boats I got to hate the very sound of their voices, so much trouble did they give us', Darwin writes in his *Journal*:

> The first and last word was 'yammerschooner'. When entering some quiet little cove, we have looked around and thought to pass a quiet night, the odious word 'yammerschooner' has shrilly sounded from some gloomy nook, and then the little signal-smoke has curled up to spread the news far and wide. On leaving some place we have said to each other, 'Thank Heaven, we have at last fairly left these wretches!' when one more faint halloo from an all-powerful voice, heard at a prodigious distance, would reach our ears, and clearly could we distinguish – 'yammerschooner'. (227)

Yammerschoonering, he said, meant 'Give me!' – but it is obvious from the record that 'give me' was a complex composite that did not fall neatly into British political economy, formal or informal. A composite of trade and gift, sometimes to be reciprocated, at other times not, it was all interwoven with a terrible insistence that the sailors came to define as outright theft – as notably suffered by poor Matthews the missionary no less than by the plump and London-tailored Fuegian Jemmy Button as soon as he was returned to his people, who stripped him clean as a whistle, and after a short while left him as thin as one. Captain Fitzroy relates in his *Journal* that he saw one Fuegian talking to Jemmy Button while another picked his pockets of a knife. Yet from the woman, Fuegia Basket, nothing was taken. (111)

Again and again this refrain of Fuegian noise, Fuegian demanding, Fuegian stealing – and perfect Fuegian equality. The beleaguered missionary lost almost everything that he hadn't hidden underground, noted Darwin in the *Journal*, and every article taken by the Fuegians, he continued, 'seemed to have been torn up and divided by the natives. Matthews described the watch he was obliged always to keep as most harassing; night and day he was surrounded by the natives, who tried to tire him out by making an incessant noise close to his head.' (225)

'They would point to almost every object of the sailors, one after the other, even the

Fig 105 The *Adelaide* in Humming Bird Cove.

buttons on the coats', Darwin remarks, 'saying their favourite word in as many intonations as possible.' It seemed as if it was the sound of the air itself, a savage melody 'vacantly repeated'. Yammerschooner. The word hangs strangely on the English ear as we hear it through Darwin's sounding it out, the same way we might try to translate a sound of nature, the sea rolling, the waves crashing, the wind shrieking alongside the glaciers and the still water beneath them. Yammerschooner!

But not everything European caught their savage eye, and Darwin found wonder in this. The whiteness of the sailors' skins surprised the Fuegians (fig. 105), and even more so the blackness of the negro cook of a sealing ship. 'Simple circumstances', Darwin said, and the term is revealing, 'such as the beauty of scarlet cloth or blue beads, the absence of women, our care in washing ourselves, excited their admiration far more than any grand or complicated object, such as our ship.'[17] (228)

Mutual aid, theft and booty

Based on his fieldwork between 1918–24, Martin Gusinde spends many pages wrestling with the difficulties that Fuegian exchange presents European political economy. Meticulous in their observation of mine and thine, and in the severe condemnation of theft, the Fuegians were scrupulous in sharing and in the practice of mutual aid no less than of a constant give-and-take of gift-giving among themselves. In addition to the exchange that occurred locally, Gusinde made the point that a visitor from near or far always brought something to give away, usually fresh meat or a beautiful skin. Then the recipient had to supply a return gift as soon as possible, the gift being given and received without a word, he noted, and without meaningful gestures expressing one's feelings. 'It is one of the inescapable obligations', he reiterated, 'of every Yámana to come now and then with a gift for someone.' Attaching considerable importance to the fact that the Yámana language has scarcely any terms for asking for gifts, but many for expecting them (Darwin's 'yammerschooner'?), Gusinde observes that 'great generosity and unselfishness are conspicuous basic features of the character of the Yámana'. Echoing themes that later acquired mighty resonance through Malinowski's description of 'primitive economics' in the Trobriands, no less than in Mauss's classic work *The Gift* and Bataille's *The Accursed Share*, Gusinde says that some Fuegians took particular pleasure in lavishly remembering neighbours with the yields from hunting and gathering – that the 'natives especially enjoy ownership in order to have the right to distribute what they have for the pleasure of being generous'.[18] Much more could be said on these important topics, but perhaps enough of an idea has been expressed so that the depth of the incongruities brought into play by the arrival of the *Beagle* into this 'system' of exchange can be appreciated. Of course the phraseology here is a little pedestrian. 'System of exchange' sounds like something out of a car gear-box manual. At stake, however, are the greatest human passions, the very nature of being a person, and the strange intimacies that giving establishes between things and personhood.

Not wanting to identify the *Beagle* and its crew with an animal of prey, let alone a beached whale, my imagination is nevertheless stimulated by the following picture provided by Gusinde with regard to booty when customary territorial boundaries of hunting are opened to all to share:

> Anyone within the widest radius who learns of the stranding of a whale may head towards the spot unmolested and remains until all the suitable parts are consumed or distributed... Alerted by dense flocks of sea birds, the Indians come pouring in to the stranded whale, even from some distance, and they all enjoy the excellent taste of the blubber. No one would dare rebuff a visiting stranger nor hinder him; if one were to do so, he would be loudly decried as a selfish human being.[19]

The spirit of the gift, the spirit of the mime

In short these Fuegians, mighty mimics of British sailors and their sea-chanties, of their dances, face-pullings, and of their very language, 'asked for everything they saw, and stole what they could', meticulously dividing the item so that 'no one individual becomes richer than another'. They were insatiable. 'It was as easy to please as it was difficult to satisfy these savages', wrote Darwin in the *Journal*, taken by that 'odd mixture of surprise and imitation which these savages every moment exhibited' face to face with the *Beagle*'s crew (218–19). With every surprise, an imitation, with every sailor's good that catches the eye, a yammerschoonering! Mimicry and yammerschoonering seem intimately connected. You can trade fish for a knife, or steal a button, but you can't so easily trade a language or steal a squint or a strange motion. But what you can do is imitate them if you want to or have to – if they're surprising, that is. Put another way, you can imitate a sailor pulling faces, but you can't so easily or convincingly imitate his buttons or knife of steel. In either event there is a way in which imitating and trading, as much as imitating and stealing, amount to the same system of gift exchange (so neatly depicted by Darwin and Fitzroy with regard to the veritable competitions of mimicry between British sailors and Fuegian men). In contemplating the analogy and the historical fact that here establishes a connection between consummately skilful miming, on the one hand, and the practice of that peculiar non-capitalist economics of exchange which Marcel Mauss called 'the spirit of the gift', on the other, are we not justified in assuming that there is more to this than analogy, that there is indeed an intimate bond between the spirit of the gift and the spirit of the mime, whose fullest flowering requires exactly the sort of 'perfect equality among individuals' that Darwin bemoaned as the Fuegian obstacle to 'improvement'?

Scarlet cloth

Before saying farewell to the Land of Fire, to Jemmy Button left desolate on the cruel shore lighting a signal fire, the smoke curling skyward as the *Beagle* stood out to sea, there is one more curious association to bear in mind concerning the mimetic faculty, a colourful association suggestive of profound links between mimetic facilty on the one hand, and non-market forms of exchange and the absence of chiefs, on the other. This can be illustrated by returning to the fiery scarlet cloth and the tricky business of Europeans exchanging gifts and entering into trade with Fuegians, having to figure anew what used to seem pretty straightforward distinctions between gift, trade, and stealing.

For this scarlet cloth is no less puzzling than valuable. First we note its success as a gift, as in the diary entry I have just requoted, reporting its spectacular success, sufficient to cause the old Fuegian man to pat the sailors' breasts and chuckle like a chicken. A month later the sailors landed among Jemmy Button's people, few of whom, wrote Darwin, could ever have seen a white man. The Fuegians were at first not inclined to be friendly. They kept their slings at the ready, but 'we soon, however, delighted them by trifling presents, such as tying red tape around their heads' (218). Yet, as we shall see, things are not so simple. Violence, or the threat of violence, seems displaced into rather than overcome by the gift and, as I read the record of these encounters of sailors and Fuegians, I feel a depressing confusion (just as I did when studying the violent incursions of the late nineteenth-century rubber traders into the Putumayo region of the Upper Amazon) as to where gifts stop and trade begins, it being obvious that objects here take on the burden of negotiating between might and right. Of course this is Mauss' great point in his essay on the gift – that the 'gift' composes an impossible marriage between self-interest and altruism, between calculated giving and spontaneous generosity. Take Darwin's account of the following joyous exchanges, with each party delighted at the other's delight, the other's silliness:

> Both parties laughing, wondering, gaping at each other; we pitying them, for giving us good fish and crabs for rags etc.; they grasping at the chance of finding people so foolish as to exchange such splendid ornaments for a good supper. It was most amusing to see the undisguised smile of satisfaction with which one young woman with her face painted black, tied several bits of scarlet cloth round her head with rushes. (227)

That was 1832, by which time the European bourgeoisie, male version, unlike the aristocracy and Middle Ages of times past, were deeply invested in grey to a degree that brilliant colours such as red took on a wild, primitive, not to mention even a revolutionary hue – obviously the perfect gift for Fuegians (whom, we are later told, had the practice of daubing their naked bodies with black, white and red). But from the beginning of European discovery and conquest, redness itself, first from a species of tree in India, called *Brasilium* on account of its fieriness, and later from Báhia (in what came to be called Brasil), and from Central and South America, fetched enormous prices in Europe into the eighteenth century. Indeed, after gold and silver and perhaps slaves, the commodity that seems to have most interested the buccaneers of the Spanish Main, those same sailor buccaneers with whom the Cuna Indians allied themselves in the famous Darién peninsula in the seventeenth century, was red dyewood.[20]

But then how curious, how absurdly convenient, that the Fuegians valued scarlet so strongly! (And the list of peoples similarly implicated seems endless, across the great Pacific, island by island, into Australia...) Martin Gusinde assures us from his work in the Land of Fire in the early twentieth century that red face- and body-paint was the most highly esteemed colour there. He notes an 'emotional preference for bright scarlet', and that the 'Indians are almost superstitiously exact in their preparation of this red pigment, for they are extraordinarily appreciative of its glowing brightness which neither dirt nor ashes impairs', and he cites late nineteenth-century ethnography affirming that 'red is the emblem of friendship and joy'.[21] In her study of the Selk'nam, Anne Chapman tells us that red, associated with the setting sun, 'is considered to be particularly beautiful and pleasing to the spirits'.[22]

Triggering endless sentient reciprocations, the sailors' welcome gift of scarlet cloth to the Fuegians thus represents not merely a profound irony – making a gift of what was in a sense a return, reissuing the exotic to the exotic from third to first, then First to Third World – but is in itself symbolic of the elusive pattern of mimesis and alterity underscoring colonialism that we have had ample opportunity to witness above. And as gift, initiating problematic distinctions and bewildering cross-connections between gift, theft, and trade – pre-eminently problems of establishing a frontier, let alone a capitalist frontier – the scarlet cloth can reveal to us subtle economic and exchange relations embedded in the mimetic faculty, beginning with certain features of property and authority.

For if, in the adamantly colonial drama of first contact, it is their very primitiveness which makes the Fuegians such great mimics, then Darwin is also at pains to elaborate that this barely human condition is consequent to their having no chiefs and no sense of property in anything remotely approaching bourgeois understandings of this term. Thus deprived of chiefs and property the Fuegians are constitutionally incapable of what Darwin called 'improvement'. He writes as conclusion to the Fuegian section of his *Journal* that it is the 'perfect equality among individuals composing the Fuegian tribes' that retards their society, and

> until some chief shall arise with power sufficient to secure any acquired advantage, such as domesticated animals, it seems scarcely possible that the political state of the country can be improved. At present, even a piece of cloth given to one is torn to shreds and distributed; and no one individual becomes richer than another. On the other hand, it is difficult to understand how a chief can arise till there is property of some sort by which he might make manifest his superiority and increase his power. (229–30)

'The perfect equality of all the inhabitants', Darwin concluded, 'will for many years prevent their civilization'. (136)

This essay is taken from *Mimesis and Alterity: A Particular History of the Senses*, first published by Routledge, Chapman and Hall, Inc. in 1993.

NOTES

1 'First contact', of course, was made at Tierra del Fuego centuries before Darwin. The Selk'nam Indians, for instance, are recorded as having first encountered Europeans, namely the Spaniard Pedro Sarmiento de Gamboa, in 1579. A Dutch commander, Olivier van Noort, landed on islands in the Estrecho de Magallanes in 1598. Haush Indians were first contacted later, in 1619, by the Nodal brothers. Captain James Cook, with scientists and sailors, met Haush Indians in 1769. See Chapman 1982.

2 Darwin 1934: 118. Subsequent references to this work appear in the text in parentheses.

3 Darwin 1896: 206. Subsequent references to this work appear in the text in parentheses.

4 Darwin 1979.

5 Ibid: 96.

6 Leahy and Crain 1937: 48.

7 Ibid: 50.

8 Gananath Obeyesekere pointed out this possibility to me.

9 Durkheim 1915: 395.

10 Ibid: 395.

11 Bridges 1951: 418.

12 Gusinde 1982. See also Gusinde 1961 and Chapman 1982 for the original characterisation of the Hain ceremony as theatre. For a comparison of these Tierra del Fuegian accounts with the central Amazon and the use of gang-rape against women to maintain the taboo against their seeing the sacred flutes kept in the men's house, see Bamberger 1974; see also Gregor 1985. For Australia, see among many sources the classic account of Baldwin Spencer and F.J. Gillen (1968); chapter five, on the sacred objects known as Churinga, begins thus: 'Churinga is the name given by the Arunta natives to certain sacred objects which, on penalty of death or a very severe punishment, such as blinding by means of a firestick, are never allowed to be seen by women or uninitiated men.'

13 Bataille 1955; 1986.

14 'It is thought that the country of Tierra del Fuego would prove suitable for cattle breeding, but the only drawback to this plan is that to all appearance it would be necessary to exterminate the Fuegians', The *Daily News*, London 1882.

15 Quoted from Gusinde 1961: 143 (vol. I). Subsequent references to this work appear in the text in parentheses.

16 Darwin 1979: 106. Subsequent references to this work appear in the text in parentheses.

17 Where the philosopher Michael Polanyi uses Evans-Pritchard's study of Zande witchcraft to show similarities between science and magic as systems impervious to empirical refutation, he cites William James as follows: 'We feel neither curiosity nor wonder concerning things so far beyond us that we have no concepts to refer them to or standards by which to measure them.' The Fuegians encountered by Darwin, notes James, wondered at the small boats but paid no attention to the big ship lying at anchor in front of them. See Polanyi 1958: 286–94.

18 Gusinde 1961: 877–8 (vol. III). See also Bataille 1990 (vol. I).

19 Gusinde 1961: 857 (vol. III).

20 Elliot Joyce 1933: lix.

21 Gusinde 1961: 92, 95 (vol. I).

22 Chapman 1982: 99.

10 Patagonian Painted Cloaks

An Ancient Puzzle

Alfredo Prieto

Elal taught the Indians how to make guanaco blankets.
He said 'take the skin of baby guanacos and make blankets to cover yourselves'[1]

Introduction

The groups that occupied the vast steppes of eastern Patagonia were known as Tehuelche or Patagon. These comprised the Gununa'Kena and Mecharnúekenk (northern Tehuelche) and the Aónikenk (southern Tehuelche); the Río Santa Cruz marked the approximate boundary between the two groups.[2] From the Río Santa Cruz to the Estrecho de Magallanes there were once perhaps as many as 2,500–3,000 Aónikenk (fig. 106). By 1905 they had disappeared from the Magellanic region and nowadays just a few descendants survive in some of the more remote parts of Argentinian Patagonia (see chapter 9). They were known above all as terrestrial hunters, who employed the bow and arrow. By far and away the most important prey was the guanaco (*Lama guanicoe*) that inhabits both the eastern and western flanks of the Andean Cordillera as far south as Isla Navarino. There may have been as many as one to two million guanaco in southern Patagonia before intensive 'commercial' hunting began in earnest towards the end of the nineteenth century.

Within two centuries of the first European contact, beginning in 1520, the Spanish had introduced the horse into the pampas to the north, and from there it spread south. By the beginning of the eighteenth century Tehuelches could be seen on horseback, having adopted the animal for both transport and hunting. This resulted in the substantial modification of their hunting techniques, and it transformed their mobility, permitting more intensive contact with the Mapuche to the north, who introduced pottery, weaving and hide armour (fig. 107).

The intensive hunting of young guanaco, and the special techniques developed for making cloaks from their skins, was a hallmark of Tehuelche artisanship both before and after European contact. The Tehuelche women were mainly responsible for the production of painted cloaks. The skills and knowledge required to treat and sew the skins as well as some of the designs applied to the finished cloaks, must have their roots far back in prehistoric times, for similar motifs are found in both rock art and on portable objects. The distinctive cut patterns created as a result of the techniques employed in making the cloaks can be seen as a practical, skilful and economical use of the skins,

Fig 106 Three Aónikenk men wearing guanaco-skin cloaks known as 'quillangos'.

although attempts have also been made to read deeper symbolic meaning into the organisation of the complex painted designs applied to the cloaks.

Guanaco-skin cloaks ('quillangos')

The introduction of the horse and the founding of the first colonial settlements in Patagonia led to a new set of trading arrangements which capitalised on traditional indigenous products, such as guanaco-skin cloaks known as 'quillangos'. The commercial trade in cloaks that sprang up acted not only as an incentive to increase their production, but also brought about significant shifts in the timing and intensity of the exploitation of guanaco and in the use of women's labour. Not least, the hunting technology itself was modified.

By the end of the eighteenth century the Tehuelche had ceased using the bow and arrow, which had been employed as far back as 1,500 BP,[3] and resumed the use of bolas, whose previous appearance in the archaeological record is dated from at least as early as 4,500 BP up to 500 BP[4] (see chapter 3). It was this combination of the horse and the bola that enabled the annual systematic hunting of the young guanaco (*chulengos*) to take place on an unprecedented scale. This ensured a regular supply of skins that far exceeded subsistence needs and responded instead to commercial demand.

Cloaks were also made using horse-hide, and more rarely fox, and even ñandú (*Rhea*) feathers. Horse-skin cloaks were the most common, although these were made of just one hide and were employed as floor coverings inside tents, or occasionally as funerary wrappings[5] (see, for example, fig. 118). During the nineteenth century the capes and cloaks rapidly became the principal item of exchange and commerce among the Tehuelche focused on the colonial settlements of Punta Arenas (Magallanes, Chile) and Carmen de Patagones (Río Negro, Argentina), 'especially during the period 1855–63 and for some time later the export of thousands of guanaco skin and *Rhea* feather cloaks stimulated an active commerce in the fledgling colony of Punta Arenas'[6] (see chapter 6). One observer, writing more than half a century later, noted that 'such robes have considerable value today and we have been told that more than half a million guanaco skins had been shipped from Patagonia by 1924'.[7]

Fig 107 Chief Kongre wearing a leather helmet and hide armour (see also colour plate 6).

As we shall see in the descriptions below, the skins of as many as thirteen young guanaco were needed to make just one cloak. The soft fur of the newborn fawns was most sought after,[8] and skins of a consistent size were needed in order to facilitate the technique of sewing them together. These very specific requirements made it imperative to hunt the guanaco immediately after they were born. Consequently, the hunting period was concentrated in the period November to December each year, when the female guanaco were giving birth. The hunting technique employed was that of encirclement, sometimes using a change of camp-site so that in the course of moving from one location to another the group of women and children would 'sweep' a predetermined area. The hunts always took place in the inland part of their territories and never on the coast, simply because this was nearly always where the young guanaco were born. Writing in the 1870s Thomas Musters described the sequence of the hunt as follows:

> Two men start off at a gallop and ride around a certain area of the country, varying according to the number of the party, lighting fires at intervals to mark their track. After the lapse of a few minutes two others are dispatched, and so on until only a few are left with the *cacique* [chief]. These spread themselves out in a crescent, closing in and narrowing the circle on a point where those first started have by this time arrived. The crescent rests on a baseline formed by the slowly-proceeding line of women, children, and baggage-horses. The ostriches [*sic*] and herds of guanaco run from the advancing party,

Fig 108 Commercial hunting of guanaco and ñandú (*Rhea*) in the Río Chico valley.

but are checked by the pointsmen, and when the circle is well closed in are attacked with the bolas, two men frequently chasing the same animal from different sides (fig. 108).[9]

According to Radburne, 'if there were enough riders, and good horses under them, few would escape, and at last the centre would be a mass of dead animals or struggling live ones, killed or entangled by boleadoras'.[10] Later he adds:

> The biggest catch I ever made when hunting was thirty-nine skins, and the biggest kill in one run was fifteen. Mulato's son used to always try and get forty skins a day but he was very light and always had such good horses, trained to run alongside the *chulengo* [newborn] at the same pace so the rider would never miss. Generally the Indians would be pleased to get enough for two *capas* [cloaks], or twenty-six skins a day.[11]

The great number of young guanaco hunted in one season underlines how the number of animals killed far exceeded the subsistence needs of the group. It is quite likely that most of the animals killed were simply skinned, leaving the rest of the animal unused. As we have noted, the hunt was concentrated in December, usually lasting a month at most. Likewise, the preparation and sewing of the skins had to be completed very quickly, in usually not more than a month, according to one source.[12] During this period all hands were devoted to processing the skins and sewing the cloaks destined for commercial ends rather than for local domestic use.

Once the skins were delivered to the women, the process of preparation began. This started with the production of the scrapers, which were their principal tool.[13] Various accounts emphasise the role of women in the production process (fig. 109). They had the knowledge and skills to cut the pattern and sew the cloaks and to apply the complex

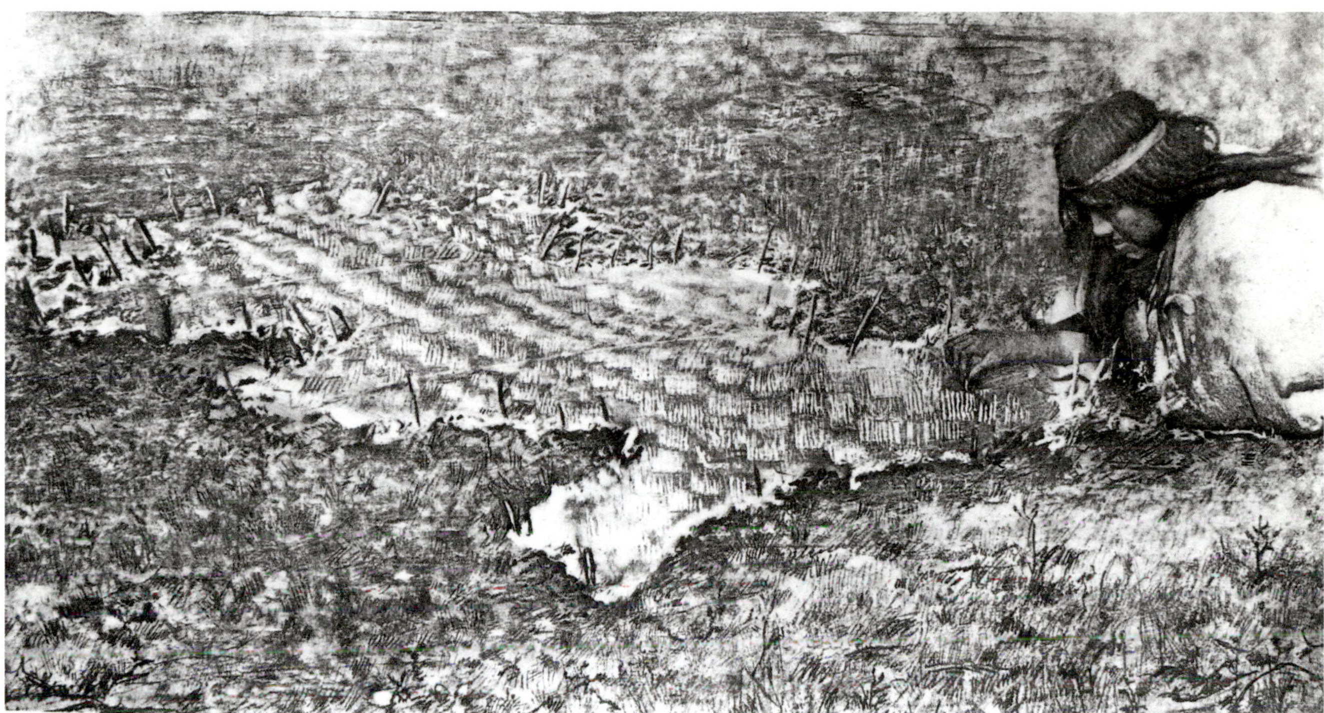

Fig 109 An Aónikenk woman painting a design in pigment on a stretched hide pegged to the ground.

designs that adorned them. They were also responsible for refining and improving the scrapers, including the methods used to affix the scraper itself to a suitable handle. The preparation process and the pattern of the cut is described as follows:

> The women clean and soften the skins and fit and sew them together into cloaks. The Indians do not believe in wetting the skins at all while working them, so the men keep them moist until they get them back to the tent by folding each along the back, hair side out, holding the nose in their teeth and squeezing the sides tight together with their hands. The women then pull the skins apart and stretch them out on the ground. They jab little holes around the edge of a skin and drive fifty-two calafate wood stakes around each skin, stretching it. They are very careful not to let the stretched skins get wet. When the skins are thoroughly dry the women scrape them with a piece of split calafate wood, heated and bent like a horseshoe to hold a curved bit of bottle glass tied into its split end with rawhide. It makes an excellent scraper. They always keep another skin under the one they are scraping. When it is well scraped they spread a paste over it made of ostrich or mare liver, roasted and whipped up with a little water. Sometimes they use a little fried mare's grease. The skins thus treated are put away to dry and whiten, after which they are taken out to be softened by rubbing two together. Then the women cut about thirteen of the skins to fit together into a big square cloak, head to tail, in a dovetail pattern.[14]

Given that they painted the skins when these were staked out and that they later had to eliminate the stake holes left in the skin, they had to match one skin to another as best as they could once they were painted. Thus it is along the line of the lower six skins, and in those that are added around the edge, that the decorative motifs sometimes become disjointed.[15] The descriptions of the techniques used differ slightly depending upon the age of the guanaco that have been hunted. Hatcher, for example, gives an extensive account of this, describing how:

> Only the skins of those that are less than two months old are employed, and the very choicest of these fur mantles are manufactured from the skins of the still unborn young. These are obtained by killing the mother a few days before the birth of the young guanaco. The season may be said to extend from 15 November to 1 February. It begins when the guanaco commence giving birth, and continues until the offspring reach an average age of about two months. As this season approaches the Tehuelches move in small companies of a half-dozen tents each to their favourite hunting grounds, where the guanaco are known to be especially abundant. A permanent camp is established in some favored spot and a relentless war is at once begun upon the young guanaco in the vicinity and kept up until they have all been killed or reach an age which renders their hides unserviceable to the Tehuelches. The work of killing and skinning is done by the men, while the drying, dressing and further care of the hides falls to the women. [...]
>
> When the young guanaco is killed, the hide is very carefully removed, even the legs, neck and head being carefully skinned out. While still green they are partially fleshed and dressed. After this they are staked out and thoroughly dried. When dry they are taken in hand by the old women and thoroughly dressed with sharp, curved, stone or glass scrapers fastened in a bit of wood or horn. Next, if the mantle or other article is to be ornamented, the skin is again staked out on the ground and, without any previously made pattern to go by, the women proceed to paint the flesh side in any one of several different patterns. In painting these skins, variously coloured mineral earths are used [figs 109 and 111]. These are usually of green, yellow and red colours and are mixed with grease and rolled into rather slender pencils. From the end of these, moistened with spittle from the mouth, the various colours are transferred directly to the skin in such a manner as often to form most intricate and not entirely inartistic patterns. When a sufficient number of skins, usually eleven or thirteen, have been thus dressed and painted, they are trimmed so that the neck of one fits nicely between the hind legs of the one in front, and the skins of the fore and hind legs between the legs on either side of adjoining skins. These skins are fitted and sewed with such skill that, when completed, there is not the slightest wrinkle anywhere in the entire mantle and the patterns painted on the different skins match as nicely as do those of the paper on the walls of a well-papered room. The really marvellous thing about the whole fabrication is that the artisan works without any visible pattern to go by, and without any better instrument than a common knife with which to cut and fit, a wooden or bone awl used as a delicate punch instead of a needle, and sinew taken from the loin of the adult guanaco for thread. The trimmings left after the manufacture of such a mantle are not wasted, but used in making still other articles (fig. 110).[16]

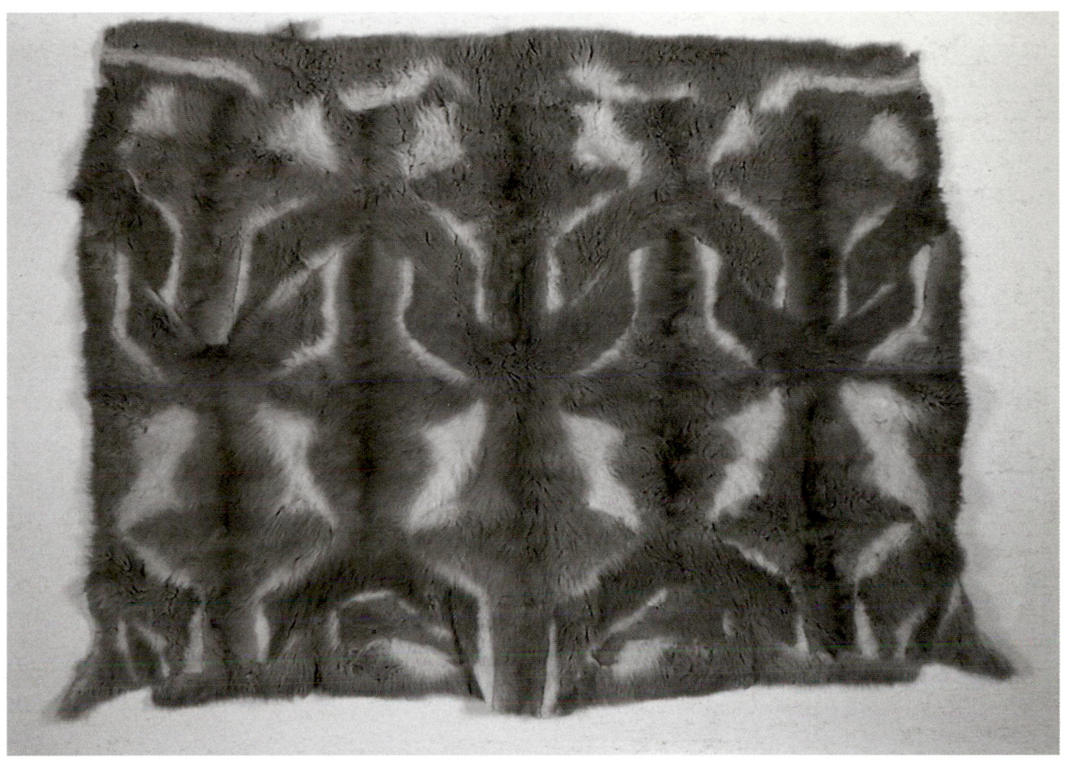

Fig 110 Aónikenk 'quillango' (front).

Fig 111 Aónikenk 'quillango' (reverse).

Historical references place the cloak tradition at least as early as the sixteenth century.[17] Perhaps the first, and most specific, in his description concerning the joining of the various skins was Sarmiento: 'they wear as garments cloaks made of skins, well matched and sewn',[18] while the first representation of decoration of the skins appears in Pernetty in 1766 (see chapter 7, fig. 94).[19] The practice of preparing and painting the skins continued well into the beginning of this century,[20] and the technique (although without painting) is still employed by shepherds in Patagonia and Tierra del Fuego to make blankets.

There is archaeological evidence to suggest that the tradition of making cloaks was practised long before contact. The pattern of the cut and its arrangement on the cloaks is clearly represented on incised stone plaques, as well as in certain painted geometric motifs in rock art that began to develop from about 500 BP onwards (fig. 112).[21] A number of scholars have noted the striking similarity between the motifs employed in both media.[22] These are hard to date directly but indicate that the tradition may go back hundreds if not thousands of years. An actual archaeological example dated to 350 ±90 BP has been found in the volcanic region of east central Magallanes.[23] This does not appear to have been made from the skin of a young guanaco, but rather that of some other adult mammal (fig. 113).

Attempts to correlate specific types of tools with preparing the skins of young guanaco are more difficult. Two types of scrapers were deployed in the preparation of the cloaks, and the Río Santa Cruz marks the approximate limit of distribution of each, corresponding to the northern and southern Tehuelche respectively (fig. 114). Towards the end of the nineteenth century stone scrapers were replaced by those made from the glass of bottles acquired by exchange from sailors, from shipwrecks or by purchasing alcohol from itinerant merchants from the colonies.[24] The handle of the northern scrapers was very similar to that employed by the Selk'nam (compare figs 114a and b), whereas the southern scrapers differed from these. Those from the north had the advantage of using the resinous gum from a shrub (*Schinus* sp.) to secure the scraper to the handle. The scraper could be repositioned or replaced by heating the resin and inserting a new one. This was not so easily done in the case of the tools used by the Aónikenk and Selk'nam, in which the scraper was attached to the handle by binding it with a leather thong. In the case of the tools from the north, the 'angle of attack' of the handle meant that in the course of being used the skin would become flattened by the handle at the front and cut into by the scraper at the back, thus increasing the speed with which the leading edge of the tool became less effective and eventually discarded. Nevertheless, the fact that the cutting edge of the scraper itself is very similar in all three instruments suggests that they were all used to prepare not only the skins of young

Fig 112 *above left* Engraved stone plaque from the Río Negro region with geometric motifs similar to those found in rock art and on painted cloaks.

Fig 113 Fragment of painted hide excavated at the archaeological site of Cerro Johnny, Magallanes, Chile.

guanaco, but also those of mature adults destined for use either as garments or in tents. The most important aspect of preparing the tool was to ensure that the cutting edge was as even as possible. Great care had to be taken to eliminate minor irregularities that might tear the delicate skins and thus create additional repair work.

We have seen that the introduction of the horse and the penetration of the market economy brought about great changes to the scale of cloak production among mainland Patagonian societies. However, this was not the case with the Selk'nam of Tierra del Fuego, who do not appear to have prepared or decorated their cloaks in the same way as the Tehuelche. Neither Gusinde nor Bridges, our principal informants, describe a technique like that employed by the Tehuelche, but Gallardo does comment that 'in the

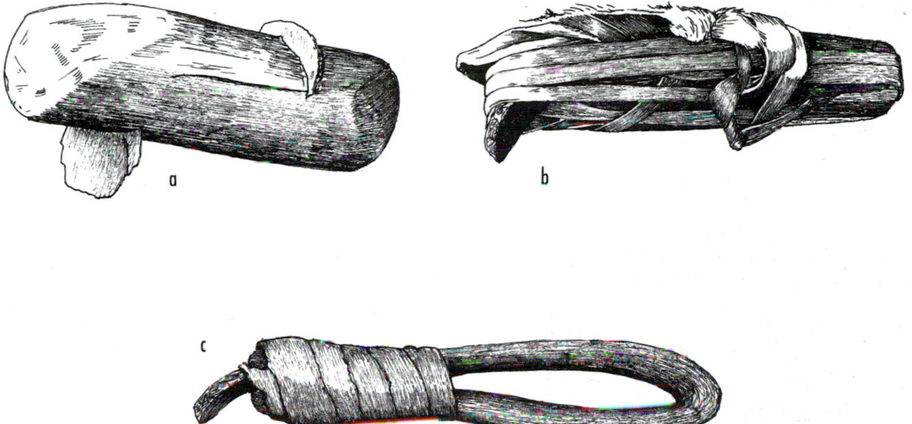

Fig 114 Scrapers used by (a) the Mecharnúekenk, (b) the Selk'nam and (c) the Aónikenk.

preparation of cloaks of guanaco or fox skin the women take great care, because over and above *joining the various skins* that make up the garment [...] (emphasis ours).[25]

Some photographs exist showing Selk'nam using cloaks, but these were probably introduced by Europeans, as noted on the back of one such image (fig. 115):

> From right to left Shoyin, an Ona youth of about 18; Aanikin, Furlong's chief Ona; Waikeeo and Otrhshoal, Aanikin's two wives. The cloak Shoyin is wearing is made by a Tehuelche woman and is composed of [the skins of] 15 very young guanaco sewn together by sinews. This belonged to Furlong and was part of his sleeping gear. The Ona cloak is a single skin with the neck and head portions cut off.[26]

There are various reasons why the production of cloaks never developed among the Selk'nam as it did among the continental groups:

1. The hunting bands were very much smaller on the island and comprised patrilocal extended families that occupied prescribed territories.[27] They are therefore unlikely to have been able to deploy sufficient numbers to use encirclement as an effective hunting technique on a regular basis.
2. Occasional larger gatherings took place for ceremonial purposes at locations often lying beyond the traditional territories. These might have offered an opportunity for collective

Fig 115 Charles Wellington Furlong's photograph showing the use of guanaco cloaks among the Selk'nam of Tierra del Fuego.

hunting, but they usually took place in autumn (February–March) when the guanaco were fit and well fed and the newborn had by this time grown speedy and agile.

3. The Selk'nam did not use the horse that would have enabled them to move rapidly and to enhance their hunting capacity.
4. They hunted with the bow and arrow that had limited effectiveness. An arrow may wound an animal and require a chase to secure the kill, while the bola immobilises the prey immediately.
5. If a Tehuelche hunter could secure between thirty to forty newborn guanaco daily, it would be difficult for a Selk'nam, by contrast, to kill more than a few animals at most. It would also have been difficult for the Selk'nam physically to move many skins at once from one camp to another. What is more, Gusinde points out that the Selk'nam reserved a specific area close to Lago Fagnano towards the south of the main island where the guanaco could reproduce without interference.
6. Hunting on foot would have demanded an exceptional group effort to provide each member of the band with the thirteen skins required for a 'quillango' and there is no historical record of the Selk'nam actually doing this.

7. Among the Tehuelche a more hierarchical political organisation is hinted at in some historical documents which speak of 'chiefs' and 'poor' Indians.[28] Because the Selk'nam were more egalitarian it is less likely that male band leaders would have worn special cloaks as a mark of distinction.

The significance of the pattern of the cut

It is worthwhile emphasising again the inventiveness and creativity employed in the pattern of the cut and the sewing of the cloak.

The Tehuelche cloak shows techniques of manufacture based on what might almost

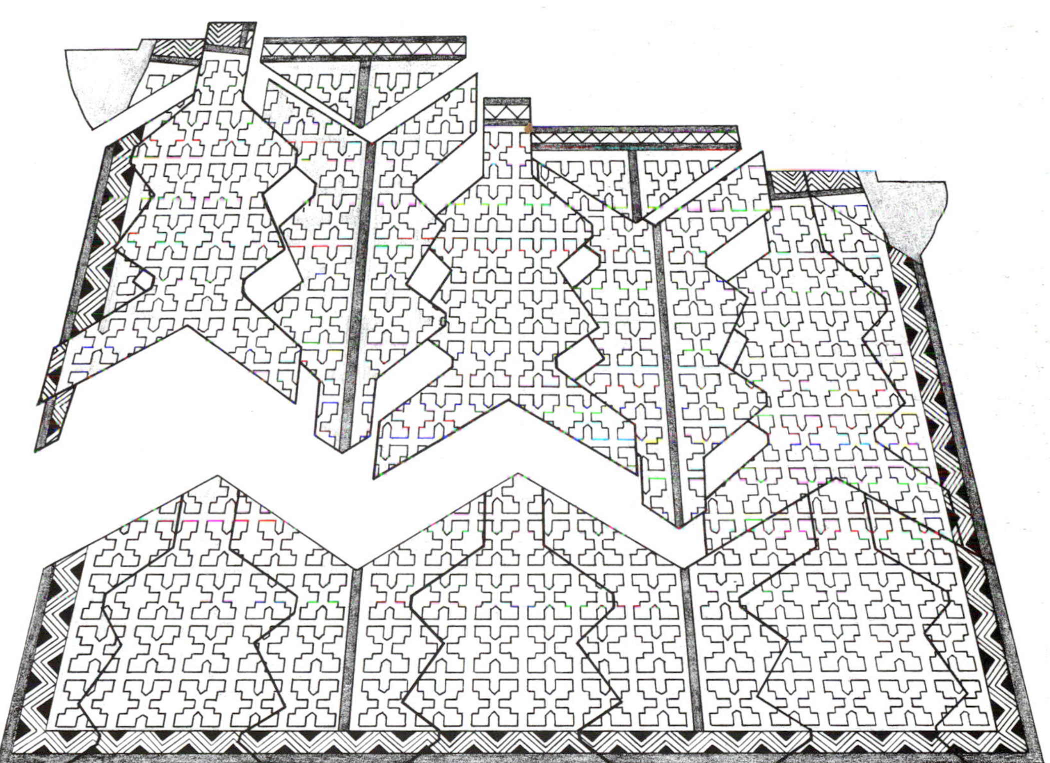

Fig 116 Drawing showing the pattern of cutting and sewing used in making 'quillangos'.

be termed an 'industrial' cut. This implies that the size of the piece is adjusted according to the requirements of the body, but could be extended *ad infinitum* given the incremental character of the pattern, just like the pieces of a puzzle (fig. 116).

Observers who witnessed the production process were inclined to believe that the cut produced a stronger garment than a simple straight seam.[29] Thus, while sewing a straight seam is undoubtedly much easier and faster, it renders the joint much more susceptible to tears and damage when in use. In contrast, the dove-tail pattern of cutting and sewing more effectively distributes the strains on the garment's seams and therefore ensures greater durability and longevity. While the sewing of rectangular units would also have been much easier, this would have entailed a lot of wastage, while the dove-tail cuts actually used required only that the strips with the stake holes and the thin chest skin be removed. It seems that this distinctive cut pattern represents the most advantageous design in order to effect the joins between skins of newborn guanaco of equal or similar size. Any attempt to add a larger adult skin would have interrupted the regularity of the pattern.

It has been proposed that the painting and organisation of the skins in the completed cloak represent an arrangement of repeated abstract human figures interpreted as 'genealogical lineages':

Fig 117 Traders of painted skins on a ship in Punta Arenas, *c.* 1889.

> One of these designs in particular I explained as a 'cutting-line' by which it must have been customary to cut through two layers of pliable material, originally, no doubt, animal skin, of contrasting colours, to produce cut-outs, which were then assembled to form a skin-mosaic of interlocking human figures, alternating in both colour and direction. [...] In fact, such reciprocal patterns may have been anthropomorphic, so to speak, from the very beginning, and they may even have provided the first impetus toward the development of what we designate generally as 'genealogical patterns'.[30]

Be that as it may, cloaks with such designs were sold in large numbers by the Tehuelches themselves, as shown in the trading scene in Punta Arenas around 1890 (fig. 117), the acquisitions made by Jorge Schythe in the 1860s and the cloak painted with the identifying marks of different ranches.[31] There are other cases of painted cloaks in which the pattern of cutting described here was not used, as in the case of the example owned by Sr. Bedrich Magas in Punta Arenas,[32] as well as the archaeological example from Cerro Johnny. This all tends to suggest that the similarity of the pattern with the human figure is merely coincidental.

Conclusion

The dramatic increase in the scale of cloak production to meet commercial demands led to the over-exploitation of both guanaco and Tehuelche women in order to sustain the incipient colonial settlements. Now the women who discovered such a distinctive and ingenious new way of fashioning these extraordinary garments are almost forgotten. The industrious artisans have disappeared, but some knowledge of their technical skills lives on in the hands of old people who still occupy the Patagonian hinterlands. Cloaks are still made following the same patterns, although they are no longer painted. All that survives are a few examples of their artistry, and the designs they painted on rock walls, leaving an enduring record of the symbols that adorned their work.

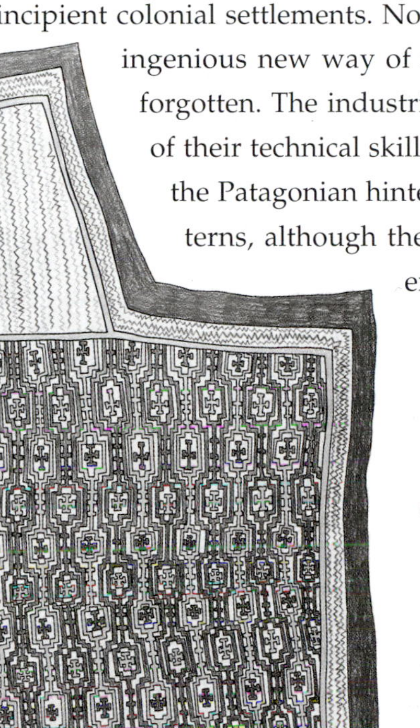

Fig 118 Drawing of a painted horse hide.

The complex polychrome motifs applied to the skins can be seen as the product of a style developed over the course of millennia, which appear throughout Tehuelche art in different media (fig. 118). Perhaps, too, they embodied a deep sense of bonds of kinship connecting succeeding generations. On the other hand, they can be admired simply for their mastery of materials and technique to use a valued resource to best effect.

NOTES

1 Wilbert and Simoneau 1984: 176.
2 Martinic 1995.
3 Massone 1981; Gómez-Otero 1986.
4 Massone 1981.
5 Martinic 1995.
6 Martinic 1995: 110–13.
7 Lothrop 1929: 14. See also Brassey 1880.
8 Brassey 1880: 103.
9 Musters, quoted in Lothrop 1929: 10.
10 Childs 1936: 160–1.
11 Ibid.
12 Ibid.
13 Musters 1964; Casamiquela 1978; Gómez-Otero 1984; Jackson 1991.
14 Childs 1936: 164–5.
15 See, for example, Martinic 1995, figs 79, 81, 82 and 83.
16 Hatcher 1903: 268–9.
17 Cooper 1946.
18 Sarmiento de Gamboa 1768.
19 Lothrop 1929.
20 Casamiquela *et al.* 1991; Martinic 1995.
21 Menghin 1957; Borrero 1976.
22 Casamiquela 1981; Echeverría 1991; Lothrop 1929; Martinic 1995.
23 Martinic 1995. See Appendix II of Borrero 1976, and his discussion of the decoration.
24 Jackson 1991; Martinic and Prieto 1985 / 86.
25 Gallardo 1910: 265. Gallardo was probably referring to the sewing of small fox skins.
26 Photograph D–11–101 from the Archivo fotográfico del Centro de Estudios del Hombre Austral, Instituto de la Patagonia.
27 Gusinde 1982.
28 Sarmiento de Gamboa 1768; Viedma 1980.
29 Musters 1964; Arms and Coan 1939; Childs 1936.
30 Schuster 1961: 434–5; Casamiquela 1981.
31 Martinic 1995: fig. 85.
32 Martinic 1995: fig. 57a and b.

BIBLIOGRAPHY

Adams, P.G., *Travellers and Travel Liars, 1660–1800*, Cambridge, 1962.

Aguerre, A.M., 'Los niveles inferiores de la Cueva Grande (Arroyo Feo). Area Río Pinturas-Provincia de Santa Cruz', *Relaciones de la Sociedad Argentina de Antropología*, XIV: 2 (1981/82), 211–39.

Aguerre, A.M., 'Informe preliminar de las excavaciones en la cueva 4 de la Martita (Depto. Magallanes, Prov. Sta. Cruz)', Trabajo presentado al VII Congreso Nacional de Arqueología Argentina, San Luis, 1982.

Alberdi, M.T. and Prado, J.L., 'El registro de *Hippidion* Owen, 1869 y *Equus* (*Amerhippus*) Hofstetter, 1950 (Mammalia, Perissodactyla) en América del Sur', *Ameghiniana*, 29: 3 (1992), 265–84.

Alfonse, J., *Les voyages adventureux du capitaine Ian Alfonce Saintonogeois*, Paris, 1559.

Aliaga Rojas, F., 'La Misión en la isla Dawson (1889–1911)', *Anales de la Facultad de Teología* (1984), Universidad Católica de Chile, Santiago.

Alonso, F., Gradín, C.J., Aschero, C.A. and Aguerre, A.M., 'Algunas consideraciones sobre recientes dataciones radiocarbónicas para el área Río Pinturas, Provincia de Santa Cruz', *Relaciones de la Sociedad Argentina de Antropología*, 16 (1984), 275–85.

Anderson, G.W., *A New, Authentic, and Complete Collection of Voyages Round the World: Undertaken and Performed by Royal Authority*, London 1781.

Anon., *Das sind die new gefunden Menschen*, Nuremberg, 1505.

Anon., *Libro segundo de Palmerín que trata de los grandes fechos de Primaleón*, Seville, 1524.

Argensola, B.L. de, *Conquista de las islas Malucas*, Madrid, 1609.

Arms, W. and Coan, T., 'Extracto de los diarios de los señores...', *Revista de la Biblioteca Nacional*, III: 9 (1939), Primer Semestre, Buenos Aires.

Aschero, C., 'Nuevos datos sobre la arqueología del cerro Casa de Piedra, sitio CCP-5', *Relaciones de la Sociedad Argentina de Antropología*, 14: 2 (1982), 267–84.

Aschero, C. 'Antecedentes arqueológicos de la cultura Tehuelche' in Massone, M., *Culturas Indígenas de la Patagonia*, Madrid, 1984, 33–6.

Aschero, C., 'Tradiciones culturales en la Patagonia Central (una perspectiva ergológica)', *Comunicaciones: Primeras Jornadas de Arqueología de la Patagonia*, Trelew, 1987, 17–26.

Aschero, C.A., Bellelli, C., Civalero de Bisset, T., Gosi, R.A., Guraieb, A.G. and Molinari, R.L., 'Cronologia y tecnologia en el parque nacional Perito Moreno: continuidad o reemplazos?', *Arqueología*, 2 (1992), 89–106.

Aschero, C., 'El area Río Belgrano-Lago Posadas (Santa Cruz): problemas y estado de problemas' in J. Gomez-Otero, *Arqueología. Solo Patagonia*, Puerto Madryn, 1996, 17–26.

Bamberger, J., 'The myth of the matriarchy: why men rule in primitive society' in M.D. Roasaldo and L. Lamphere (eds), *Women, Culture, and Society*, Stanford, 1974.

Barent, J., *Kort ende waerachtigh Verhael van't gheene seeckere vijf Schepen, van Rotterdam in't jaer 1598 den 27 Junij nae de Straet Magaljanes varende, over-ghekomen is, tot den 21 Januarij 1600 toe, op welcken*, Amsterdam, 1703.

Barth, F., 'Cultural development in southern South America: Yahgan and Alakaluf vs. Ona and Tehuelche', *Acta Americana*, 6 (1948), 192–9.

Bataille, G., *Lascaux, or the Birth of Art*, Switzerland, n.d. [1955?].

Bataille, G., *Erotism: Death and Sensuality*, trans. M. Dalwood, San Francisco, 1986.

Bataille, G., *The Accursed Share*, vol. 1, New York, 1990.

Bataillon, M., 'Acerca de los Patagones, "Retractatio"', *Filología*, VIII (1962).

Bate, L.F., 'Primeras investigaciones sobre el arte rupestre de la Patagonia chilena', *Anales del Instituto de la Patagonia*, 1 (1970), 15–25.

Bate, L.F., *Origenes de la Comunidad Primitiva en Patagonia*, Mexico, 1982.

Bate, L.F., 'Comunidades primitivas de cazadores recolectores en Sudamérica' in *Historia General de América*, vol. 2, Caracas, 1983.

Beer, G., 'Four bodies on the "Beagle": touch, sight and writing in a Darwin letter' in J. Still and M. Worton (eds), *Textuality and Sexuality*, Manchester, 1993.

Belardi, J., Borrero, L.A., Campán, P., Carballo Marina, F., Franco, N.V., García, M.F., Horwitz, V.D., Lanata, J.L., Martín, F.M., Muñoz, A.S., Muñoz, F.E. and Savanti, F., 'Intensive archaeological survey in the upper Santa Cruz basin, southern Patagonia', *Current Anthropology*, 33 (1992), 451–4.

Belardi, J., 'Cuevas, aleros, distribuciones y poblamiento' in J. Gomez-Otero (ed.), *Arqueología. Sólo Patagonia*, Puerto Madryn, 1996, 43–8.

Bettinger, R., 'Explanatory/predictive models of hunter-gatherer adaptation' in Schiffer (ed.), *Advances in Archaeological Method and Theory*, vol. 3, New York, 1980, 189–255.

Bird, J., 'Antiquity and migrations of the early inhabitants of Patagonia', *Geographical Review*, 28 (1938), 250–75.

Bird, J., 'The archaeology of Patagonia' in J. Steward (ed.), *Handbook of South American Indians*, vol. 1, Washington, D.C., 1946.

Bird, J., 'A comparison of South Chilean and Ecuadorian "fishtail" projectile points', *The Kroeber Anthropological Society Papers*, 40 (1969), 52–71.

Bird, J., 'Investigaciones arqueológicas en la Isla Isabel, Estrecho de Magallanes', *Anales del Instituto de la Patagonia*, 11 (1980), 75–88.

Bird, J., *Travels and Archaeology in South Chile* (ed. John Hyslop), Iowa, 1988.

Borella, F., Borrero, L.A. and Martin, F.M., 'Taphonomy, Analogy, and the Fossil Record: An Introduction to Scavenging Opportunities in Fuego-Patagonia', paper presented at the 61st Annual Meeting of the Society for American Archaeology, New Orleans, 1996.

Bórmida, M. and Siffredi, A., 'Mitología de los Tehuelches Meridionales', *Runa*, XII: 1 and 2 (1970), 199–269.

Borrero, L. 'Un enterramiento con ocre y cueros pintados en estancia Brazo Norte (Chile): Analisis Preliminar', *Anales del Instituto de la Patagonia*, 7 (1976), 102–3.

Borrero, L.A., 'La extinción de la megafauna: su explicación por factores concurrentes. La situación en Patagonia austral', *Anales del Instituto de la Patagonia*, 8 (1977), 81–93.

Borrero, L.A., 'La economía prehistórica de los habitantes del Norte de la Isla Grande de Tierra del Fuego', Ph.D. thesis, Universidad de Buenos Aires (1986).

Borrero, L.A., Lanata, J.L. and Borella, F., 'Reestudiando huesos: nuevas consideraciones sobre sitios de Ultima Esperanza', *Anales del Instituto de la Patagonia* (Serie Ciencias Sociales), 18 (1988), 134–56.

Borrero, L.A., 'Replanteo de la arqueología patagónica', *Interciencia,* 14: 3 (1989a), 127–35.

Borrero, L.A., 'Spatial heterogeneity in Fuego-Patagonia' in S. Shennan (ed.), *Archaeological Approaches to Cultural Identity*, London, 1989b, 258–66.

Borrero, L.A., Lanata, J.L. and Cárdenas, P., 'Reestudiando cuevas: nuevas consideraciones sobre sitios de Ultima Esperanza', *Anales del Instituto de la Patagonia* (Serie Ciencias Sociales), 20 (1991), 101–10.

Borrero, L.A., 'El registro arqueológico del Contacto: enfermedad y discontinuidad poblacional', paper presented at the symposium "Encuentro de Dos Culturas", Centro Cultural General San Martín, Buenos Aires, 1992.

Borrero, L.A., 'The extermination of the Selk'nam' in E.S. Burch and L.J. Ellanna (eds), *Key Issues in Hunter-Gatherer Research*, Oxford, 1994, 247–61.

Borrero, L.A., 'Arqueología de la Patagonia', *Palimpesto*, 4 (1994/95), 9–69.

Borrero, L.A. and Franco, N.V., 'Early Patagonian Hunter-Gatherers: Subsistence and Technology', paper presented at the 60th Annual Meeting of the Society for American Archaeology, Minneapolis, 1995.

Borrero, L.A. and Martin, F., 'Tafonomía de carnívoros: un enfoque regional' in J. Gómez Otero (ed.), *Arqueología. Sólo Patagonia*, Puerto Madryn, 1996, 189–98.

Borrero, L.A., 'The Pleistocene-Holocene transition in southern South America' in L.G. Straus, B.V. Eriksen, J.M. Erlandson and D.R. Yesner (eds), *Humans at the End of the Ice Age: The Archaeology of the Pleistocene-Holocene Transition*, New York, 1996, 339–54.

Borrero, L.A., 'Magallania. Divergent Evolution on the Strait of Magellan', MS (1997a).

Borrero, L.A., 'Faunal extinctions in Fuego-Patagonia: a supra-regional approach', *L'Homme et l'Animal*, (1997b, in press).

Boschín, T., 'Arqueología del Area Plicaniyeu, sudoeste de Río Negro, Argentina', *Cuadernos del Instituto Nacional de Antropología*, 11 (1986), 99–119.

Bougainville, L.A. de, *Voyage autour du monde, par la frégate du roi la Boudeuse, et la flute l'Etoile; en 1766, 1767, 1768 & 1769*, Paris, 1771, 2nd enlarged edn, Paris, 1772.

Brassey, A.A., *A Voyage in the 'Sunbeam'*, London, 1880.

Braun Menendez, A., *Pequeña Historia Fueguina*, Buenos Aires, 1971.

Bridges, E.L., 'Supersticiones de los Onas', *Argentina Austral*, 73 (1935), 33–9.

Bridges, E.L., *Uttermost Part of the Earth*, London, 1951, 1987.

Bridges, Revd T., *Yámana-English. A Dictionary of the Speech of Tierra del Fuego*, ed. F. Hestermann and M. Gusinde, 2nd edn, Buenos Aires, 1987.

Brosses, C. des, *Histoire des navigations aux terres australes*, Paris, 1756.

Browne, J., *Charles Darwin Voyaging. Volume 1 of a Biography*, London, 1995.

Bryan, A.L., *Early Man in America*, Alberta, 1978.

Buck-Morss, S., *The Origin of Negative Dialectics*, New York, 1977.

Buffon, G.L.L., comte de, *De l'Homme. Œuvres complètes de Buffon*, enlarged by M. Cuvier, Paris, 1834.

Burger, R., 'Concluding remarks: early Peruvian civilization and its relation to the Chavín Horizon' in Donnan (ed.), *Early Ceremonial Architecture in the Andes*, Dumbarton Oaks, 1985, 269–89.

Byron, J., *A Voyage Round the World in His Majesty's Ship* The Dolphin, *Commanded by the Honourable Commodore Byron... by an Officer on Board the Said Ship*, London, 1767a.

Byron, J., *Voyage autour du monde fait en 1764 & 1765, sur le Vaisseau de guerre Anglois le Dauphin, commandé par le Chef d'Escadre Byron*, trans. from the English by M.R., Paris, 1767b.

Byron, J., *The narrative of the Honourable John Byron containing an account of the great distresses suffered by himself and his companions on the coast of Patagonia, from the year 1740 till their arrival in England, 1746*, 2nd edn, London, 1768.

Byron, J., *Byron's Journal of his Circumnavigation* (ed. R.E. Gallagher), Cambridge 1964.

Caldenius, C.C., 'Las glaciaciones cuaternarias en la Patagonia y Tierra del Fuego', *Geografisak Annaler*, 14 (1932), 1–64.

Canals-Frau, S., 'Expansion of the Araucanians in Argentina' in J. Steward (ed.), *Handbook of South American Indians*, vol. 1, Washington, D.C., 1946, 761–6.

Canals-Frau, S., *Poblaciones indígenas de la Argentina*, Buenos Aires, 1953.

Canto, H.J., 'Posible presencia de una variedad de Smilodon en el pleistoceno tardío de Magallanes', Appendix I in Prieto 1991; 96–9.

Cardich, A., Cardich, L. and Hajduk, A., 'Secuencia arqueológica y cronología radiocarbónica de la cueva 3 de Los Toldos', *Relaciones de la Sociedad Argentina de Antropología*, 7 (1973), 85–123.

Cardich, A., Tonni, E. and Kriscautzky, N., 'Presencia de *Canis familiaris* en restos arqueológicos de Los Toldos', *Relaciones de la Sociedad Argentina de Antropología*, 11 (1977), 115–19.

Cardich, A. and Flegenheimer, N., 'Descripción y tipología de las industrias líticas más antiguas de Los Toldos', *Relaciones de la Sociedad Argentina de Antropología*, 12, n.s. (1978), 225–42.

Cardich, A., Mansur-Franchomme, M.E., Giesso, M. and Duran, V.A., 'Arqueología de las cuevas de El Ceibo', *Relaciones de la Sociedad Argentina de Antropología*, 14 (1981/82), 173–209.

Cardich, A. and Miotti, L., 'Recursos faunísticos en los cazadores recolectores de Los Toldos', *Relaciones de la Sociedad Argentina de Antropología*, 15 (1983), 145–57.

Cardich, A., 'Una fecha radiocarbónica más de la cueva 3 de Los Toldos', *Relaciones de la Sociedad Argentina de Antropología,* 14 (1985), 269–73.

Cardich, A., Paunero, R. and Castro, A., 'Análisis de los conjuntos líticos de la cueva 2 de Los Toldos (Santa Cruz, Argentina)', *Anales del Instituto de la Patagonia* (Serie Ciencias Sociales), 22 (1993/94), 149–73.

Cardich, A. and Paunero, R., 'Mid-Holocene herding in central Patagonia', *Research and Exploration*, 10: 3 (1994), 368–9.

Carr, C., 'Why didn't the American Indians domesticate sheep?' in Reed (ed.), *Origins of Agriculture*, The Hague, 1977, 637–91.

Carter, P., *The Road to Botany Bay: An Essay in Spatial History*, London, 1987.

Casamiquela, R., 'Dos nuevos yacimientos patagónicos de la cultura Jacobaccense', *Revista del Museo de La Plata*, 5 (1961), 171–8.

Casamiquela, R., *Un Nuevo Panorama Etnológico del Area Pan-Pampeana y Patagónica Adyacente*, Santiago, 1969.

Casamiquela, R., 'Alacalufes, canoeros occidentales y pueblos marginales o metamórficos', *Relaciones de la Sociedad Argentina de Antropología*, 7 (1973), 125–43.

Casamiquela, R., 'Temas patagónicos de interés arqueológico III: La técnica de la talla de vidrio', *Relaciones de la Sociedad Argentina de Antropología*, 12, n.s. (1978).

Casamiquela, R., *El Arte Rupestre de la Patagonia*, Neuquén, Argentina, 1981.

Casamiquela, R. and Dillehay, T.D., 'Vertebrate and invertebrate faunal analysis' in T.D. Dillehay (ed.), *Monte Verde. A Late Pleistocene Settlement in Chile*, Washington, D.C., 1989, 205–10.

Casamiquela, R., Mondelo O., Perea E. and Martinic, M., *Del mito a la realidad. Evolución iconográfica del pueblo tehuelche meridional*, Viedma, 1991.

Casamiquela, R., *Del Mito a la Realidad*, Videma, Argentina, 1992.

Caviglia, S.E., 'Sobre la presencia de un cetáceo en asociación con *Hippidion-Onohippidion* (s.l.) y ground sloth en la cueva Las Buitreras', *Relaciones de la Sociedad Argentina de Antropología*, 10 (1976), 313–14.

Caviglia, S.E. and Figuerero Torres, M.J., 'Material faunístico de la cueva "Las Buitreras" (Dto. Guer Aike, Santa Cruz)', *Relaciones de la Sociedad Argentina de Antropología*, 10 (1976), 315–19.

Caviglia, S.E., 'Nuevos restos de cánidos tempranos en sitios arqueológicos de Fuego-Patagonia', *Anales del Instituto de la Patagonia*, 16 (1986), 85–93.

Ceballos, R., 'El sitio Cuyin Manzano', Centro de Investigaciones Cientifícas de Río Negro, Viedma, *Series y Documentos*, 9 (1982), 1–66.

Chapman, A., *Selk'nam Chants of Tierra del Fuego, Argentina*, vol. 1, Folkways Records Album FE 4176, Smithsonian Institution, 1972.

Chapman, A., *Selk'nam Chants of Tierra del Fuego, Argentina*, vol. 2, Folkways Records Album FE 4179, Smithsonian Institution, 1978.

Chapman, A., *Drama and Power in a Hunting Society: The Selk'nam of Tierra del Fuego*, Cambridge, 1982.

Chapman, A., *El Fin de un Mundo. Los Selk'nam de Tierra del Fuego*, Buenos Aires, 1990.

Chapman, A., 'Economía y estructura social de la sociedad Selk'nam (Tierra del Fuego)' in J.R. Bárcenas (ed.), *Culturas Indígenas de la Patagonia*, Spain, 1992, 171–200.

Chapman, A., *At the Back of Beyond: The Indians of Cape Horn and Adjacent Areas, their Encounters with Europeans from 1578 to 1997*, MS (1997).

Childs, H., *El Jimmy: Outlaw of Patagonia*, Philadelphia, 1936.

Cigliano, E.M., *El Ampajanguense*. Facultad de Filosofia y Letras, Instituto de Antropología, Publicación Número 5, Rosario, 1962.

Clapperton, C.M., 'The glaciation of the Andes', *Quaternary Science Review*, 2 (1983), 85–155.

Clapperton, C.M., 'Asymmetrical drumlins in Patagonia, Chile', *Sedimentary Geology*, 62 (1989), 387–98.

Clapperton, C.M., 'La última glaciación y deglaciación en el Estrecho de Magallanes: implicaciones para el poblamiento en Tierra del Fuego', *Anales del Instituto de la Patagonia*, 21 (1992), 113–28.

Clapperton, C.M., *The Quaternary Geology and Geomorphology of South America*, Amsterdam, 1993.

Clapperton, C.M., 'The quaternary glaciation of Chile: a review', *Revista Chilena de Historia Natural*, 67 (1994), 369–83.

Clapperton, C.M., Sugden, D.E., Kaufman, D.S. and McCulloch, R.D., 'The last glaciation in Central Magellan Strait, southernmost Chile', *Quaternary Research*, 44 (1995), 133–48.

Clapperton, C.M., Hall, M., Mothes, P., Hole, M.J., Still, J.W., Helmens, K.F., Kuhry, P. and Gemmell, A.M.D., 'A Younger Dryas icecap in the equatorial Andes', *Quaternary Research*, 47 (1997), 13–28.

Clark, G., 'Migration as an explanatory concept in Paleolithic Archaeology', *Journal of Archaeological Method and Theory*, 1 (1994), 305–43.

Cocilovo, J., 'Estudio sobre discriminación y clasificación de poblaciones prehispánicas del N.O. Argentino', *Publicación Ocasional*, 36 (1981), Museo Nacional de Historia Natural, Santiago.

Cocilovo, J. and Guichón, R., 'Propuesta para el estudio de las poblaciones aborígenes del extremo austral de Patagonia', *Anales del Instituto de la Patagonia* (Serie Ciencias Sociales), 16 (1985/86), 111–23.

Cocilovo, J. and Guichón, R., 'La variación geográfica y el proceso de microdiferenciación de las poblaciones aborígenes de Patagonia austral y de Tierra del Fuego', paper presented at the Symposium "Los sistemas naturales subantárticos y su ocupación humana", Madrid, 1991.

Colección Fotográfica del Instituto de la Patagonia, Universidad de Magallanes, Punta Arenas.

Constantinescu, F. and Aspillaga, E., 'Paleopatología y anatomía funcional de la columna de una muestra de indígenas Chonos', *Actas del XI Congreso Nacional de Arqueología Chilena*, III (1990), 237–41.

Cooper, J.M., 'Analytical and critical bibliography of the tribes of Tierra del Fuego and adjacent territory', *Bulletin*, 63, Bureau of American Ethnology, Smithsonian Institution, Washington, D.C., 1917.

Cooper, J.M., 'The Patagonian and Pampean Hunters' in J.H. Steward (ed.), *Handbook of South American Indians*, vol. I: *The Marginal Tribes*, Washington, 1946.

Coppinger, R.W., *A Two Years' Cruise of the*

Allert, *in Patagonian and Polynesian Waters*, London, 1883.

Coronato, A., Salemme, M. and Rabassa, J., 'Palaeoenvironmental conditions during the early peopling of southernmost South America (late Glacial-early Holocene, 14–8 14C KA BP)', *Quaternary International* (1997, in press).

Crivelli, E.A., 'La industria Casapedrense', *Runa*, 13: 1–2 (1980), 35–57.

Crivelli, E.A., Curzio, D. and Silveira, M.J., 'La estratigrafía de la cueva Traful 1 (Provincia del Neuquén)', *Prehistoria*, 1 (1993), 9–160.

Crivelli, E.A., Pardiñas, U., Fernández, M.M., Bogazzi, M., Chauvin, A., Fernández, V. and Lezcano, M., 'Cueva Epullan Grande (Pcia. del Neuquén). Informe de avance', *Prehistoria*, 2 (1996), 185–265.

Curry, P., 'Distribución de sitios e implicaciones para la movilidad de los canoeros en el canal Messier', *Anales del Instituto de la Patagonia*, 20 (1991), 145–54.

Darwin, C., *Charles Darwin's Diary of the Voyage of H.M.S. 'Beagle'*, ed. Nora Barow, Cambridge, 1934.

Darwin, C., *Journal of Researches...*, New York, 1896.

Darwin, C., *The Beagle Record*, ed. R.D. Keynes, Cambridge, 1979.

Dennell, R., *Prehistoria Económica de Europa*, Barcelona, 1987.

Denton, G.H. and Hendy, C., 'Younger Dryas age advance of Franz Josef glacier in the Southern Alps of New Zealand', *Science*, 264 (1994), 1434–7.

Diaz, Cristián and Garretón, M., 'El poblamiento prehispánico del área insular septentrional chilena', *Actas del VI Congreso de Arqueología Chilena*, Santiago, 1973, 559–84.

Dillehay, T. (ed.), *Monte Verde. A Late Pleistocene Settlement in Chile*, vol. I, Washington, D.C., vol. I (1989), vol. II (1997).

Dillehay, T.D. and Collins, M.B., 'Monte Verde, Chile: a comment on Lynch', *American Antiquity*, 56 (1991), 333–41.

Dillehay, T.D., Calderón, G., Politis, G. and Coutinho, M. da C., 'Earliest hunters and gatherers of South America', *Journal of World Prehistory*, 6 (1992), 145–204.

Drake, F., 'Voyage of M. John Winter into the South Sea, by the Straits of Magellan, in concert with M. Francis Drake, begun in the year 1577... written by Eduard Cliffe' in Sir F. Drake, *Drakes' World Encompassed*, The Hakluyt Society, 1854: 278.

Dubois, J., Chapman, A., Barthe, C. and Revols, P., *Cap Horn 1882–83: Rencontres avec les indiens Yahgan*, collection de la photothèque de Musée de l'Homme, Paris, 1995.

Duchet, M., *Anthropologie et histoire au Siècle de Lumières*, Paris, 1971.

Dumont-d'Urville, J.C., *Voyage au Pôle Sud et dans l'Oceanie sur les corvettes* L'astrolabe *et* La Zelée, *1837–40*, vol. I, Paris, 1846.

Dunnell, R.C., 'Methodological impacts of catastrophic depopulation on American Archaeology and Ethnology' in D.N. Thomas (ed.), *Columbian Consequences. The Spanish Borderlands in Pan-American Perspective*, Washington, D.C. and London, 1991, 561–80.

Durkheim, E., *The Elementary Forms of Religious Life*, trans. J.W. Swain, London, 1915.

Duviols, J.P., *L'Amérique espagnole vue et rêvée: Les livres de voyages de Christophe Colomb á Bougainville*, Paris, 1985.

Echevarría Valeta, M., *Kai Ajnun*, Río Gallegos, 1991.

Elliot Joyce, L.E., 'Introduction' in L. Wafer, *A New Voyage and Description of the Isthmus of America*, Oxford, 1933.

Emperaire, J., *Los Nómadas del Mar*, Chile, 1956, 1963.

Emperaire, J., Laming-Emperaire, A. and Reichlen, H., 'La Grotte Fell et autre sites de la region volcanique de la Patagonie chillenne', *Journal de la Société des Americanistes*, 52 (1963), 167–254.

Fairbanks, R.G., 'A 17,000-year glacio-eustatic sea level record: influence of glacial melting rates on the Younger Dryas event and deep ocean circulation', *Nature*, 347 (1989), 637–47.

Federman, N., *Indianische Historia*, Hagenaw, 1557.

Fernández, J., 'Roedores, guanacos, huevos, semillas de araucaria y almeja fluvial: estacionalidad, subsistencia y estrategia locacional en Haichol, cordillera andina del Neuquén', paper presented at the ninth Congreso Nacional de Arqueología Argentina, Buenos Aires, 1988.

Figuerero Torres, M.J. and Mengoni Goñalons, G.L., 'Excavaciones arqueológicas en la Isla El Salmón, Parque Nacional Tierra del Fuego', *Informes de Investigación*, 4 (1986), PREP-CONICET.

Figuerero Torres, M.J., 'Biological and archaeological information in coprolites from an early site in Patagonia', *Current Research in the Pleistocene*, 3 (1986), 73–4.

Fischer, A., '¿Existe la Industria Jacobaccense?' *Relaciones de la Sociedad Argentina de Antropología*, 17: 1 (1987), 81–94.

Fitzroy, R., 'Narrative of the Surveying Voyages of his Majesty's ships 'Adventure' and 'Beagle', between the years 1826 and 1836, describing their examination of the southern shores of South America and the 'Beagle' circumnavigation of the globe', *Proceedings of the Second Expedition, 1831–36, under the command of Captain Robert Fitz-Roy*, vol. II, London, 1839.

Franco, N.V. and Borrero, L.A., 'Bifaces, guanacos and other resources. The evolution of Patagonian populations', paper presented at the Annual Meeting of the Society for American Archaeology, Minneapolis, 1995.

Franco, N.V., 'Excavaciones arqueológicas en Paso Verlika, Santa Cruz', MS (1997).

Franklin, W.L., 'Biology, ecology, and relationship to man of the South American camelids' in M.A. Mares and H.H. Genoways (eds), *Mammalian Biology in South America*, Pittsburgh, 1982, 457–89.

Frézier, A., *Relation du Voyage de la Mer du Sud aux côtes du Chily et du Pérou fait pendant les années 1712, 1713 et 1714*, Paris, 1716.

Froger, F., *Relation d'un voyage fait en 1695, 1696 et 1697 aux côtes d'Afrique, détroit de Magellan, Brézil, Cayenne et Isles Antilles par une escadre de vaisseaux du Roy, commandée par M. de Gennes*, Paris, 1698 and Amsterdam, 1715.

Gallardo, C.B., *Tierra del Fuego. Los Onas*, Buenos Aires, 1910.

Gamble, C., *Timewalkers. The Prehistory of Global Colonization*, Cambridge, Mass., 1994.

García de Nodal, B. and G., *Relación del viage que por orden de Su Maj. y acuerdo del Real Consejo de Indias hicieron los capitanes Bartolomé García de Nodal y Gonzalo de Nodal hermanos, naturales de Pontevedra, al descubrimiento del Estrecho nuevo de S. Vicente y reconocimiento del Magallanes*, Madrid, 1621.

García, L.C. and Pérez de Micou, C., 'Aproximación a un análisis funcional de parapetos pertenecientes al complejo patagoniense en la meseta de Somuncura, Pcia. de Río Negro', *Sapiens*, 4 (1982), 1–13.

Gerbi, A., *La Disputa del Nuevo Mundo*, Mexico, 1960.

Glaser, G.M. and Fernández, H.N.F., *Arte Rupestre Chileno*, Colección Historia del Arte Chileno, published by the Departamento de Extensión Cultural de Educación, 1983.

Gómez-Otero, J., 'Un raspador de vidrio confeccionado por una tehuelche meridional', MS (1984).

Gómez-Otero, J., 'Investigaciones arqueológicas en el alero Potrok Aike: una revisión de los períodos IV y V de Bird', *Relaciones de la Sociedad Argentina de Antropología*, 17, n.s. (1986).

Gómez-Otero, J., 'Posición estratigráfica particular de puntas de los periodos IV y V de Bird en el alero Potrok-Aike, Santa Cruz', *Comunicaciones: Primeras Jornadas de Arqueología de la Patagonia*, Trelew, 1987.

Gómez-Otero, J., 'Reseña sobre la arqueología en la Provincia de Chubut', *Guía de Campo*, Séptima Reunión de Campo Cadinqua, Puerto Madryn, 1994, 93–5.

Gómez-Otero, J., 'Bases para una arqueología de la costa patagónica central (entre el Golfo San José y Cabo Blanco)', *Arqueología*, 5 (1995), 61–103.

Goñi, R., 'Arqueología de momentos tardíos en el Parque Nacional Perito Moreno (Santa Cruz, Argentina)', *Precirculados, X Congreso Nacional de Arqueología Argentina*, Buenos Aires, 1988, 140–51.

Gordillo, S., Bujalesky, G., Pirazzoli, P., Rabassa, J. and Saliege, J.F., 'Holocene raised beaches along the northern coast of the Beagle Channel, Tierra del Fuego, Argentina', *Palaeogeography, Palaeoclimatology, Palaeoecology*, 99 (1992), 41–54.

Gordillo, S., Coronato, A. and Rabassa, J., 'Late quaternary evolution of a subantarctic palaeofjord, Tierra del Fuego, Argentina', *Quaternary Science Review*, 12 (1993), 889–97.

Gradín, C., 'Parapetos de piedra y grabados de piedra de la meseta del Lago Buenos Aires', Actas IV Congreso Nacional de Arqueología Argentina, *Rev. Museo Hist. Nat. Sn. Rafael*, 3: 1/4 (1976), 315–37.

Gradín, C., Aschero, C. and Aguerre, A.M., 'Investigaciones arqueológicas en la Cueva de las Manos, Estancia Alto Río Pinturas', *Relaciones de la Sociedad Argentina de Antropología*, X (1976), 201–50.

Gradín, C., 'Las pinturas del Cerro Shequen', *Revista del Instituto de Antropología*, Univ. Nac. de Córdoba, 6 (1978), 63–92.

Gradín, C., Aschero, C. and Aguerre, A.M., 'Arqueología del Area Río Pinturas', *Relaciones de la Sociedad Argentina de Antropología*, 13 (1979), 183–227.

Gradín, C., 'Secuencias radiocarbónicas del sur de la Patagonia Argentina', *Relaciones de la Sociedad Argentina de Antropología*, 14: 1 (1980), 177–94.

Gradín, C., 'El arte rupestre de la cuenca del Río Pinturas, Provincia de Santa Cruz, República Argentina', *Acta Prehistórica*, 2: 87 (1983), 149.

Gradín, C., Aschero, C. and Aguerre, A.M., 'Primeros niveles culturales en el Área Río Pinturas (Provincia de Santa Cruz, Argentina)', *Estudios Atacameños*, 8 (1987), 118–41.

Gradín, C. and Aguerre, A.M., *Contribucion a la arqueología del Río Pinturas. Provincia de Santa Cruz*, Concepción del Uruguay, 1994.

Graham, R. and Lundelius, E., 'Coevolutionary disequilibrium and Pleistocene extinctions' in R. Klein and P.S. Martin (eds), *Quaternary Extinctions*, Tucson, Arizona, 1984, 223–49.

Gregor, T., *Anxious Pleasures: The Sexual Lives of Amazonian People*, Chicago 1985.

Guichón, R., 'Antropología biológica en Tierra del Fuego', Ph.D. thesis, University of Buenos Aires (1995).

Guidón, N., Pessis, A-M., Parenti, F., Fontugue, M. and Guerin, C., 'Nature and Age of the Deposits in Pedra Furada, Brazil: Reply to Meltzer, Adovasio and Dillehay', *Antiquity*, 70 (1996), 408–21.

Gusinde, M., *Die Feuerland-Indianer*, Mödling bei Wien, 1931.

Gusinde, M., *Fueguinos. Hombres Primitivos en la Tierra del Fuego*, Sevilla, 1951.

Gusinde, M., *The Yámana: The Life and Thought of the Water Nomads of Cape Horn*, trans. F. Shutze, 5 vols, New Haven, 1961.

Gusinde, M., *Los Indios de Tierra del Fuego*, tome I: *Los Selk'nam*, 2 vols, Buenos Aires 1982.

Gusinde, M., *Los Indios de Tierra del Fuego*, tome II: *Los Yámana*, 3 vols, Buenos Aires, 1986.

Hammel, E.A. and Howell, N., 'Research in population and culture: an evolutionary framework', *Current Anthropology*, 28 (1987), 141–60.

Hatcher, J.B., *Reports of the Princeton University Expeditions to Patagonia (1896–1899)*, vol. I: *Narrative and Geography*, Princeton and Stuttgart, 1903.

Haynes, C.V., 'The earliest Americans', *Scientific American*, 214: 6 (1969), 104–12.

Haynes, C.V., 'Clovis origin update', *The Kiva*, 52: 2 (1987), 83–92.

Hedges, R.E.M., Housley, R.A., Bronk, C.R. and van Klinken, G.J., 'Radiocarbon dates from the Oxford AMS system: archaeometry datelist 15', *Archaeometry*, 34 (1992), 337–57.

Herbst, G., Palacios, T. and Scheinsohn, V., 'Primera aproximación al estudio de las propiedades mecánicas de las materias primas óseas utilizadas en Tierra del Fuego, Argentina' in J.L. Lanata and L.A. Borrero (eds), *Arqueología de Cazadores-Recolectores. Límites, Casos y Aperturas*, *Arqueología Contemporánea*, 5 (1994).

Hernández, M., 'Morfología craneal de las etnias de la Tierra del Fuego: diferencias sexuales e intergrupales', *Anales del Instituto de la Patagonia* (Serie Ciencias Sociales), 21 (1992), 81–98.

Heusser, C.J. and Streeter, S., 'A temperature and precipitation record of the past 16,000 years in southern Chile', *Science*, 210 (1980), 1345–7.

Heusser, C.J., 'Late-Quaternary climate of Chile' in J.C. Vogel (ed.), *Late Cainozoic Palaeoclimates of the Southern Hemisphere*, Rotterdam, 1984, 59–83.

Heusser, C.J., 'Fire history of Fuego-Patagonia', *Quaternary of South America and Antarctic Peninsula*, 5 (1987), 93–109.

Heusser, C.J. and Rabassa, J., 'Cold climate episode of Younger Dryas age in Tierra del Fuego', *Nature*, 328 (1987), 609–11.

Heusser, C.J., 'Climate and chronology of Antarctica and adjacent South America over the past 30,000 years', *Palaeogeography, Palaeoclimatology, Palaeoecology*, 76 (1989a), 31–7.

Heusser, C.J., 'Late Quaternary vegetation and climate of southern Tierra del Fuego', *Quaternary Research*, 31 (1989b), 396–406.

Heusser, C.J., 'Chilotan piedmont glacier in the southern Andes during the last glacial maximum', *Revista Geológica de Chile*, 17 (1990), 3–18.

Heusser, C.J., 'Late-glacial of southern South America', *Quaternary Science Review*, 12 (1993), 345–50.

Heusser, C.J., 'Palaeoindians and fire during the late Quaternary in southern South America', *Revista Chilena Historia Natural*, 67 (1994), 435–43.

Heusser, C.J., 'Three late Quaternary pollen diagrams from southern Patagonia and their palaeoecological implications', *Palaeogeography, Palaeoclimatology, Palaeoecology*, 118 (1995), 1–24.

Hollin, J.T. and Shilling, D.H., 'Late Wisconsin-Weichselian mountain glaciers and small ice caps' in G.H. Denton and T.J. Hughes (eds), *The Last Great Ice Sheets*, New York, 1981: 179–220.

Horwitz, V.D., 'Maritime settlement patterns in southeastern Tierra del Fuego (Argentina)', unpublished Ph.D. dissertation, University of Kentucky, Lexington (1990).

Horwitz, V.D., 'Maritime settlement patterns: the case from Isla de los Estados (Staten Island)', *Arqueología Contemporánea*, 4 (1993), 149–61.

Höss, Matthias, Dilling, Currant and Pääbo, 'Molecular phylogeny of the extinct ground sloth *Mylodon darwinii*', *Proceedings of the National Academy of Science*, 93 (1996), 181–5.

Humphrey, P.S., Péfaur, J.E., Rasmussen, P.C., 'Avifauna of three Holocene cave deposits in southern Chile', *Occasional Papers of the Museum of Natural History*, The University of Kansas, Lawrence, 154 (1993), 1–37.

Imbelloni, J., 'El poblamiento de América', *Revista de la Universidad de Buenos Aires* (Cuarta Epoca), 1:1 (1947), 9–35.

Imbelloni, J., 'Los Patagones: características corporales de una población que agoniza', *Runa*, 11 (1949).

Islebe, G.A., Hooghiemstra, H., and van der Borg, K., 'A cooling event during the Younger Dryas chron in Costa Rica', *Palaeogeography, Palaeoclimatology, Palaeoecology*, 117 (1995), 73–80.

Jackson, S.D., 'Componente lítico del sito arqueológico Tres Arroyos', *Anales del Instituto de la Patagonia* (Serie Ciencias Sociales), 17 (1987), 67–72.

Jackson, S.D. 'Raspadores de vidrio Dinamarquero: reflejo de una encrucijada cultural', *Anales del Instituto de la Patagonia* (Serie Ciencias Sociales), 20 (1991), 57–67.

Jackson, Douglas and Trejo, 'Cánidos patagónicos: identificación taxonómica de mandíbulas y molares del sitio arqueológico Cueva Baño Nuevo 1 (alto Ñirehuao, XI Región)', unpublished MS sent to the *Revista Chilena de Historia Natural*.

Joppien, R. and Smith, B., *The Art of Captain Cook's Voyages. Vol. 1: The Voyage of the Endeavour 1768–1771*, New Haven and London, 1985.

Keegan, W.F. and Diamond, J.M., 'Colonization of islands by humans: a biogeographical perspective', *Advances in Archaeological Method and Theory*, 10 (1987), 49–92.

Keynes, R.D. (ed.), *The Beagle Record: Selections from the Original Pictorial Records and Written Accounts of the Voyage of HMS Beagle*, Cambridge, 1979.

Kligmann, D.M., 'Reconstrucción de las cadenas operativas de los recursos líticos del sitio Río Pipo 17 (Tierra del Fuego)', unpublished Masters dissertation, University of Buenos Aires (1991).

Kluge, A., 'On new German cinema art, enlightenment and the public sphere', *October*, 46 (1988).

Koppers, W., *Unter Feuerland-Indianern*, Stuttgart, 1924.

Lalueza, C., Perez-Perez, A., Prats, E., Moreno, P., Pons, J. and Turbon, D., 'Ausencia de la deleccion 9 bp COII/tRNA ^{Lys} en aborígenes de Fuego-Patagonia mediante análisis de DNA antiguo', *Anales del Instituto de la Patagonia*, 22 (1993/94), 181–91.

Lalueza, C., Pérez-Pérez, A., Prats, E. and Turbón, D., 'Linajes mitocondriales de los aborígenes de Tierra del Fuego y Patagonia', *Anales del Instituto de la Patagonia* (Serie Ciencias Sociales), 23 (1995), 75–86.

Laming-Emperaire, A., 'Los sitios arqueológicos de los archipiélagos de Patagonia Occidental', *Anales del Instituto de la Patagonia*, 3: 1–2 (1972a), 87–95.

Laming-Emperaire, A., 'Pêcheurs des archipels et chasseurs des pampas', *Objets et Mondes*, 12 (1972b), 167–184.

Laming-Emperaire, A., Lavallée, D. and Humbert, R., 'Le site de Marazzi en Terre de Feu', *Objets et Mondes*, 12 (1972), 225–44.

Lanata, J.L., 'Diversidad en el registro arqueológico del S. E. de Tierra del Fuego', Ph.D. dissertation, University of Buenos Aires (1996).

Lanata, J.L., 'The Haush puzzle', *Revista do Museu Paulista*, 1997 (in press).

Laszlo, E., *Evolution: The Grand Synthesis*, Boston, 1987.

Le Testu, G., 'Cosmographie Universelle', MSS Ministère de la Défense Nationale, Paris, 1556.

Leahy, M. and Crain, M., *The Land That Time Forgot*, New York and London, 1937, 48.

Lefevre, C., 'L'avifaune de Patagonie australe et ses relations avec l'homme au cours des six derniers millenaires', Ph.D. thesis, University of Paris (1989).

Legoupil, D., 'Indígenas en el mar de Otway: arqueología y etno-historia', *Actas del Primer Congreso de Historia de Magallanes*, Punta Arenas, 1983, 107–21.

Legoupil, D., 'Los indios de los archipiélagos de la Patagonia. Un caso de adaptación a un ambiente adverso', *Anales del Instituto de la Patagonia*, 16 (1985/86), 45–52.

Legoupil, D., 'Un recién nacido de 17 siglos descubierto en la isla Englefield (Seno de Otway, Magallanes)', *Anales del Instituto de la Patagonia*, 16 (1987), 45–52.

Legoupil, D., 'Ultimas consideraciones sobre las dataciones del sitio de isla Englefield (Seno de Otway)', *Anales del Instituto de la Patagonia*, 18 (1988), 95–8.

Legoupil, D., *Ethno-Archéologie dans les archipels de Patagonie: les nomades marins de Punta Baja*, Paris, 1989.

Legoupil, D., 'El archipiélago de Cabo de Hornos y la costa sur de la isla Navarino: poblamiento y modelos económicos', *Anales del Instituto de la Patagonia*, 22 (1993/94), 101–21.

Levillier, R. (ed.), *El Mundo Nuevo*, Buenos Aires, 1951.

Lista, R., *Viaje al país de los Onas*, Buenos Aires, 1887.

Lothrop, S.K., *Polychrome Guanaco Cloaks of Patagonia*, New York, 1929.

Lothrop, S.K., *Essays in Pre-Columbian Art and Archaeology*, Cambridge, Mass., 1961.

Lowell, T.V., Heusser, C.J., Andersen, B.G., Moreno, P.I., Hauser, A., Heusser, L.E., Schluchter, C., Marchant, D.R. and Denton, G.H., 'Interhemispheric correlation of Late Pleistocene glacial events', *Science*, 269 (1995), 1541–9.

Lundelius, E., 'The implications of disharmonious assemblages for Pleistocene extinctions', *Journal of Archaeological Science*, 16 (1989), 407–17.

Lynch, T.F., 'Glacial-age man in South America? A critical review', *American Antiquity*, 55 (1990), 12–36.

MacArthur, R.H. and Wilson, E.O., *The Theory of Island Biogeography*, Princeton, 1967.

Malkiel, M.R.L. de, 'Para la toponimía argentina: Patagonia', *Hispanic Review*, XX (1952).

Mansur-Franchomme, M.E., 'Traces d'utilisation et technologie lithique: exemples de la Patagonie', Doctoral dissertation, University of Bordeaux I (1983).

Manusr-Franchomme, M.E., 'Outils ethnographiques de Patagonie: emmanchement et traces d'utilisation' in *La Main et l'Outil: manches et emmanchements prehistoriques*, vol. 15, Lyon, 1987, 300–1, figs 4, 5, 6.

Marden, C.J. and Clapperton, C.M., 'Fluctuations of the South Patagonian Icefield during the last glaciation and the Holocene', *Journal of Quaternary Science*, 10 (1995), 197–210.

Marden, C.J., 'Late-glacial fluctuations of the South Patagonian Icefield, Torres del Paine National Park, southern Chile', *Quaternary International*, 38/39 (1997), 61–8.

Markgraf, V. and Bradbury, P., 'Holocene climatic history of South America', *Striae*, 16 (1982), 40–5.

Markgraf, V., 'Late and postglacial vegetational and paleoclimatic changes in subantarctic, temperate and arid environments in Argentina', *Palynology*, 7 (1983), 43–70.

Markgraf, V., 'Late Pleistocene and Holocene vegetation history of temperate Argentina: Lago Morenito, Bariloche', *Dissertationes Botanicae*, 72 (1984), 235–54.

Markgraf, V., 'Late Pleistocene faunal extinctions in Southern Patagonia', *Science*, 228: 4703 (1985), 1110–12.

Markgraf, V., 'Paleoclimates in Central and South America since 18000 BP based on pollen and lake-level records', *Quaternary Science Review*, 8 (1989), 1–24.

Markgraf, V., 'Paleoenvironments and paleoclimates in Tierra del Fuego and southernmost Patagonia, South America', *Palaeogeography, Palaeoclimatology, Palaeoecoloy*, 102 (1993), 53–68.

Martin, P., 'The discovery of America', *Science*, 179 (1973), 969–74.

Martinic, M., 'Panorama de la colonización en Tierra del Fuego entre 1881 y 1900', *Anales del Instituto de la Patagonia*, 4 (1973a), 5–69.

Martinic, M., *Crónica de las Tierras del Sur del Canal Beagle*, Buenos Aires and Santiago de Chile, 1973b.

Martinic, M., 'Hallazgo y excavación de una tumba Aónikenk en Cerro Johnny (Brazo Norte), Magallanes', *Anales del Instituto de la Patagonia*, 7 (1976), 95–8.

Martinic, M., *Historia del Estrecho de Magallanes*, Santiago de Chile, 1977.

Martinic, M., 'La política indígena de los gobernadores de Magallanes, 1843–1910', *Anales del Instituto de la Patagonia*, 10 (1979), 7–58.

Martinic, M. and Moore, D.M., 'Las exploraciones inglesas en el Estrecho de Magallanes, 1670–71. El mapa manuscrito de John Narborough', *Anales del Instituto de la Patagonia*, 13 (1982), 7–20.

Martinic, M., 'El Reino de Jesús. La efímera y triste historia de una governación en el Estrecho de Magallanes', *Anales del Instituto de la Patagonia*, 14 (1983), 7–32.

Martinic, M., 'San Gregorio, centro tehuelche meridional', *Anales del Instituto de la Patagonia*, 15 (1984), 11–25.

Martinic, M. and Prieto, A., 'Dinamarquero, encrucijada de rutas australes', *Anales del Instituto de la Patagonia*, 16 (1985/86), 53–83.

Martinic, M., 'El genocidio Sélknam: nuevos antecedentes', *Anales del Instituto de la Patagonia* (Serie Ciencias Sociales), 19 (1989/90), 23–8.

Martinic, M., *Los Aónikenk. Historia y Cultura*, Punta Arenas, 1995.

Marx, K., *The Economic and Philosophic Manuscripts of 1844*, ed. D. Struik, trans. M. Milligan, New York, 1964.

Massone, M., 'Panorama etnohistórico y arqueológico de las ocupaciones Tehuelches y Prototehuelches en la costa del Estrecho de Magallanes', *Anales del Instituto de la Patagonia*, 10 (1979), 63–107.

Massone, M., 'Arqueología de la región volcánica de Palli-Aike', *Anales del Instituto de la Patagonia*, 12 (1981), 95–124.

Massone, M., 'El poblamiento humano aborigen de Tierra del Fuego', *Culturas Indígenas de la Patagonia*, 12 (1984), 95–124.

Massone, M., 'Los cazadores paleoindios de Tres Arroyos (Tierra del Fuego)', *Anales del Instituto de la Patagonia* (Serie Ciencias Sociales), 17 (1987a), 47–60.

Massone, M., 'Las culturas aborígenes de Chile austral en el tiempo' in *Hombres del Sur*, Museo Chileno de Arte Precolombino & Congragación Salesiana, Santiago, 1987b, 10–46.

Massone, M., Jackson, D. and Prieto, A., *Perspectiva Arqueológica de los Selk'nam*, Centro de Investigaciones Diego Barros Anaña, Santiago de Chile, 1993.

Mayer-Oakes, W.J., 'Early man projectile points and lithic technology in the Ecuadorian sierra' in A.L. Bryan (ed.), *New Evidence for the Pleistocene Peopling of the Americas*, Orono, Maine, 1986, 133–56.

McCulloch, R.D., 'Palaeoenvironmental evidence for the Late Wisconsin/Holocene transition in the Strait of Magellan, southern Patagonia', unpublished Ph.D. thesis, University of Aberdeen (1994).

McCulloch, R.D. and Bentley, M.J., 'Late-glacial ice advances in the Strait of Magellan', *Quaternary Science Review*, in press.

Meglioli, A., 'Glacial geology of southernmost Patagonia, the Strait of Magellan, and northern Tierra del Fuego', unpublished Ph.D. thesis, Lehigh University, USA (1992).

Meltzer, D.J., 'Was stone exchanged among eastern North American paleoindians?' in C.J. Ellis and J. Lothrop (eds), *Eastern Paleoindian Lithic Resource Use*, Boulder, 1989, 11–39.

Meltzer, D.J., Adovasio, J. and Dillehay, T., 'On Pleistocene Human Occupation at Pedra Furada, Brazil', *Antiquity*, 68 (1994), 694–714.

Mena, F., 'Excavaciones arqueológicas en Cueva Las Guanacas (R1–16) XI Región de Aisén', *Anales del Instituto de la Patagonia*, 14 (1983), 67–75.

Mena, F., 'Alero Entrada Baker: Faunal Remains and Prehistoric Subsistence in Central Patagonia', unpublished MA thesis, University of California, Los Angeles (1986).

Mena, F., 'Cazadores recolectores en el area Patagónica y tierras bajas aledañas (Holoceno medio y tardío)', *Revista de Arqueología Americana*, 4 (1988), 134–67.

Mena, F., 'Prehistoric Resource Space and Settlement at the Río Ibañez Valley (Central Patagonian Andes)', unpublished Ph.D. dissertation, University of California, Los Angeles (1991).

Menegaz, A., Salemme, M. and Miotti, L., 'Extinciones pleistocénicas: un aporte zooarqueológico' in M. Iriondo and C. Cerrutti (eds), *Resumenes Expandidos*, Paraná, 1990, 154–8.

Menghin, O., 'Fundamentos cronológicos de la prehistoria de Patagonia', *Runa*, 5 (1952), 23–43.

Menghin, O., 'Estilos del arte rupestre de Patagonia', *Acta Prehistórica*, 1 (1957).

Mengoni Goñalons, G.L. and Silveira, M., 'Análisis e interpretación de los restos faunísticos de la Cueva de las Manos, Estancia Alto Río Pinturas', *Relaciones de la Sociedad Argentina de Antropología*, 10 (1976), 261–70.

Mengoni Goñalons, G.L., 'Modificaciones culturales y animales en los huesos de los niveles inferiores del sitio Tres Arroyos 1 (Tierra del Fuego, Chile)', *Anales del Instituto de la Patagonia*, 17 (1987), 61–6.

Mengoni, G., 'Investigaciones arqueológicas en el noroeste de la Meseta Central de Santa Cruz', *Comunicaciones: Primeras Jornadas de Arqueología de la Patagonia*, Trelew, 1987, 171–5.

Mengoni, G., 'Patagonian prehistory: early exploitation of faunal resources (13,500–8,500 BP)' in Bryan (ed.), *New Evidence for the Pleistocene Peopling of the Americas*, Orono, 1986, 271–9.

Mercer, J.H., 'The last glaciation in Chile: a radiocarbon-dated chronology', *Actas del Primer Congreso Geológico Chileno*, 1 (1976), 55–8.

Mercer, J.H., 'Glacial history of southernmost South America', *Quaternary Research*, 6 (1976), 125–66.

Mercer, J.H. and Sutter, J., 'Late Miocene-earliest Pliocene glaciation in southern Argentina: implications for global ice sheet history', *Palaeogeography, Palaeoclimatology, Palaeoecology*, 38 (1981), 185–206.

Miotti, L. and Berman, W.D., 'Mamíferos del Holoceno tardío de Punta Bustamante, Provincia de Santa Cruz, Argentina', *Resumenes V Jornadas de Paleontología de Vertebrados*, La Plata, 1988, 68–9.

Miotti, L., Salemme, M. and Menegaz, A., 'El manejo de los recursos faunísticos durante el Pleistoceno final y Holoceno temprano en Pampa y Patagonia', *Precirculados*, IX (1988), Congreso Nacional de Arqueología Argentina, Universidad de Buenos Aires, 102–18.

Miotti, L., 'Paleoindian occupations at Piedra Museo Locality, Santa Cruz Province, Argentina', *Current Research in the Pleistocene*, 9 (1992), 30–1.

Miotti, L., 'Piedra Museo: nuevos datos zooarqueológicos para la interpretación de la ocupación paleoindia en Patagonia', *Resumenes*, Taller Internacional 'El Cuaternario en Chile' (1993a), 54.

Miotti, L., 'La ocupación humana de la Patagonia austral durante el Holoceno' in M. Iriondo (ed.), *El Holoceno en la Argentina*, vol. 2, CADINQUA, 1993b, 94–130.

Miotti, L., 'Piedra Museo (Santa Cruz), nuevos datos para la ocupación pleistocénica en Patagonia' in J. Gómez-Otero (ed.), *Arqueología. Solo Patagonia*, CENPAT-CONICET, (1996), 27–38.

Miotti, L. and Salemme, M., 'Biodiversity, taxonomic richness and specialists-generalists during late Pleistocene/early Holocene times in Pampa and Patagonia (Argentina, southern South America)', *Quaternary International* (1997, in press).

Mires, F., *El Discurso de la Naturaleza. Amerinda Estudios*, Santiago de Chile, 1990.

Moore, D., *Flora of Tierra del Fuego*, Oswestry, 1983.

Moore, P.D., Webb, J.A. and Collinson, M.E., *Pollen Analysis*, Oxford, 1991.

Morner, N.A. and Sylwan, C., 'Magnetostratigraphy of the Patagonian moraine sequence at Lago Buenos Aires', *Journal of South American Earth Science*, 2 (1989), 385–90.

Morner, N.A., 'Holocene sea-level changes in the Tierra del Fuego region', *Boletim IG-USP, Publicação Especial*, 8 (1991), 133–51.

Moseley, M., *The Maritime Foundations of Andean Civilization*, California, 1975.

Musters, J.G.C., *Vida entre los Patagones*, Buenos Aires, 1964.

Musters, J.G.C., *At Home with the Patagonians*, London 1871.

Nacuzzi, L. and Perez de Micou, C., 'Los recursos vegetales de los cazadores de la cuenca del Río Chubut', *Cuadernos del Instituto Nacional de Antropología*, 10 (1985), 407–23.

Nami, H.G., 'Algunos datos para el conocimiento de la tecnología de industrias talladas de las sociedades cazadoras y recolectoras de Tierra del Fuego', *Anales del Instituto de la Patagonia*, 16 (1985/86), 125–36.

Nami, H.G., 'Experimentos para el estudio de la tecnología bifacial de las ocupaciones tardías en el extremo sur de Patagonia continental', *Informes de Investigación*, 5 (1986), PREP-CONICET.

Nami, H.G., 'Cueva del Medio: Perspectivas arqueológicas para la Patagonia Austral', *Anales del Instituto de la Patagonia* (Serie Ciencias Sociales), 17 (1987), 73–106.

Nami, H.G. and Menegaz, A., 'Cueva del Medio: aportes para el conocimiento de la diversidad faunística hacia el Pleistoceno-Holoceno en la Patagonia austral', *Anales del Instituto de la Patagonia* (Serie Ciencias Sociales), 20 (1991), 117–32.

Nami, H.G., 'Observaciones sobre desechos de talla procedentes de las ocupaciones tempranas de Tres Arroyos (Tierra del Fuego, Chile)', *Anales del Instituto de la Patagonia* (Serie Ciencias Sociales), 22 (1993/94), 175–80.

Nami, H.G. and Nakamura, 'Cronología radiocarbónica con AMS sobre muestras de hueso procedentes del sitio Cueva del Medio (Ultima Esperanza, Chile)', *Anales del Instituto de la Patagonia* (Serie Ciencias Sociales), 23 (1995), 125–33.

Nassau-Siegen, Prince N.O. de, 'Journal du voyage autour du monde', MS in the possession of the Ministry of Foreign Affairs, Paris.

Noort, O. van, *Beschrijvinge van dee Schipvaerd by de Hollanders ghedaen onder't beleydt ende Generaelschap van Olivier van Noort, door de Straet oft Engte van Magallanes*, Amsterdam, 1601.

Nordenskiöld, E., 'Lakttagelser ach fynd, grottor vid Ultima Esperanza i sydustra Patagonien', *Kongliga Svenska Vetenskaps-Akademiens Handlingar* (Stockholm), 33: 3 (1990), 1–24.

Núñez, L. and Santoro, C., 'Cazadores de la Puna Seca y salada, norte de Chile', *Estudios Atacameños*, 9 (1988), 11–60.

Ocampo, C. and Aspillaga, E., 'Breves notas sobre una prospección arqueológica en los archipiélagos de las Guaitecas y los Chonos', *Revista Chilena de Antropología*, 4 (1984), 155–6.

Ocampo, C. and Aspillaga, E., 'Problemas del registro arqueológico de los sitios del archipiélago de los Chonos y las Guaitecas', *Resumenes del XII Congreso Nacional de Arqueología Chilena*, 1991, 17–18.

Ocampo, C. and Rivas, P., 'Caracterización arqueológica preliminar del suroeste de la Tierra del Fuego', *Anales del Instituto de la Patagonia*, 24 (1996), 125–51.

Ochsenius, C., 'Late Pleistocene aridity in the neotropic as extinction causes of the South American land megafauna', *Zbl. Geol. Paläeont. Teil*, Stuttgart, 11/12 (1985a), 1619–9.

Ochsenius, C., 'Pleniglacial desertization, large-animal mass extinction and Pleistocene-Holocene boundary in South America', *Revista de Geografía Norte Grande*, 12 (1985b), 35–47.

Ohlsen, T.H., *Druck van Meisenbach*, Berlin, 1884.

Orbigny, A. d', *L'Homme américain*, Paris, 1839.

Orquera, L.A. and Piana, E.L., 'Adaptación marítima prehistórica en el litoral magallánico-fueguino', *Relaciones de la Sociedad Argentina de Antropología*, 15 (1983), 225–35.

Orquera, L.A., 'Tradiciones culturales y evolución en Patagonia', *Relaciones de la Sociedad Argentina de Antropología*, 16 (1985), 249–66.

Orquera, L.A. and Piana, E.L., 'Composición tipológica y datos tecnomorfológicos y tecnofuncionales de los distintos conjuntos arqueológicos del sitio Tunel 1 (Tierra del Fuego)', *Relaciones de la Sociedad Argentina de Antropología*, 17: 1 (1987), 201–39.

Orquera, L.A., 'Advances in the archaeology of the Pampa and Patagonia', *Journal of World Prehistory*, 1:4 (1987), 333–413.

Orquera, L.A. and Piana, E.L., 'La adaptación al litoral marítimo en la región del canal Beagle y adyacencias', MS presented to Borrero and Stuart (eds), *Tierra del Fuego: Settlement and Subsistence on Mankind's Southern Frontier.*

Ortíz-Troncoso, O., 'Los yacimientos de Punta Santa Ana y Bahía Buena', *Anales del Instituto de la Patagonia*, 6: 1/2 (1975), 93–122.

Ortíz-Troncoso, O., 'Arqueología del Estrecho de Magallanes y canales del sur de Chile' in *Culturas Indígenas de la Patagonia*, Madrid, 1984.

Pagano, M.I., 'Determinacion de edad en mandibulas de guanaco arqueologicas – cueva 4 la Martita – Santa Cruz' in J. Gomez-Otero (ed.), *Arqueología. Sólo Patagonia*, Puerto Madryn, 1996, 279–91.

Pagden, A., *European Encounters with the New World: From Renaissance to Romanticism*, New Haven, 1993.

Palavecino, E., 'Las protoculturas de Sudamérica', *Relaciones de la Sociedad Argentina de Antropología*, 2: 2 (1971), 9–34.

Parenti, F., Fontugue, M. and Guerin, C., 'Pedra Furada in Brazil and its "presumed" evidence: limitations and potential of the available data', *Antiquity*, 70 (1996), 416–21.

Pauw, C. de, *Recherches philosophiques sur les Américains*, Berlin, 1770.

Peillard, L. (ed.), *Relation du premier voyage autour du monde*, Paris, 1964.

Perez de Micou, C., Bellelli, C. and Aschero, C.A., 'Vestigios minerales y vegetales en la determinacion del territorio de explotacion de un sitio' in L.A. Borrero and J.L. Lanata (eds), *Analisis Espacial en Arqueología Patagonia*, Buenos Aires 1992, 53–82.

Pernetty, A.J., *Journal historique d'un voyage fait aux îles Malouines en 1763 et 1764*, Berlin 1769.

Pernetty, A.J., *Journal historique d'un voyage fait aux îles Malouines*, tome II, Paris, 1780.

Pertuiset, E., *Expédition Pertuiset à la Terre de Feu*, Paris 1876.

Piana, E., 'Arrinconamiento o adaptación en Tierra del Fuego' in Belgrano (ed.), *Ensayos de Antropología Argentina*, Buenos Aires, 1984.

Pigafetta, A., *Navigation et découvrement de la Indie supérieure*, 1519.

Pisano Valdes, E., 'Fitogeografía de Fuego-Patagonia chilena. Communidades vegetales entre las latitudes 52° y 56° S.', *Anales del Instituto de la Patagonia*, 8 (1977), 121–250.

Polanyi, M., *Personal Knowledge*, Chicago, 1958.

Popper, J., 'Exploración de la Tierra del Fuego', *Boletín del Instituto Geográfico Argentino*, 8 (1887), 74–93, 97–115.

Porter, S.C., Stuiver, M. and Heusser, C.J., 'Holocene sea-level changes along the Strait of Magellan and Beagle Channel, southernmost South America', *Quaternary Research*, 22 (1984), 59–67.

Porter, S.C., Clapperton, C.M. and Sugden, D.E., 'Chronology and dynamics of deglaciation along and near the Strait of Magellan, southernmost South America', *Sveriges Geologiska Undersokning*, 81 (1992), 233–9.

Pratt, M.L., *Imperial Eyes: Travel Writing and Transculturation*, London, 1992.

Prichard, J., *The Natural History of Man; Comprising Inquiries into the Modifying Influence of Physical and Moral Agencies on the Different Tribes of the Human Family*, London, 1987.

Prieto, A., 'Cazadores-recolectores del Istmo de Brunswick', *Anales del Instituto de la Patagonia*, (Serie Ciencias Sociales), 18 (1988), 113–32.

Prieto, A., 'Cazadores tempranos y tardíos en cueva del Lago Sofía 1', *Anales del Instituto de la Patagonia* (Serie Ciencias Sociales), 20 (1991), 75–99.

Purísima Concepción 1765. 'Diario de Navegación y Acaecimientos del navío nombrado La Purísima Concepción en su viaje desde el Puerto de Cádiz a la Mar del Sur que dió principio en enero de 1764', copy of the manuscript deposited in the Museo del Fin del Mundo, Ushuaia.

Quesada, C., *Histoire hypothétique et idéologie anti-indienne au XVIIIè siècle*, Paris, 1982.

Rabassa, J. and Clapperton, C.M., 'Quaternary glaciations of the southern Andes', *Quaternary Science Review*, 9 (1990), 153–74.

Rabassa, J., Bujalesky, G., Meglioli, A., Coronato, A., Gordillo, S., Roig, C. and Salemme, M., 'The Quaternary of Tierra del Fuego: the status of our knowledge', *Sveriges Geologiska Undersvkning*, ser. ca., 81 (1992), 249–56.

Rabassa, J., Heusser, C. and Stuckenrath, R., 'New data on Holocene sea transgressions in the Beagle Channel: Tierra del Fuego', *Quaternary of South America and Antarctic Peninsula*, 4 (1996), 291–309.

Ramirez, C., 'Macrobotanical remains' in T.D. Dillehay (ed.), *Monte Verde. A Late Pleistocene Settlement in Chile*, Washington, D.C., 1989, 147–69.

Renfrew, C. and Bahn, P., *Archaeology*, 2nd edn, London, 1996.

Restif de la Bretonne, *La Découverte australe par un Homme-volant...*, Leipsick, Paris, no date.

Rick, J., *Cronología, Clima y Subsistencia en el Precerámico Peruano*, Instituto Andino de Estudios Arqueológicos, Lima, 1983.

Roig, C., Heusser, C.J. and Rabassa, J., 'Late Quaternary Palaeoenvironmental Reconstruction of Tierra del Fuego. Part I: Pollen Data', XIV Inqua Congress, 1995, Terra Nostra Abstracts, Berlin.

Romero, H., *Geografía de Chile: geografía de los climas*, Santiago, 1985.

Rouse, I., *Migrations in Prehistory: Inferring population movement from cultural remains*, New Haven and London, 1986.

Sahlins, M., *Islands of History*, London, 1987.

Salemme, M., Heusser, C., Roig, C., Coronato, A. and Rabassa, J., 'Fire in Tierra del Fuego, southern South America. Charcoal particles from the late Glacial/early Holocene and their relationship with the regional peopling', unpublished Spanish MS, XIV Inqua Congress, Terra Nostra Abstracts (237), Berlin.

Salemme, M., Roig, C., Coronato, A. and Rabassa, J., 'Early peopling in Tierra del Fuego: aboriginal fires from the late Glacial/early Holocene', XIII U.I.S.P.P. Congress, Abstracts, Forli, Italy.

Sanguinetti, A.C., 'Excavaciones prehistóricas en la Cueva Las Buitreras', *Relaciones de la Sociedad Argentina de Antropología*, 10 (1976), 271–92.

Sarmiento de Gamboa, P., 'Sumaria relación fechada en el Escorial acerca de las poblaciones hechas en el Estrecho' in *Viage al Estrecho de Magallanes*, Madrid, 1768.

Savanti, F., *Las aves en la dieta de los cazadores-recolectores terrestres de la costa fueguina*, Programa de Estudios Prehistóricos, Buenos Aires, 1994.

Saxon, E.C., 'La prehistoria de Fuego-Patagonia: colonización de un hábitat marginal', *Anales del Instituto de la Patagonia*, 7 (1976), 63–73.

Saxon, E.C., 'Natural prehistory: the archaeology of Fuego-Patagonian ecology', *Quaternaria*, 21 (1979), 329–56.

Schiffer, M.B., *Formation Processes of the Archaeological Record*, Albuquerque, 1987.

Schobinger, J., *Prehistoria de Sudamérica*, Barcelona, 1969.

Schobinger, J., 'La Patagonia en el marco de la más antigua prehistoria americana', *Comunicaciones, Primeras Jornadas de Arqueología de la Patagonia* (1987), 279–93.

Schuster, C., 'Observations on the painted designs of Patagonian skin robes' in S.K. Lothrop (ed.), *Essays in Pre-Columbian Art and Archaeology*, Cambridge, Mass., 1961, 421–83.

Schuster, C. and Carpenter, E., *Patterns that Connect: Social Symbolism in Ancient and Tribal Art*, New York, 1996.

Senatore, X., 'Tecnología cerámica en el área de piedra del Aguila, Plias de Río Negro y Neuquén', *Prehistoria*, 2 (1996), 127–45, PREP-CONICET, Buenos Aires.

Serrano Montaner, R., 'Diario de la excursión a la isla grande de la Tierra del Fuego durante los meses de enero i febrero de 1879', *Anuario hidrográfico de la marina de Chile*, 6 (1880), 151–204.

Silveira, M., 'Análisis e interpretación de los restos faunísticos de la Cueva Grande de Arroyo Feo', *Relaciones de la Sociedad Argentina de Antropología*, 13 (1979), 229–53.

Singer, B., Ton-That, T., Vincze, Y., Rabassa, J., Roig, C. and Brunstad, K., 'Timescales of late cenozoic climate change in the southern hemisphere from 40AR/39AR dating of Patagonian lavas', *Terra Abstracts*, European Union of Geosciences, 9 (1997).

Skottsberg, C., 'Observations on the natives of the Patagonian Channel region', *American Anthropologist*, 15 (1913), 578–616.

Smith, B., *European Vision and the South Pacific*, 2nd edn, New Haven, 1988.

Snow, W. Parker, *A Two Years' Cruise off Tierra del Fuego, the Falkland Islands, Patagonia and the River Plate*, vol. 2, London, 1857.

Soddy, F., *Cartesian Economics. The Bearing of Physical Science upon State Stewardship*, London, 1992.

Soto-Heim, P., 'Paleo-Indian human remains of Patagonia-Chile', *Current Research in the Pleistocene*, 11 (1994), 55–7.

Spencer, B. and Gillen, F.J., *The Native Tribes of Central Australia*, 1899, reprinted New York, 1968.

Stern, C. and Prieto A., 'Obsidiana verde de los sitios arqueologicos en los alrededores del Seno Otway, Magallanes, Chile', *Anales del Instituto de la Patagonia* (Serie Ciencias Sociales), 20 (1991), 139–44.

Stocking, G.W., *Victorian Anthropology*, London, 1987.

Sutcliffe, A.J., *On the Track of Ice Age Mammals*, Cambridge, Mass., 1985.

Thevet, A., *La Cosmographie universelle*, Paris, 1575.

Thompson, L.G., Mosley-Thompson, E., Davis, M.E., Lin, P-N., Henderson, K.A., Cole-Dai, J., Bolzan, J.F. and Liu, K-B., 'Late glacial stage and Holocene tropical ice core records from Huascaran, Peru', *Science*, 269 (1995), 46–50.

Todorov, T., *The Conquest of America: The Question of the Other*, trans. Richard Howard, New York, 1984.

Tonni, E. and Politis, G., 'Un gran cánido del Holoceno de la Provincia de Buenos Aires y el registro prehispánico de *Canis (canis) familiaris* en las áreas Pampeana y Patagónica', *Ameghiniana*, 18: 3–4 (1981), 251–65.

Turner, C.G., 'New World origins: new research from the Americas and the Soviet Union' in D.J. Stanford and J.S. Day (eds), *Ice-Age Hunters of the Rockies*, Denver Museum of Natural History and University Press of Colorado, 1992, 7–50.

Valdés, C., Sánchez, M., Inostroza, J., Sanzana P. and Navarro, X., 'Excavaciones arqueológicas en el alero Quillén 1, Provincia de Cautín, Chile', *Actas del IX Congreso Nacional de Arqueología*, La Serena, 1982, 399–435.

Van der Hammen, T. and Hooghiemstra, H., 'The El Abra stadial, a Younger Dryas equivalent in Colombia', *Quaternary Science Review*, 14 (1995), 841–52.

Vargas y Ponce, J. de, *Relación del último viage al estrecho de Magallanes de la fragata de S.M. Santa María de la Cabeza en los años de 1785 y 1786*, Madrid, 1788.

Vayda, A.P. and Rappaport, R.A., 'Island cultures' in F.R. Fosberg (ed.), *Man's Place in the Island Ecosystem*, Honolulu, 1963, 133–42.

Veblen, T. and Lorenz, D., 'Recent vegetation changes along the forest/steppe ecotone of northern Patagonia', *Annals of the Association of American Geographers*, 78: 1 (1988), 93–111.

Velasco, J. de, *Historia Natural del Reino de Quito*, Quito, 1735 and 1927.

Vidal, H., 'Primeros lineamientos para una arqueología etnográfica de Península Mitre', *Comunicaciones, Primeras Jornadas de Arqueología de la Patagonia* (1987), 303–10.

Viedma, A. de, 'Descripción de la Costa Meridional del Sur, llamada vulgarmente Patagónica, etc.' in O.O. Amaya (ed.), *Diario de...*, Argentina, 1980.

Vignati, M.A., 'Arqueología y Antropología de los conchales fueguinos', *Revista del Museo de La Plata*, 30 (1927), 79–143.

Wilbert and Simoneau, *Folk Literature of the Tehuelche Indians*, Los Angeles, 1984.

Wilbert, J. (ed. and trans.), *Folk Literature of the Selk'nam Indians. Martin Gusinde's Collection of Selk'nam Narratives*, Los Angeles, 1975.

Winter, Capt, *The Famous Voyage of Sir Francis Drake into the South Sea, and there Hence about the Whole Globe of the Earth*, London, 1577/79.

Winterhalder, B., 'Optimal foraging strategies and hunter-gatherer research in anthropology: theory and models' in Winterhalder and Smith (eds), *Hunter-Gatherer Foraging Strategies*, Chicago, 1981, 13–35.

Yacobaccio, H.D. and Guraieb, G., 'Tendencia temporal de contextos arqueológicos: Area del Río Pinturas y zonas vecinas' in C.J. Gradín and A.M. Aguerre (eds), *Contribución a la arqueología del Río Pinturas*, Uruguay, 1994, 13–28.

Yesner, D., 'Maritime hunter-gatherers: ecology and prehistory', *Current Anthropology*, 21: 6 (1980), 727–50.

Yesner, D., 'Fuegians and other hunter-gatherers of the subantarctic region: "cultural devolution" reconsidered' in B. Meehan and N. White (eds), *Hunter-Gatherer Demography. Past and Present*, Sydney, 1991, 1–22.

INDEX

Figures are indicated by their page numbers in *italics*, while colour plates are indicated by plate number in **bold**. References to the notes are given by page number with the suffix n.

PICTURE ACKNOWLEDGEMENTS

Adriana Meirelles: 21 and 29 (after Glaser and Fernandez 1983: 8, 18), 31, 58, 59 and 66 (after Gusinde 1931 and 1982); American Museum of Natural History, New York: 22 (after Bird 1988: 166); Anne Chapman: 60; Anthropos-Museum und Institut, Germany: 53, 57, 61–8, 70–3, 86 (after Gusinde 1931, 1982 and 1989); British Library: 76, 117 (after the *Illustrated London News*, July 1889); the Trustees of the British Museum: 26, 32, 35 (after Schuster & Carpenter 1996: fig. 256), 36 (after Lothrop 1961, essay 27: fig. 18); 40, 42, 43, 45, 54, 80 (drawing by Bayot, after Dumont-d'Urville 1846), 82 (after Brassey 1880: 135), 88, 94 (after Pernetty 1780), 95–9 and 101 (drawings by C. Martens), 100 (drawing by W. Sculp after Anderson 1781: pl. 14b), 102, 104, 105 (drawings by P.P. King after Fitzroy 1839), 103 (after Snow 1857: II: 45), 107 (drawing by Goupil and Le Breton after Dumont-d'Urville 1846: pl. 14a), 108 (after Musters 1871); Centro de Estudios del Hombre Austral, Magallanes: 103; David Williams: 23 (after Nami 1987: 91), 28 (after Crivelli 1980: pl. 1), 33 (after Orquera 1987: 402), 112 (after Aschero 1984: 36) and 118 (Museum of Mankind); Instituto de la Patagonia, Universidad de Magallanes, Chile: 18, 75, 78 (drawing by Ohlsen [1884], after Druck van Meisenbach), 79, 106, 115; Jean-Paul Duviols: 90, 91, 92, 93 (all after Duviols 1985); Liz Errington: 1, 5, 6, 10, 11, 12, 13, 14, 17, 36, 77; Luis Alberto Borrero: 30; Musée de l'Homme, Paris: 44, 46–9, 74 (after Dubois *et al.* 1995: 2637, 2640, 2638, 2702, 2665, respectively); Museo Nazionale della Montagna 'Duca Degli Abruzzi', Turin: frontispiece, photo by Alberto Agostini; Museum für Völkerkunde, Berlin: 110, 111; National Museum of Ethnography, Sweden: 51; Natural History Museum, London: 16 (after Sutcliffe 1985: 177); Princeton University: 109 (after Hatcher 1903: 1: fig. 42); Pitt-Rivers Museum, Oxford: 41 (after Coppinger 1883); Rhonda Klevansky: 2, 3, 4, 7, 8, 9, 15, 19, 20, 25, 27, 34, col. pls 1a and 1b; Rodrigo Cárdenas: 104a, 104b (after Mansur-Franchomme 1987), 104c (after Gusinde 1931), 106; Royal Geographical Society, London: 38, 55, 69, 87, 89 (photos by Wellington Furlong, *c.* 1906–7), 39, 52, 81, 84, 85 (photos by W.S. Barclay, *c.* 1901–3); South American Missionary Society, Kent: 50, 83.